Men's
Secret
Wars

PATRICK A. MEANS

Fleming H. Revell
A Division of Baker Book House Co
Grand Rapids, Michigan 49516

Published by Fleming H. Revell
a division of Baker Book House Company
P.O. Box 6287, Grand Rapids, MI 49516-6287

Paperback edition published 1999

Fifth printing, July 2002

Printed in the United States of America

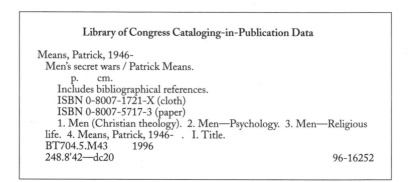

Library of Congress Cataloging-in-Publication Data

Means, Patrick, 1946-
  Men's secret wars / Patrick Means.
      p.   cm.
  Includes bibliographical references.
  ISBN 0-8007-1721-X (cloth)
  ISBN 0-8007-5717-3 (paper)
  1. Men (Christian theology). 2. Men—Psychology. 3. Men—Religious
life. 4. Means, Patrick, 1946- . I. Title.
  BT704.5.M43   1996
  248.8'42—dc20   96-16252

Unless otherwise marked, Scripture quotations are from the New American Standard Bible, © the Lockman Foundation 1960, 1962, 1963, 1968, 1971, 1972, 1973, 1975, 1977.

Scripture quotations marked LB are taken from *The Living Bible,* copyright © 1971 by Tyndale House Publishers, Wheaton, Illinois. Used by permission.

Scripture quotations marked NEB are from *The New English Bible.* © The Delegates of the Oxford University Press and The Syndics of the Cambridge University Press 1961, 1970. Reprinted by permission.

Scripture quotations marked NIV are taken from the HOLY BIBLE, NEW INTERNATIONAL VERSION®. NIV®. Copyright © 1973, 1978, 1984 by International Bible Society. Used by permission of Zondervan Publishing House. All rights reserved.

Scripture quotations marked KJV are taken from the King James Version of the Bible.

The Life Rating Scale in chapter 4 is from *Your Money or Your Life* by Vicki Robin and Joe Dominguez. Copyright © 1992 by Vicki Robin and Joe Dominguez. Used by permission of Viking Penguin, a division of Penguin Books USA Inc.

Portions of this book originally appeared in *STEPS* magazine, the magazine of the National Association for Christian Recovery. Used by permission.

For current information about all releases from Baker Book House, visit our web site:
http://www.bakerbooks.com

Contents

110199

Contents

For Sarah and David, with love
and with gratefulness to God
for who he's made you to be

Acknowledgments

To all the men whose stories appear in this book, for their courage in battling their own secret wars, and their willingness to share their stories with other men. Thank you.

To Roy Carlisle, Ron Halvorson, and Jack McGinnis, for their guidance and encouragement at critical times in my recovery journey.

To Dale and Juanita Ryan, for taking a risk and for modeling what it means to have "grace in your guts."

To the men in our men's group: Jon, Dave, Dick, Van, and Craig, for helping to create a safe place where we all experienced the joys and terrors of true honesty.

To my parents, Mancel and Lola Means, for their unconditional love and unflagging support when I needed it most.

And most of all, to my wife, Marsha, God's grace-gift to me, and my best friend. I can't imagine life without you.

Introduction

Nine years ago my world turned upside down. I was attending a ministry leadership conference in central Europe. In the middle of the night the phone rang. Even half asleep I could hear the strain in my supervisor's voice: "I need you to come to my room immediately. It's serious."

The next four hours were the start of a nightmare: a confrontation over the discovery of my extramarital affair, immediate dismissal from the ministry in which I had served for almost twenty years, and the beginning of a wilderness period that eventually included divorce and the loss of my family.

The journey back toward spiritual and emotional healthiness has been long and difficult. With the help of therapists and caring Christian leaders I've had to go back in and rebuild the breaches in the walls of my life, as Nehemiah did in ancient Jerusalem. As I worked on my personal recovery, I searched for answers to the question, How could this have happened? I've been a Christian since I was a young boy. I was raised in a Christian home and a Bible-believing church. As an adult I'd been exposed to some of the best theological teaching and leadership training the Christian world could offer. Despite all that, I had made a series of wrong choices. The result was sin, and the fallout hurt many people.

I did find answers to my question, but I found more than that. Along the way, I met scores of pastors and Christian laymen who shared with me the stories of their own secret wars. Clear patterns began to emerge. Certain predictable factors that lead to crisis showed up again and again in the lives of each of these men.

Several years into my rebuilding period, I wanted nothing more than to quietly get on with my life. God had graciously allowed me to remarry. I was able to pursue my love of writing as editor of a national magazine for Christians in recovery. A lot of healing was going on, and life was satisfying again.

But almost against my will a new ministry began to emerge. Pastors referred men to me who were struggling with destructive behavior. I began to sense—with some anxiety—that God was calling me back into the ministry, but a different kind of ministry, a ministry to help Christian men who are under fire on the front lines of spiritual warfare. As I've sought to follow that calling, a seminar and retreat ministry to men has taken shape.

In these Manhood Without Models seminars, we talk about the early warning signs of personal crisis. We look at the key steps we can take to strengthen our personal lives and our marriage and family relationships. And though I've spoken to many audiences in the past, I've never experienced the electric response from an audience that I have from the men in these seminars. Many of the men say they appreciate the honesty they hear; others talk about feeling hope for the first time in certain defeated areas of their lives. Much of that hope is reflected in the pages that follow.

The need to talk honestly about the real issues facing Christian men has never been greater. For the last three years, I've taken a Men's Confidential Survey during our retreats and workshops, and several hundred have participated in it. These men are the "cream of the crop" of the Christian community—the most dedicated laymen, the most successful pastors. The results of the survey are sobering. Serious burnout affects one in five. Two-thirds struggle with secret sexual sin or addictive behavior. Twenty-five percent of the married men admit to having had an extramarital affair since they've become Christians. Many say they have never sought help even though they knew what they were doing was wrong. They were embarrassed, they said, and were afraid of what others would think.

In this book we will look at several of the most destructive battles that can erupt in the life of a Christian man. We'll hear the stories of courageous men* who have worked through issues like stress, burnout, unhealthy relationship styles, temptation, and sexuality. We'll look at both the causes and the cures.

My hope is that through the broken experiences of many other Christian men you will find the insight and inspiration you need to grow stronger. Together we *can* chart a safe path through the minefields that surround us.

---

*All the stories of the men in this book are true. Names and certain details in each story have been changed to protect the privacy of the individuals involved.

Part 1

The Secret Wars

What you live with, you learn.
What you learn, you practice.
What you practice, you become.
What you become has consequences.

Anonymous

Choose your rut carefully. You'll be in it for the next 200 miles.

Sign on Alaska highway

White Knights, Black Hats

Men and the Hero Subculture

If only there were evil people somewhere insidiously committing evil deeds, and it were necessary only to separate them from the rest of us and destroy them. But the line dividing good and evil cuts through the heart of every human being. And who is willing to destroy a piece of his own heart?
Aleksandr Solzhenitsyn, *The Gulag Archipelago*

Show me a hero and I will write you a tragedy.
F. Scott Fitzgerald, *Notebooks*

By all accounts Rich Chollet had every-thing. Born the son of struggling French immigrants, he rose to head Brookstone, a hugely successful national mail order business. He was good looking, happily married, loved by his employees—and as it turned out, deeply depressed. One March morning, seemingly out of the blue, Chollet took his life. He simply locked the garage door of his New Hampshire house, climbed into his BMW, and turned on the engine. When they found him, they also found the note he'd written to his family. "Please forgive me," he wrote, "but the thought of going through the torture of living is just too much to bear."

13

His wife, Susan, later revealed that Chollet had been depressed for half of his adult life. People had put him on such a pedestal, she said, that he had constantly feared letting them down. "He swung from feeling totally powerful to totally helpless."[1]

In another part of the country a few months earlier, members of Atlanta's respected Wieuca Road Baptist Church were shocked when their longtime pastor, Dr. William Self, announced he was resigning because the stress of the job was more than he could handle. "Unless I quit now," he told them, "my obituary will read, 'Bill Self today sank like a rock—beat up, burned out, angry and depressed, no good to himself, no good to the people he loved.'"

For more than twenty-five years, Dr. Self had been a highly successful preacher, teacher, administrator, and fundraiser. It was not a lack of talent that eventually caused him to leave the ministry. Instead, he says, it was because he found himself "subconsciously navigating into the age-old 'walk on water' syndrome—the notion that, because you're a preacher, you can accomplish anything. . . ."

"It's almost impossible for the leaders of a congregation to accept that their pastor needs pastoring," Self said later. "So I began to strangle on my anger, finding myself unable to sleep and even losing interest in the studies that I love. . . . The church is the only army that shoots its wounded, but I refused to let that happen to me. Instead, I fell on my sword."[2]

White Knights

Men from all walks of life are under unprecedented pressure—and more and more are falling on their swords, either literally or figuratively. The suicide rate for men is two-and-a-half times higher than that of women. And the incidence of stress related diseases such as high blood pressure, stroke, and heart disease is two to four times higher for men than for women.

The "walk on water" syndrome that Bill Self described is one reason that many men experience killer levels of stress. We take on too much and try too hard to play the Hero role in all our responsibilities. We're expected to be successful breadwinners, loving husbands, devoted fathers, good sons to our aging parents, and to do all this while actively involved in the church and community.

Multiple responsibilities might not, in themselves, be bad. But many of us find it hard to accept anything less than perfection from ourselves in each of our roles. This push toward perfectionism is fueled by society's emphasis on men being successful.

Society evaluates the worth of men and women by two completely different, but equally unfair, standards. In our society, women's worth is judged on the basis of beauty. Numerous studies have proven that more-attractive women are given preferential treatment over less-attractive women. Men, on the other hand, are judged on the basis of their success, as measured by money, power, and prestige. Society even has a special set of pejorative terms it uses exclusively for men who are judged to be unsuccessful; the terms *loser, deadbeat,* and *bum* are never used for women. These terms of derision are reserved exclusively for men—men whom society has judged to have low worth, based on their apparent lack of success.

I learned early that society rewards the strong, confident hero-types—the "white knights"—and brushes aside the wimps. (A wimp is anyone who commits the unforgivable sin of looking weak.) So I invested tons of energy in perfecting the hero image. And I was rewarded for it. I was student body president and picked Most Likely to Succeed in high school. I started and led a campus-wide ministry in college, and then spent the next several years climbing the ranks of professional Christian leadership.

White knights specialize in grandiose achievements, especially the kind that are accomplished at great personal cost. For most of my life, my biggest thrills came from trying to achieve the impossible. By age thirty I had written a best-selling book and become the national field director of a large Christian organization, with responsibility for three thousand staff.

Not that there's anything wrong with aiming high in life. But with absolute perfection and superhuman achievement as my standards, like Rick Chollet, I lived with an almost constant sense of failure. And that sense of failure activated a caustic chorus inside my head. Like a row of bleacher bums at a baseball game, the chorus would mock and jeer whenever I fell short of perfection. As I bulldozed toward achievement in my vain attempts to drown the chorus out, I ignored the warning flags along the way: the anger or depression that inevitably followed a public mistake or a criticism from a coworker or a failure to get a coveted promotion. If I'd looked more closely, I could have seen the evidence of unhealthiness within me. But I had bought society's belief that personal worth is determined by success, and my self-critical drivenness was the result.

My friend, Pastor Van Savell, recently told me a true story that perfectly illustrates society's obsession with success. Van's son, Van Jr., was a standout distance runner in high school. Football-crazy Denham Springs (Louisiana) High School wasn't much for track. But when Van Jr. moved into town his senior year, they knew how to embrace a winner.

Savell had run on three state champion cross-country teams at Astronaut High School in Titusville, Florida. He had also won both the 1600 meter and 3200 meter championships at the Louisiana AAA State Track Championships while a sophomore at Westlake, Louisiana.

During his senior year Savell won every track race he ran until the state AAA meet. The Denham Springs fans were electric in their support of the young runner. But at the state meet, despite a strong effort, Savell finished second in the 1600 and second in the 3200. The races were very fast with winning times among the top five in the United States in 1982.

The headline in the *Denham Springs News* the next Tuesday was classic. Eight columns wide in sixty-four-point type, it said simply, SAVELL LOSES. Van Jr. was one of the best distance runners in the country and went on to become a Division 2 all-American in college. But there is no grace in society's hero subculture. You must win every time, or you're labeled a loser.

But there's a high cost to being a winner. For many men that high cost is fatigue and burnout. These are not only dangers to us physically, but they also rob us of the joy of living and dull our effectiveness in all the roles we play.

High levels of stress carried for long periods of time can eventually lead to burnout. Pastor Charles Perry tells the story of a fellow pastor from his midwestern city who went through a period of severe burnout. This pastor went so far as to fake a suicide and become a homeless drifter, all because every aspect of his life had become so painful. Perry's initial response was to label and dismiss his friend's aberrant behavior as spiritual weakness. But that was before he himself went through the personal devastation of burnout, despite a strong walk with the Lord. Perry eventually recovered from his bout with burnout, returned to the ministry, and wrote a book to help other Christians dealing with the effects of stress and fatigue. In his book *Why Christians Burn Out*, Perry offers a list of symptoms of burnout. (They're summarized at the end of this chapter for your reflection.)

Black Hats

Even more sobering than society's emphasis on success is the degree to which we have adopted the hero subculture in the church today.

A pastor friend of mine told me a story recently that illustrates the attitude of many in the church. For some time he's felt a burden to develop an extensive small group ministry in his church. He wants to create safe places where wounded or struggling Christians can go to heal and to grow. But he's meeting resistance from some church members. One member worried that such groups would attract too many divorced and otherwise broken people. "What will 'normal' people like me do then?" he asked.

The implication was clear: "Normal" Christians don't ever struggle with anything serious. This attitude minimizes the negative power of our dark side. So we continue to feel shock and disbelief when "good" people do bad things—when seemingly wise, mature, gracious Christian leaders are caught in behaviors that are terribly inconsistent with their callings.

Far too often in the Christian community we overfocus on strength and external success and scorn weakness and failure. If we ever do struggle with temptation or failure, we're expected to replace it with instant victory. A popular book sold in Christian bookstores a few years ago was *Now Is Your Time to Win!* In bold letters under the title, the jacket trumpeted: "*You* can bounce back from failure to success in 30 seconds!" I don't know about you, but the failures that have troubled me the most are not the kind I can "bounce back" from in thirty seconds.

Men who live in this kind of hero subculture are especially vulnerable. In my own case I had assumed that because I'd been a Christian since I was a child, knew the Bible well, and loved the Lord, I could never fail the way that I did. Many other Christian men now tell me they feel the same way. What's at work here is a false sense of security—the "it could never happen to me" syndrome.

But this overemphasis on success and strength is actually the opposite of the biblical value system. Over and over Scripture warns us against relying on our human strength. Repeatedly we're exhorted to own our weaknesses, rather than cover them up.

Second Chronicles 26 sketches the story of one of history's greatest leaders. Uzziah became king of Judah when he was sixteen. He went on to become a great statesman and warrior, an inventor of armaments, and an agricultural engineer. For decades Uzziah experienced the Lord's blessing in all that he did. But then the writer of Chronicles punctuates the king's list of accomplishments with this sobering comment: "Hence his fame spread afar, for he was marvelously helped *until he was strong*. But when he became strong, his heart was so proud that he acted corruptly, and he was unfaithful to the Lord his God. . . ."[3]

Uzziah's strength and success were his undoing. In my own experience, success often leads to false pride, which inevitably leads to personal disaster, as it did with Uzziah. In his pride he decided he could break one of God's laws with impunity. It wasn't enough that he was a renowned statesman and warrior and inventor. He coveted the one task reserved for the high priest alone—the burning of incense in the temple to the Lord. Ultimately Uzziah was confronted in the midst of his rebellious act by Azariah, the high priest. When Uzziah reacted with anger, he was struck with leprosy and removed from the kingship. The linkage in Scripture is clear: We're helped by the Lord as long as we remember that we are weak. But when we think that we are strong, that we are beyond weakness and failure, we're on the same dangerous ground as Uzziah.

This same false pride afflicted the Laodicean church in the New Testament. Jesus rebukes them for thinking they are "rich" and "have need of nothing." The truth, Jesus tells them, is this: "You do not know that you are wretched and miserable and poor and blind and naked."[4] It's bad enough to be wretched and miserable and poor and blind and naked. But to be all those things and not know it, is disastrous. Jesus' point is clear: The wise man views himself as deeply needy, regardless of his outward appearance or circumstances.

Perhaps the most ringing denunciation of our obsession with strength and success comes from the apostle Paul himself. Paul had an impressive theological pedigree as a "Pharisee of the Pharisees." He had communed with God face-to-face in a vision. But when he asked God to take away one of his weaknesses—his "thorn in the flesh"—this great follower of Christ received an unequivocal response from the Lord. No, Paul, I won't take away your weakness, the Lord said. Rather, "My grace is sufficient for you, for power is perfected in weakness."[5]

And the great apostle got it. "Most gladly, therefore," he said, "I will rather boast about my weaknesses, that the power of Christ may dwell in me . . . for when I am weak, then I am strong."[6]

I came across a chilling news account not long ago. The article told the story of a New Jersey family named Olson who bought a wolf dog for their sixteen-month-old son, Tyler. "Completely domesticated," they'd been told. "Safe as a collie." But without warning, the wolf dog reverted to his wild roots and savagely attacked young Tyler, severing his arm and nearly killing him.

When I came across that news report, I was struck by its parallel to our own situation as Christians. Even though Christ lives in us and we are indeed new creatures, we will remain hybrids until the day we die. Alongside our new nature lies our old nature—our dark side. Our dark side is that part of us that we would rather no one ever knows about, the side that seems determined to pull us toward sinful, self-destructive behavior.

The Olsons thought the wolf dog was now tamed—safe. And that assumption brought tragic results. But we Christians do the same thing! We give lip service to the belief that we still possess a sinful nature. But we're quite sure that it's a domesticated sinful nature now that we're committed Christians. We say, "I've left my wolf days behind me. I've gone to dog obedience school, and I'm no longer capable of doing anything really bad or wild and savage."

But the sobering reality remains. We Christians *do* possess a dark side, a propensity toward unhealthiness that will never be eradicated in this life. In fact, in his letter to the church at Ephesus, Paul warns that even after we become Christians, our dark side (the "old self") actually becomes *more* corrupt, not better![7] The sad truth is, we Christians are just as capable of horrific deeds as anyone else.

John, in his first epistle, puts it plainly: "If we say that we have no sin, we are deceiving ourselves, and the truth is not in us."[8] And you can almost hear the anguish in the apostle Paul's voice as he confesses his own struggle with his dark side in the seventh chapter of Romans: "For the good that I wish, I do not do; but I practice the very evil that I do *not* wish."[9]

"There, but for the grace of God, go I" should be more than a motto at the Union Gospel Mission; it should be a sober statement of our personal theology, expressed with deepest humility. We will be wolf dogs until the day we die.

Approval Junkie

Several years ago, author and songwriter John Fischer wrote a profoundly whimsical little booklet called *Dark Horse*. It tells the story of a black-and-white-spotted horse who longed to be all white. He was sent to a special ranch to learn how to think, walk, and prance like white horses. There, said the horse, "We learned how to make the most of our white parts; even how to pose to show the most amount of white (without looking unnatural)."

The highlight of every year was when the white horse show came to the ranch. This was their chance to see real white horses in all their splendor as they performed. "I used to dream of being in that spotlight," said the horse, "because I knew that with its help, even though I wasn't, I could still look like a white horse. All of us at the ranch shared that one burning dream—to one day join a white horse show."

It was during one of these shows that the horse had an encounter that would change his life. A stallion from outside the ranch, "wild as a prairie storm, dark as the night plains," approached as the spotted horse watched the show.

"Have you ever seen a white horse?" the dark stallion asked.

"Well, of course," the spotted horse answered. "Isn't this a white horse show?"

"But have you ever seen a white horse?"

"I see the white horses that come in the show. And some of us here at the ranch are almost all white."

Now the stallion was starting to rattle something in the horse's thinking. True, he had only seen the real white horses from a distance. When they were through showing they were whisked away to the separate stables where they were always quartered. He thought of all the horses he knew and had to admit, he had never walked completely around a white horse.

"Look at that horse right now in the spotlight," the dark stallion said. "Do you see all of him?"

"No."

"Of course you don't. And watch—when he's through posing he'll walk off in the darkness. Do you see? The light only shines on the pose, not the real horse."

The horse turned toward the stage and tried to collect his thoughts. He watched the horses come and go in the spotlight, striking their poses with casual grace. They'd all been through this many, many times before.

And then with a new light that was already illuminating his thoughts, he saw in an instant the folly of this whole procedure. "How foolish," he thought, "that it never occurred to me before! I'm not going to get any whiter by being at this ranch—only more clever at appearing white!"

The horse looked back again at the dark stallion and his eyes were dancing with excitement. Without even speaking the stallion was willing the horse to ask the ultimate question. The question had already asked itself in his mind and there was nothing that could keep it from falling out of his mouth.

"Do you mean to tell me . . . there are no white horses?"

"No," he replied. "There is one."

"You mean the White One?"

"Of course. He is the only white horse there ever was or ever will be."

"But aren't we to be like the White One?" It was another horse from the ranch speaking, for there was now a small group listening in on the conversation.

"Yes," said the dark horse. "But whiteness is not on the outside. It is in the heart. You cannot change a hair on your body, but he can change your heart and shine his light in your eyes. It all starts when we stop pretending to be something we're not.

"There are thousands of horses out there who need the help of the White One and there is an enemy afoot— crouching at the door—while you waste your time striking poses and comparing whiteness."

At that he reared back and his cry was a mighty thing. "If you would follow the White One, then follow me!" And with that, the dark horse vaulted the fences and disappeared

23

into the night with the other horses from the ranch following close behind.[10]

Many of us have spent our lives at ranches like the one in Fischer's story, practicing how to preen and posture so that we would hide our dark sides and show only our white. But as the spotted horse finally realized, that kind of environment doesn't help us become whiter, but only "more clever at appearing white." God wants to do the real work inside us and transform our character, but we're too busy expending our energy on looking good.

One of my all-time favorite movies is the Bill Murray comedy *Groundhog Day*. Murray plays the part of a TV weatherman who finds himself trapped in a time warp, doomed to repeat one day of his life—Groundhog Day— over and over again in the same small Pennsylvania town. Murray eventually finds out where and when every accident is going to happen in town that day—the boy who falls from the tree, the man choking on a piece of meat—and places himself in the right spot at the right time to rescue each and every one of them. He also uses his endless repetition of the same day to become a virtuoso jazz pianist, a skilled marriage counselor, and a respected physician. All his altruism and talent finally peak in a town-wide party where Murray is the star. He is cheered for his performance on the keyboard, swarmed by hordes of grateful people whom he's helped, and dazzles the woman he's trying to woo.

I both laughed and cried when I saw the movie. I laughed because it is a funny movie and cried because it perfectly captured all my fondest fantasies as a lifelong approval junkie. For forty years I drove my life by the assumption that I would receive unending praise, affirmation, and approval from others if I dedicated myself to rescuing and pleasing everyone I met. By the time I reached midlife, my drivenness and unhealthiness had burnt me to a crisp and led me down several destructive, dead-end paths. The irony was, I received a lot of praise along the way, but it was never enough.

The first-century Pharisees were the approval junkies of Jesus' day. John 12:43 says of the Pharisees, "They loved the approval of men rather than the approval of God." Healthiness begins when we wean ourselves from worrying about what other people think of us.

At least five significant problems develop from a lifestyle of people pleasing and approval seeking.

1. We can never say no. Pleasers let others dictate their agendas. The result is emotional and physical exhaustion and a growing reservoir of resentment and rage.
2. Our activity becomes guilt driven. We do things because we fear the consequences, rather than because we really want to. We constantly operate from a sense of obligation and feel "in deficit."
3. We don't experience the affirmation of our true self. The commodities we strive to earn with people-pleasing activities—approval and affirmation—are the very things we never receive. As people pleasers, our true identity lies trapped behind a false self; what's hidden cannot be approved or affirmed.
4. We don't discover the wonderful, unique person God created us to be. We spend our lives trying to be someone else.
5. People pleasing is a form of idolatry. We are making other people, rather than God, the center of our universe.

For further insight on this area, fill out the Personal Assessment on People Pleasing and Approval at the end of this chapter.

Steps to Healthiness

As in almost all areas of the Christian life, the pendulum can swing too far in either direction. On one extreme are those who believe in living a self-centered existence, running roughshod over everyone in their lives. These men don't struggle with people pleasing. They have the opposite problem: narcissism, excessive concern for oneself. But for many of us, the pendulum is stuck on the opposite extreme: We overfocus on other people's opinions and deny personal needs and limitations. The balance is found in the middle—a lifestyle that includes appropriate self-care and an openness to help others.

Two New Testament passages capture this balance well. Philippians 2:4 encourages us, "Do not merely look out for your own personal interests, but also for the interests of others." Notice that both interests are important. Galatians 6:2 says, "Bear one another's burdens," but that's balanced two verses later by the admonition "But let each one examine his own work. . . . For each one shall bear his own load."

How do men caught in the hero trap find freedom from the endless struggle for success and affirmation? They start by dismantling the trap itself, piece by piece, and building a new model grounded in God's view of them. Here are the steps.

1. Anchor Your Self-Worth to God's View of You

The motive behind our drive to please others is the need to shore up our flagging self-worth. If enough people say they like us (or at least need us), we feel good about ourselves. But because this drive is coming from our shame core—our inner sense that we are defective and not good enough—it is like carrying water in a sieve. It runs out quickly.

In *Tired of Trying to Measure Up* Jeffrey Van Vonderen explains the difference between guilt and shame. "Guilt," he says, "is a healthy thing. Because guilt comes as a result of something you and I do, we can do something about it—change our behavior—and the guilty feeling will go away.

"Shame, on the other hand, is the belief . . . that something is wrong with *you*. It's not that you feel bad about your behavior, it's that you believe you are deficient, defective or worthless as a human being."[11]

If in your childhood you were raised with the message that you were worthless or stupid or, conversely, that you were special and needed to overachieve to be acceptable, or if the adults in your life consistently disregarded your feelings and your personal boundaries, you probably developed a toxic shame core. Below are characteristics of the shame core that show up in adult life.

Shame core

- Low self-esteem, negative self-concept
- Highly performance conscious
- Unawareness of personal boundaries
- Sacrifice of personal needs
- Frequent unawareness of own feelings
- Perfectionism
- Frequent or persistent fatigue
- Addictive behavior
- Distrust of people
- Possessiveness in relationships
- High need for control

Clearly, God alone can heal our shame core with its damaged self-worth. Only his view of us fills the need we have for a parent to affirm and accept us unconditionally. In short, we need to stop looking to others—our wives, friends, children, bosses—to give us a sense of personal worth, and instead claim God's view of us as reflected in his Word.

Psalm 139 is a beautiful celebration of God's high esteem for us, his children. David confirms that we have been designed by the Master Creator himself, and that his workmanship is superb: "I will give thanks to Thee, for I am fearfully and wonderfully made; Wonderful are Thy works, and my soul knows it very well."

David captures two realities here: (1) God did a magnificent job in making you and me, and he knows it and values us highly; (2) *David* "knows it very well" himself. *David* knows, and is not afraid to say, that he has been made "fearfully and wonderfully." As Mahalia Jackson loved to say, "God don't make no junk!"

That second reality is the one we need to pray for the grace to experience: a full acceptance and belief, deep in our souls, that we are each wonderful examples of God's creation, that he has done a *good* job on us. (You might find the Scripture for Meditation page at the end of this chapter to be helpful.)

2. Give Up the Compulsive Need to Be Perfect

Someone has said that a perfectionist is one who takes great pains . . . and gives them to others. I've been one of those pain givers for most of my life, primarily because that's what I thought God expected of me. After all, doesn't Jesus say, "You are to be perfect, as your heavenly Father is perfect"?[12]

It's astounding, but God's plan throughout history has been to use imperfect people. David failed miserably and was still called the apple of God's eye. Moses failed and was still honored as one of the great leaders in the Bible. Peter failed and was still entrusted with the leadership of the early church.

That doesn't mean that we can ever justify failure, moral or otherwise. It simply means that fear-driven perfectionism is unhealthy; the need to look perfect often makes it difficult to admit neediness or to ask for help. And when we cut ourselves off from help, we're usually only a couple of steps away from disaster.

A team of Christian men and I recently conducted a Manhood Without Models seminar at Seattle Pacific University. Each of us on the presentation team—two pastors and three laymen—honestly shared our own stories, stories that included both failures and victories, and the lessons we'd learned from them. The seminar was open to men from the community, and one who attended, named Dwight, was an elder from a prominent evangelical church in Seattle.

"I've never heard honesty like this before," Dwight said in one of the small discussion groups. He went on to share his own story of private pain about his rebellious son, who had run away from home twice in the last year.

"I haven't told anyone else about this before today," he said quietly, "especially anyone at church. I was too afraid of what they'd think. But hearing you men share honestly about your own struggles has helped me see that I need to reach out for help, too."

I called Dwight a couple of weeks after the seminar just to ask him how he was doing.

"I'm doing great!" he exuded. "My son and my wife and I have started working with a family counselor, and it's going really well! In fact I told our counselor that this is going so well I'd like to start marriage counseling, too, to work on some issues in our marriage. But she recommended I slow down a little," he said, laughing. "She said I don't have to solve everything overnight. But I can't thank you and the other men enough for modeling that it's okay to reach out for help!"

When we give up our need to be perfect, we open the door to deep healing.

Personal Assessment:

People Pleasing and Approval

To evaluate whether you fit the pleaser profile, answer each of the questions as honestly as possible. First, answer all the questions as they pertain to your relationship with your wife or your life at home. Check the boxes in the left-hand column that come closest to your experience—whether the behavior occurs often, sometimes, or never. When you have finished, go through the questions a second time, answering them as they pertain to your relationship with your boss or your experience at work. Check the appropriate boxes in the right-hand column.

When you are done, total your at-home score and your at-work score separately, and read the interpretive material at the end. It's important that you not answer the questions according to what you think the "right" answer should be (there are no right answers), but rather what is most often true for you.

At home or with wife				At work or with boss		
often	*sometimes*	*never*		*often*	*sometimes*	*never*
☐	☐	☐	I have a deep fear of anger, rejection, or abandonment.	☐	☐	☐
☐	☐	☐	I feel a strong responsibility to help the people around me be happy.	☐	☐	☐
☐	☐	☐	I tend to be conscious of my behavior around others, as well as highly aware of others' behavior around me.	☐	☐	☐
☐	☐	☐	I anticipate others' needs before they express them.	☐	☐	☐
☐	☐	☐	I have difficulty saying no, even when it would be best for me.	☐	☐	☐
☐	☐	☐	I am burdened by "shoulds" and "oughts" and feel guilty about my performance.	☐	☐	☐

At home or with wife				At work or with boss		
often	*sometimes*	*never*		*often*	*sometimes*	*never*
☐	☐	☐	I avoid confrontations.	☐	☐	☐
☐	☐	☐	I wonder what other people are saying or thinking about me.	☐	☐	☐
☐	☐	☐	I am afraid others will find out who I really am.	☐	☐	☐
☐	☐	☐	I tend to overcommit myself.	☐	☐	☐

Total each column, giving 2 points to each answer marked "often," 1 point to "sometimes," and 0 for "never." Record your totals below.

Total points:　　at home　_____
　　　　　　　　at work　_____

Score	Interpretation
0–4	*Low.* You have little problem with people pleasing or unhealthy approval seeking. Your needs may be on the narcissistic end of the spectrum.
5–7	*Medium.* Certain situations trouble you more than others. Check the questions on which you scored the highest, and try to identify your problem areas.
8–11	*High.* Your people pleasing and approval seeking are damaging your relationships and undercutting your satisfaction. Working on these issues should be among your highest priorities.
12 and above	*Highest.* You are in a lot of pain in your relationships. You must give this area immediate and serious attention, possibly with the help of a trained therapist, before you experience a life-damaging blowout.

The Signs of Burnout

Read the following questions and note the ones you answer yes.

1. Are you weary of your work?
Does it drain you emotionally?
Do you dislike waking up in the morning because you have to go to your job again?

31

Does your job frustrate you?
Do you constantly feel at your wits' end at work?
Do you ever think about death as a way of escape?

2. Are you callous toward other people?
Do you think of the people with whom you work as objects?
Do you notice a definite hardening of your attitude toward your fellow workers?
Do you rejoice to see a colleague endure a hardship, especially if that person has caused you stress?
Do you blame others for your problems and failures?

3. Are your dreams gone?
Do you blame others for hindering your success?
Have you stopped making plans to do great things?
Do you consider your career a treadmill?
Do you consider life to be one big disappointment?

4. Are you a loner?
Do you find yourself avoiding people who make your life stressful?
Do you feel as if other people, especially your supervisors, have taken something of great value from you?
Do you constantly blame others for your problems?
Do you want to be left alone?

If you answered yes to the majority of these questions, you could be entering—or already experiencing—burnout.[13]

Scriptures for Meditation:

The Truth about You

For Thou didst form my inward parts;
Thou didst weave me in my mother's womb.
I will give thanks to Thee, for I am fearfully and wonder-
fully made;
Wonderful are Thy works,
And my soul knows it very well. My frame was not hidden
from Thee,
When I was made in secret,
And skillfully wrought in the depths of the earth.
Thine eyes have seen my unformed substance;

And in Thy book they were all written,
The days that were ordained for me,
When as yet there was not one of them.

How precious also are Thy thoughts to me, O God!
How vast is the sum of them!
If I should count them, they would outnumber the sand.
When I awake, I am still with Thee.

Psalm 139:13–18

How precious it is, Lord, to realize that you are thinking about me constantly! I can't even count how many times a day your thoughts turn towards me. And when I waken in the morning, you are still thinking of me!

verses 17–18 LB

If the Genes Fit

Rewriting Your Lifescript

Pain from our past that is unresolved is pain we're condemned to repeat.

Terry Kellogg

[God visits] the iniquity of the fathers upon the children unto the third and fourth generation.

Exodus 20:5 KJV

In many ways, the human brain is just
a highly sophisticated garbage dump. Composed of over 12
billion nerve cells, with the analytical ability of a room full
of Pentium-equipped computers, the brain indiscriminately
receives and stores every kind of information thrown its
way—truth, trash, and trivia alike.

For instance, researchers tell us the average adult in North
America is bombarded by 560 advertising messages a day,
and the person's brain stores 76 of these. That's more than
500 slogans, ditties, and jingles of dubious value stored every
week. In addition, the average adult absorbs another twenty
to thirty thousand words per day from newspapers, magazines, books, and television.[1] This mountain of infobits
shapes the way we view life.

But the thousands of hours of messages we received
growing up in our childhood homes exert a much greater

34

influence on us. Some experts believe more than twenty-five thousand hours of these parental messages are stored in the average adult's mind.[2] Together, these messages form the "lifescript" we carry from childhood into adult life.

This lifescript affects every aspect of our lives: the way we see ourselves, the marriage partners we pick, our work-style. As adult men, a major step in being conformed to the image of Christ occurs when we take responsibility for rewriting our lifescripts, instead of blindly following them.

One of my best friends in the Seattle area is an artist and an active Christian layman. Craig has worked for years to develop his entrepreneurial venture into a viable business. Recently he received a series of encouraging phone calls about three exciting new projects. His wife saw the break-throughs as validation for all the hard work he'd done, but Craig quickly became depressed.

Behind the depression was some important family history. Craig has had to fight two generations of fear and negative scripting to move in these new directions, for both his father and grandfather tried and failed in entrepreneurial ventures. He grew up hearing stories of their failures and of the depri-vations they experienced during the Great Depression.

It's no wonder, then, that his body began to tie itself up in knots, producing severe stomach pains that his doctor described as "a migraine in the stomach." Craig couldn't stand up and he couldn't lie down.

"I had that reaction," Craig explained later, "because by opening the door to those new projects, I was going against all the old family rules: Don't risk; don't overextend your-self; keep everything moderate and balanced; and above all, don't draw attention to yourself. Well, two of the three ven-tures involved national exposure, and the third involved self-promotion. Of course my body rebelled."

We have all been significantly influenced by the scripts given to us by our parents—both for good and for bad.

35

These scripts and a warehouse full of memories are stored in that extraordinary organ called the brain. That's why Scripture repeatedly tells us that the spiritual battles that result in change are fought primarily in the darkened streets and back alleys of the mind.

Scripture teaches that sin is intergenerational in its impact. Exodus 20:5 says the sins of our fathers affect us as children "unto the third and fourth generation." But let me be clear. We all have a will, and when we exercise our wills to commit sins or to carry out destructive behaviors, we are fully responsible for our actions. But part of living on a fallen planet, even for the most fortunate among us, is having imperfect parents. Many of us carry a whole sackful of unhealthy behaviors and attitudes from our childhood homes into our adult lives.

The Bible offers many examples of how one generation sets up the next for unhealthy patterns of living. Even though King David repented of his adultery with Bathsheba, his broken sexual behavior cast a shadow across the generation that followed him. His son Amnon committed rape, and another son, Solomon, collected more than a thousand foreign wives and concubines, undermining his walk with God. Both sons were eventually brought down by their obsession with sex.

The patriarch Jacob's dark side—lying and deceit—had been modeled for him by his forefathers. When his grandfather Abraham first moved into the land of Gerar with his beautiful wife, Sarah, Abraham feared King Abimelech would kill him to take his wife. So he lied. He told Abimelech that Sarah was his sister and let Abimelech take her for his wife. God intervened with Abimelech in a dream before any harm was done, but the sad legacy remained—Abraham had lied and abandoned his wife to save his own skin.

One generation later, in a scenario worthy of *Ripley's Believe It or Not,* Abraham's son, Isaac, committed virtually the same transgression. Isaac brought his beautiful bride, Rebekah, home to Gerar. He too feared the men would kill him to get his wife. So he dusted off the same old lie his father had used and told King Abimelech and the men of Gerar that Rebekah was his sister.

Another generation later, Jacob, the Deceiver, was born and began following a well-worn lifescript. The sobering truth is, most of us swear that when we reach adulthood we won't emulate any of our parents' negative qualities—but the opposite usually happens.

Some men are uncomfortable identifying unhealthy patterns in their families. For some, this discomfort flows from a need to idealize their parents and grandparents. They fear that admitting imperfection either reflects negatively on themselves or dishonors their parents. After all, they say, their parents did the best they could. Other men express concern that this activity amounts to blaming others for their sin and excusing or justifying themselves.

But biblical repentance involves telling the truth about our weaknesses, which inevitably includes telling the truth about our past. In the Old Testament, when Ezra the priest led the children of Israel through a process of national repentance in connection with their return to Jerusalem from exile in Babylon, he had them confess not only their own sins but also "the iniquities of their fathers."[3]

This resembles Isaiah's repentant response following his overwhelming vision of God's holiness. "Woe is me, for I am ruined!" Isaiah cried. "Because I am a man of unclean lips, and I live among a people of unclean lips."[4] We simply can't talk in meaningful ways about our own behavior without honestly acknowledging the societal and familial context in which we learned that behavior. Many of the habits and attitudes that give us the most trouble have several generations of momentum and modeling behind them. Facing our history honestly helps us see clearly the scope of the problem we must address in our own lives.

When God commanded us to honor our parents, he was not telling us to lie about them, nor to pretend they had no faults. Honoring our parents involves representing them fairly, presenting a balanced picture that includes both good and bad traits. On the other hand, we dishonor our parents when we slander them or talk about them maliciously. If we feel bitter toward them, it's easy to talk in ways that dishonor. But if we have forgiven them and made our peace with who they are, we can tell the truth without dishonoring them.

After one of our seminars, a man told me, "I have Jesus now, and he's changing all these areas in my life. I don't have to dig around in the past to be changed. Jesus is in there working on me whether I'm in touch with all those issues or not."

To an extent I agree; the Holy Spirit's transforming work within us is indeed beyond our ability to understand or manage. But God has established a process for change, and that process involves repentance. Repentance begins by seeing our sin clearly, then taking responsibility for it. In his New Testament epistle, James uses the imagery of a mirror to explain how we avoid character change. "For if any one is a hearer of the word and not a doer, he is like a man who looks at his natural face in a mirror; for once he has looked at himself and gone away, he has immediately forgotten what kind of person he was."[5]

Our parents can often act as such a mirror for us. I struggle with impatience and anger. Both my parents struggle with the same qualities. Somehow seeing those patterns acted out in them provides one more way for me to break my denial and see myself clearly. That's invaluable help as

I continue to work toward being conformed to the image of Christ.

Lifescripts: The Three *R*s

The lifescript we carry into adulthood is based on the three Rs of our early family environment: rules, roles, and recordings.

Rules

All homes have rules. Some are healthy and appropriate; some are not. Examples of unhealthy rules are:

Don't talk about anything that upsets the parents or about opinions your parents disagree with.
Don't think for yourself or form your own convictions. The adults will tell you what to believe.
Don't feel any "bad" emotions such as anger or sadness or disappointment (or if you do feel them, keep them to yourself).

Other unhealthy family rules include: Be perfect; don't make mistakes; don't think about yourself; never embarrass the family; don't reveal family secrets; live your life according to "What will others think?"; be loyal to the family system and its rules, even in adulthood.

Roles

In some shame-based families, members are influenced to play certain roles. Some roles serve to meet the parents' needs; others cover the family's secrets or the sense of family shame—of not being good enough.

Here are three common roles, along with the tasks that usually go with the role in childhood and the adult behavior that results. See if you can find yourself in any of these.

Role	Tasks assigned in childhood	Adult behaviors
Hero	Achieve success at school. Uphold family name. Cover family shame. Provide vicarious experience of success for parents.	Overachieving Perfectionism Drivenness Difficulty with honesty, vulnerability, and intimacy Sense of hollowness Lack of authenticity Fear of being known
Rebel (Scapegoat)	Take focus away from other family members' unhealthy behaviors by getting into trouble.	Underfunctioning Irresponsibility Passiveness Difficulty with commitment and perseverance in work and relationships Addictions
Caretaker (Little Parent)	Take care of family. Be super-responsible, self-sacrificing, serious, hard-working. Cover for absence or passivity of one of the parents.	Overfunctioning Over-responsibility for others Rules orientation Workaholism Controlling behaviors Difficulty with relaxing Frequent exhaustion Secret resentment of serving others

Other possible roles include Mascot (gets by in life by being cute and charming), Surrogate Spouse (sides with Mom against Dad, takes care of Mom's emotional needs), Saint (a Hero whose arena is religion and spirituality), Mediator-Peacemaker, Dad's Buddy. Some children play a combination of two or more roles.

Recordings

In addition to the rules we learned and the roles we play, we may have shame-based parental messages recorded in our minds. As one friend told me recently, "When I make a mistake, I immediately hear either my mother's voice saying, 'You should be ashamed of yourself!' or my father's voice saying, 'You'll never amount to anything.'"

Men raised to be Heroes may hear messages like "You can do anything you set your mind to," which equates to "There's no excuse for being less than number one." Some common shame messages given to boys in childhood:

You'll never learn.
Who do you think you are?
Just look what you're doing to your mother!
Stop acting like a baby.
I'll give you something to cry about!
You're good for nothing.
Why didn't you get all As? I know you can do better!
You're just like (some despised relative).
Why can't you be more like (your sibling)?
You're so stupid.
You're just a little sissy.

If, in addition, you experienced physical or sexual abuse growing up, you received additional destructive messages about your self-worth. If this is true for you, I strongly encourage you to work on these issues with the help of a trained therapist.

Steps to Healthiness

1. Rewrite the Rules

The unhealthy family rules we learned in childhood demand allegiance long after we've grown up. Craig, my artist friend, wrestled with a fear of failure that was a legacy from his father and grandfather. The fear eventually became so paralyzing that he realized he was emotionally unavailable to his family. So he began to work with a therapist to untie these generational knots.

Over several months, he and his therapist identified seven patterns from his childhood family that he had unconsciously retained as an adult. All were negatively affecting his attitudes and relationships. Determined to break free, Craig took a courageous step; he wrote a Personal Declaration of Disloyalty to the toxic patterns from his past.

In part, Craig's declaration stated, "I am about the process of identifying and then intentionally declaring war on loyalties to family patterns, expectations, and actions that are unhealthy and binding. Believing that Jesus Christ came to set the captives free, I state the following . . ." Craig then listed and described the unhealthy attitudes he carried from childhood into adulthood: fear, worry, shame, isolation, selfishness, restraint, and powerlessness.

I recently asked Craig what specific steps he was taking to change in these areas.

"Money has always been linked to fear in my mind," Craig replied, "and that fear originated in my childhood family. So my therapist and I talked about it, and I decided to bring my mother into the counseling session with me. [Craig's father is deceased.] My counselor felt it's one thing to say your new insights in a private counseling session, but it's another to say it to family members. For me it was a kind of rite of passage—dragging my new philosophy into the light.

"It went really well," Craig continued. "I discussed with my mother the fear base of my life, especially my fear about money, and my decision to unhook from the old system. I was very nonconfrontive. My parents set me up for this, but I'm the one perpetuating it.

"Rewriting lifescripts demands disloyalty to the unhealthy family rules," Craig explained. "If we were taught to always be loyal, any threat of disloyalty will feel like a threat to the core of your being. That's why my body went ballistic when I had the business breakthroughs. But the core is exactly what needs to be changed."

As a first step in this process, many men find it helpful to talk honestly about their childhoods with their wives, mentors, or friends. Other men have found it helpful to journal about these issues, listing the traits—both positive and negative—they feel they share with their parents.[6]

It's tough work rewriting the old rules, and we can expect a period of turmoil and even opposition, possibly—as with Craig—from within ourselves. But the payoff is knowing that we're being "transformed by the renewing of [our] minds"[7] instead of remaining bound by generations of fear.

2. Rescript the Roles

Playing a role helps us cover our shame by pretending we're either more or less than human. But the truth is, we are neither supermen, nor are we worthless bums. We are much loved, highly valued, but fallible children of God. In Romans 12:3 the apostle Paul exhorts, "I say to every man among you not to think more highly of himself than he ought to think; but to think so as to have sound judgment, as God has allotted to each a measure of faith."

Paul tells us not to think too highly of ourselves, as the Hero does. But he also tells us not to swing the pendulum to the other extreme, but rather to have sound judgment about who we are. We are valuable, as evidenced by God's granting to each of us a measure of faith and our own set of spiritual gifts, as itemized by Paul in verses 4–8.

Neither the grandiose Hero role nor the self-deprecating Scapegoat role is God's desire for us. Sound judgment

43

calls us to give up our false roles on either end of the spectrum and to accept our redeemed humanity in the middle.

THE HERO: ADDICTED TO RECOGNITION

The Hero has become addicted to achievement, recognition, and praise, given in exchange for superhuman accomplishment. To give up the Hero role means a decision to live without the regular fix of public praise. It means giving up the grandiosity that comes with believing you have no limits.

Not all the qualities cultivated by the Hero are bad, however. Heroes generally are long on courage and are undaunted by big challenges. These qualities are open to abuse, but they can also be used to good advantage by a recovering Hero when he changes his focus from conquering external mountains to climbing the mountains within himself toward Christlike virtue.

The apostle Paul exemplifies the driven, high-achieving Hero (he described himself as "a Pharisee of the Pharisees") who eventually surrendered his false role to become a "bond-servant of Christ Jesus."[8]

Not long ago I called on a pastor in his office. As I waited in the outer office, the young secretary began to talk about the pastor in glowing terms—his preaching, his selflessness, his loving nature. "He's absolutely the most wonderful pastor in the entire world!" she gushed.

A red light went on inside me as I heard her go on and on. I don't know what this pastor is made of, but few men can handle such 100-proof praise in a healthy way—especially men in leadership positions. It's seductive and addictive and perpetuates the kind of hero image that ultimately becomes a prison for the man receiving the idolization. It's fine to receive affirmation, but adulation and hero worship create a dangerous atmosphere. I've experienced it.

During a recent move I came across a number of mementoes, trophies, and plaques that were gifts from previous coworkers when I was still cultivating a hero image. To my embarrassment I saw that several were inscribed with superlatives: "To the World's Best . . . ," "To the Greatest. . . ." I had actively cultivated unhealthy levels of praise from those I worked with to pump up my own self-esteem.

If you've been a practicing Hero, but you're ready to turn in your Masters of the Universe costume, you'll need to take deliberate steps to turn that image around. The most important step is to take yourself off the pedestal as often as anyone tries to put you on it. Once again our recovering Hero, the apostle Paul, gives us a dramatic example.

Toward the end of Paul's first missionary journey, in the dusty highlands of Asia Minor, he and Barnabas healed a lame man in the city of Lystra. What happened next is a case study for recovering Heroes. "And when the multitudes saw what Paul had done, they raised their voice, saying in the Lycaonian language, 'The gods have become like men and have come down to us.' And they began calling Barnabas, Zeus, and Paul, Hermes, because he was the chief speaker."[9]

The apostles' immediate response was to step down from the pedestal before the people. "When the apostles, Barnabas and Paul, heard of it, they tore their robes and rushed out into the crowd crying out and saying, 'Men, why are you doing these things? We are also men of the same nature as you, and preach the gospel to you in order that you should turn from these vain things to a living God.'"[10]

What a great metaphor for how to live a transparent life! Paul and Barnabas literally *ripped their garments* to show these men who tried to worship them that "we are also men of the same nature as you." That's exactly what it takes to dismantle the unhealthy Hero role. We must rip our garments, figuratively speaking, and let people see our humanity. Let them know we are not in a special category above them. We make mistakes and we fail. We are subject to the same temptations. We can't be their heroes, but we can be their brothers, walking with them through the challenges of life.

THE REBEL: THE DELIBERATE UNDERACHIEVER

The Rebel, or Scapegoat, works hard to lower everyone's expectations of his performance. With twisted logic, the Rebel believes his substandard behavior will take the pressure off him and allow him to be irresponsible. ("Hey, I'm only doing what everyone expects.")

Giving up the Rebel role means turning in all our excuses about underfunctioning and stepping back onto the playing field with the rest of the human race.

The Rebel, too, has qualities worth redeeming. He has an ability to identify and understand society's outcasts, people in trouble, and the common man. Matthew, the despised tax collector, is a biblical example of a Scapegoat who was invited by Jesus to give up his old identity, his old role, and take a responsible place in the inner circle of disciples.

Recently a friend from my men's group told me he's been making excuses all his married life. "I don't know how to love," he'd told his wife, "because there was no love in my home when I was growing up." But on several occasions lately his wife has told him how much she has appreciated his loving actions. That realization encouraged him, but he also found it disturbing. He can no longer use his well-worn excuse! Now, in a sense, the pressure is on.

That's a normal response for any of us who have been deliberately underfunctioning. As we step back onto the playing field, as husbands, fathers, or in some other role, we need to remember the promise of Philippians 2:13, "For it is God who is at work in you, both to will and to work for His good pleasure." All we can do is turn in our Rebel role as a deliberate step of obedience and ask God to begin building a new sense of responsibility in us.

THE CARETAKER: THE VELVET-COVERED CATTLE PROD

The Caretaker lives for the appreciation of those he is helping and rescuing. Focusing too much on others and their neediness becomes a good way to avoid focusing on his own neediness. For all his talk about loving and caring for others, the Caretaker actually becomes quickly resentful and bitter when he fails to receive the appreciation he believes he deserves for his altruism.

Caretakers automatically organize their environment and everyone in it. They believe they know what's best for others and on that basis justify their intrusion into others' affairs. In that sense, Caretakers are really just Controllers with a velvet covering, looking for ways to manage others' lives in the name of helping them.

Healthiness begins for the Caretaker when he stops taking responsibility for everyone else and begins to accept responsibility for his own issues. His qualities of dedication and discipline can serve him well as he and the Lord work on his new project—himself.

In Luke 10:38–42 Jesus confronts a classic Caretaker in the person of Martha, the sister of Mary and Lazarus. In just three verses he paints a clear picture of the highly efficient, overworked, and resentful Caretaker. Jesus gently rebukes her for her worry and her uptightness ("you are worried and bothered about so many things") and encourages her to let go of her role and join Mary in a simpler, less frantic focus on relationships.

3. Reprogram Your Recordings

For several months I worked with a young man named Jerry in our Mentor Leadership Training course. I grew to appreciate Jerry's deep insights, as well as his honesty and openness. He was bright and gifted but struggled with low self-esteem. As we worked through the lifescript material,

47

Jerry quickly identified three shaming messages he had received growing up.

The first involved an incident at school when he was twelve. Mathematics came hard for Jerry, and although he'd studied long hours for one particular math test, he did poorly. The next day, the teacher passed out the graded exams. He held up Jerry's test and with scorn in his voice called Jerry stupid in front of his classmates. Jerry has never forgotten the feeling of shame.

The second incident happened while working a summer job when he was fourteen. He made a simple mistake, and his boss labeled him stupid. He worked hard on that job and performed well overall. But that one shaming comment remains, years later, burned into his memory.

But the most shaming messages of all came from his father. One typical incident happened when he was ten. While playing outside one day, Jerry fell and skinned his knee. The scrape hurt, and he cried. When his father saw his tears, he mocked him, calling him a sissy and a crybaby. Twenty years later, those words still sting.

In response to these and similar shaming messages, Jerry adopted the Rebel role. He decided to deliberately become irresponsible so people would expect less from him. That, he felt, was the best way to avoid future criticism. He also distanced himself emotionally from his parents and siblings. He lacked self-confidence and feared letting anyone *really* know him. And his feelings accompanied him into adulthood; he feared intimacy, even with his wife, and his friendships with men were superficial.

Over the months of our mentoring relationship, Jerry began to confront the old shame messages echoing in his head. And he started the hard work needed to reprogram them. When he made a mistake and the critical chorus inside him yelled, "You're so stupid! You don't ever get anything right!" he silenced the old voices and forced them out of his mind. In their place he developed a new, positive response. "I have certain giftings and strengths," he'd remind himself. "I'm a good worker, and I'm kindhearted. I may not have the highest IQ in the world, but I am not unintelligent, and I won't accept the label 'stupid.'" I wanted to stand up and cheer when I heard that.

Jerry also confronted the echoes of the emasculating taunts from his father. His response was simple but powerful: "As for the 'sissy' label—I am sensitive by nature, but more often than not, that's a strength, not a sign of weakness."

Proverbs 23:7 says, "As he thinks within himself, so he is." Sorting through the old, distorted messages that play in our minds and steal our joy ranks among the most liberating acts of spiritual obedience we can perform. When we discard the old messages and plug in the truth, we sense new freedom and experience fresh growth. Many of our current behaviors—our reactions, defensiveness, depression—have little to do with our immediate circumstances and everything to do with old voices we have allowed to resonate in our minds for decades.

Try these simple exercises this week to still the critical chorus inside you.

1. Monitor your thoughts and your self-talk. When you make a mistake or are criticized, notice what message plays in your head.
2. As often as the negative, critical voices intrude, take those thoughts captive in the spirit of 2 Corinthians 10:5 and forcibly shove them out of your mind. Replace them with statements like those above that reflect God's view of you as a much-loved but fallible child of God.[11]
3. Meditate on Scriptures that reflect God's gracious attitude toward you. See Scriptures for Meditation at the end of this chapter.

4. Jesus commanded, "Love your neighbor as your-self."[12] It is appropriate and healthy for us to love and appreciate those qualities God has produced in our lives. (This is not the same as the self-centered narcissism condemned in the Bible.) To nurture healthy self-appreciation, list in the space below, or in your journal, the five honors, affirmations, or com-pliments you have received in your life that have been the most meaningful to you. (For some, childhood training makes it difficult to receive a compliment. If this is true for you, make a special effort to open yourself to the affirmations you record, letting your-self take in and enjoy the positive feelings.)
5. Finally, other people can speed our healing from toxic shame. Continue to ask God to lead you into rela-tionships with other men who will give grace and encouragement as you seek to rewrite your lifescript.

Scriptures for Meditation:

The Truth about You

There is therefore now no condemnation for those who are in Christ Jesus.

Romans 8:1

For you have not received a spirit of slavery leading to fear again, but you have received a spirit of adoption as sons by which we cry out, "Abba! Father!"

Romans 8:15

If God is for us, who is against us?
Romans 8:31

For as high as the heavens are above the earth,
So great is His lovingkindness toward those who fear Him.

As far as the east is from the west,
So far has He removed our transgressions from us.
Just as a father has compassion on his children,
So the Lord has compassion on those who fear Him.
For He Himself knows our frame;
He is mindful that we are but dust.

Psalm 103:11–14

Can a mother forget her little child and not have love for her own son? Yet even if that should be, I will not forget you. See—I have tattooed your name upon my palm.

Isaiah 49:15–16 LB

The LORD your God is with you,
he is mighty to save.
He will take great delight in you,
he will quiet you with his love,
he will rejoice over you with singing.

Zephaniah 3:17 NIV

Come to Me, all who are weary and heavy-laden, and I will give you rest. Take My yoke upon you, and learn from Me, for I am gentle and humble in heart; and you shall find rest for your souls.

Matthew 11:28–29

The Elusive Father Blessing

Manhood without Models

When you coming home, Dad, I don't know when. But
we'll get together then; You know we'll have a good time
then.

Harry Chapin, "Cat's in the Cradle"

A father to the fatherless . . . is God in his holy dwelling.

Psalm 68:5 NIV

For Kevin, the desperate desire to connect with his father is like a dull ache that never quite goes away. Kevin's dad has been a classic workaholic all his life, laboring long hours as a mechanic in the garage underneath the family's apartment. Kevin remembers times when he and his brother would go downstairs just to be close to their father, only to be chased out of the garage with a stick. "Get out of here and stop bothering me!" his father would yell. When Kevin went to bed at night, his father was still working. He rarely saw him.

Kevin grew up with a hole in his heart where his father's love was meant to be. Thirty years later he still longs for his father's approval. He's confused about what it means to be a man. That in turn is causing problems in his marriage.

Unfortunately Kevin's not alone.

In *Fatherless America* sociologist David Blankenhorn demonstrates that the "Missing Father Syndrome" is getting worse. "Tonight, about 40% of American children will go to sleep in homes in which their fathers do not live. Before they reach the age of 18, more than one-half of our nation's children are likely to spend at least a significant portion of their childhoods living apart from their fathers. Never before in this country have so many children . . . grown up without knowing what it means to have a father."[1]

These underfathered men inevitably drag a wounded masculinity into their relationships with their wives and with all other women.

Perhaps more than anything else, sons need a sense of approval from their fathers. It is God's plan that a son receive the "Father Blessing" from his father as part of his transition to manhood. The Father Blessing was a deeply respected tradition in Old Testament times. Patriarchs like Abraham, Isaac, and Jacob conferred their blessing—their sign of approval on their sons—as a rite of passage into adulthood.

The Father Blessing was also modeled for us by God the Father in Matthew 3 at Jesus' baptism—his rite of passage into adult life and ministry. "After his baptism, as soon as Jesus came up out of the water, the heavens were opened to him and he saw the Spirit of God coming down in the form of a dove. And a voice from heaven said, 'This is my beloved Son, in whom I am well-pleased.'"[2]

That succinct benediction captures the heart of what all sons need from their fathers. They need two things: a sense that they are beloved and that their fathers are well-pleased with who they are as men. The model for the Father Blessing given in Matthew 3 is all the more striking in that the Father gave his blessing before Jesus had even begun his ministry, before he "proved" himself or "accomplished" anything. When given in this kind of healthy, unconditional spirit, the Father Blessing affirms the son's unique personhood, rather than requiring him to be made over in his father's image before the blessing can be given.

In addition to validating the son's personhood, the Father Blessing plays a crucial role in affirming the son's masculinity. There is a core of truth to the saying "A boy is not a man until his father says he is." When a father fails to affirm his masculinity, the son will most often try to get that validation in unhealthy ways from women. But no woman will be able to fill the father-shaped void inside a man.

Like many men, I grew up feeling I'd never received my father's blessing. Dad has always been a "man's man" in the old-fashioned sense. Three months before his fifteenth birthday, he dropped out of school and ran away from home to escape his abusive taskmaster of a father. He never went back. A physically powerful man, he worked with his hands all his life as a cowboy, truck driver, and rancher. Now eighty-six, Dad has spent the last forty years turning sagebrush and desert into fertile farmland in a corner of the vast Columbia River Basin in eastern Washington state.

I grew up on that farm, spending summers herding sheep by horseback and wrestling hay bales onto a sled behind the hot exhaust of a tractor. We were literally on the frontier, and I revelled in the wild freedom and limitless horizons of the plains around our farm.

And yet, as much as I enjoyed growing up on the farm, I knew I wasn't cut out to be a farmer. I didn't have my father's innate sense of the natural rhythms of the land nor his fierce protective streak toward animals, whose needs always took priority over the needs of humans.

In fact, the high point of each week for me (aside from sitting by the pastor's daughter at church on Sunday) was the sound of the horn of the big white and blue bookmobile that served our rural area. Every week I'd run down our dusty drive to the waiting van and return with my arms laden with books. Those books opened up fascinating new worlds to me, worlds far beyond the horizons of our quiet farm community.

Dad was horrified. By his lights, a real man doesn't become involved in the world of books, the intellectual world; he becomes involved in the physical world. Manhood is proven by raw strength and by prowess with man-tools: wrenches and fishing rods and rifles. When it became apparent I would not be taking over the family farm, Dad was deeply disappointed. As I slid into adolescence, our relationship was increasingly characterized by conflict. At some point during those years, a wall of hurt and disapproval went up between us that lasted for more than thirty years.

Despite that wall, I desperately wanted my father's approval, especially his approval of my manhood. I turned out for track in high school, pushing my skinny body to letter all four years, because track was the sport Dad had turned out for thirty-five years earlier. I wanted what adolescent boys have wanted for thousands of years: an opportunity to prove myself as a man, to hear from my father, "Well done. I'm proud of you, Son," and to receive admission into full fellowship with the other warriors of the tribe. But for whatever reasons, Dad's blessing always seemed to elude me.

Like so many men of my generation, I carried that father wound with me into my adult relationships. In retrospect, I see that I have operated out of an insecure masculinity for most of my adult life, gravitating toward emotionally needy women and "rescuing" them, trying to substitute cheap strokes for the Father Blessing I really desired.

But no amount of female attention can fix a man's wounded masculinity. Many men confuse the temporary anesthetic of female attention for true healing. But the anesthetic always wears off, and the need inevitably returns. True healing is work that can only be done between a man and his heavenly Father.

Harmful Fathering Styles

The first step in that healing work begins as we identify the kind of father wound we have experienced. There are at least three fathering styles that leave wounds: the Abusive Father, the Absent Father, and the Critical or Controlling Father.

Abusive Father

During one of our Manhood seminars some months ago, I showed a video clip to a roomful of men. The clip dramatically portrayed a verbally abusive father bullying and taunting his young son in front of the family at dinner. The moment the lights came up, a mountain of a man near the front jumped to his feet and literally ran from the room.

I hesitated a moment, unsure whether to go on with the presentation or to see if he needed help. Almost immediately, however, the retching sounds of someone being violently ill carried clearly into the room. Several men rushed out to see if they could help, and after a few moments I went on with the presentation.

At the next break, shaken and white, the big man came back in. I took the chair next to him and asked him what happened. The man, whose name was Rudy, explained that he'd grown up with a violently abusive stepfather. Between the ages of two and twelve, Rudy was frequently beaten by this man.

"When you showed the movie clip, I suddenly had this flashback. I felt like I was twelve years old again, and I was about to get beaten by my stepdad. Then I began to feel sick, and I knew I had to get out of here."

"Would you rather not talk about it, Rudy?" I asked.

"No, I need to talk about it," he said, gulping. "That one particular scene has terrorized me for twenty years."

I nodded and waited.

"It was when I was twelve," Rudy went on. "Some piddly little thing I'd done had made my stepdad mad; I don't even remember what it was now. But all of a sudden he cocked his fist back to slug me full force in the face. Right when he threw the punch, I ducked." Rudy squeezed his eyes shut for a moment, his lower lip trembling.

"What I didn't realize," he went on, "was that my mom was standing right behind me. When I ducked, my stepdad hit her full in the mouth. He knocked out all her front teeth." Rudy was quietly sobbing now, drawing in great gulps of air.

I didn't know what to say. Rudy's pain seemed to fill the room. I put my hand on his shoulder, and we both sat in silence for several long minutes. Finally I managed, "That must be incredibly painful. I bet you've felt guilty all these years for what happened to your mother, even though it obviously wasn't your fault."

Rudy nodded miserably.

"But surely your mother understood it wasn't your fault. Didn't she let you know that she didn't blame you?"

"Not really," he said, looking at the floor. "She just said, 'I don't know why you have to make him so mad.'"

Using a son for a punching bag leaves scars for life. Rudy was living with the replay of that scene and others like it as if they happened only yesterday. It's with good reason that the Book of Ephesians warns, "And, fathers, do not provoke your children to anger."[3] Or as the New English Bible translates that passage, "Fathers, you must not goad your children to resentment." Abuse is inexcusable.

Absent Father

The second kind of father wound comes from the father who simply isn't there. There are many reasons a father may be absent today: Death, divorce, illness, and work all can take a dad away during the critical years when a son is trying to put together what it means to be a man. Or a father may be physically present but not emotionally available to his son. The latter was true for Kevin, whom we met earlier in this chapter.

Kevin and I worked in a mentoring relationship for several months. We spent quite a bit of that time working on issues related to authentic manhood and the father wound. Kevin doesn't remember experiencing any affection or emotional nurturing from his dad. His mother told Kevin that when he and his little brother were babies, Kevin's father refused to even hold them. He would hold their baby sister, but not the two little boys. Evidently his father's behavior was rooted in an almost paranoic homophobia.

Even though Kevin is grown now with four children of his own, the lack of affection and emotional nurturing from his father still grieves him. "I'd give anything to be hugged by Dad," Kevin told me. "Even now as an adult I've tried to hug Dad a couple of times. But he always pulls away. One time he said, 'Don't do that. If someone sees us, he'll think we're homosexuals.' I've actually bawled like a baby when I hear other men talk about being hugged by their dads."

Sons need emotional support from their fathers. And they need to know their fathers care enough about them to actually be involved with them.

But some men have experienced a father wound on the flip side of this issue. Not long ago I spoke at a men's retreat in the Seattle area. During one of the sessions a spirited interaction erupted as several men talked honestly about their absent fathers and the loss they felt. One man talked about playing on his high school football team for three straight years without his father coming to see him play even once. "Me, too," one man said. "Same for me," another added.

In the back of the room a man in his thirties raised his hand. "Not all of us see that issue the same way," he said, his eyes flashing anger. "My dad came to every one of the matches I wrestled in—and every practice, too. And I wish he hadn't!" The other men looked at him as if he were crazy.

The man went on bitterly, "My father was there because wrestling had been *his* pick for my life, not mine. I got all the attention any boy could ever want, but it was the wrong kind."

Some fathers, indeed, are not so much attentively involved in their sons' lives as they are intrusively involved. This is the Critical or Controlling Father style.

Controlling Father

I met Frank in the little Northwest logging town my wife and I moved to soon after our marriage. Frank had served as pastor of the community church for three years. He came to the church fresh from seminary and brimming with enthusiasm. I liked Frank, and we began meeting weekly for lunch, eventually developing a solid friendship. We'd only been meeting for a few weeks when Frank began to talk honestly about his sense of calling to the church.

"The first twelve months weren't so bad here," Frank said. "I guess it was the honeymoon period. But the last year and a half have been rough. I'm working fifteen- and sixteen-hour days. And I'm getting more and more criticism from church members. I don't know—I guess I'm starting to question my calling."

I asked Frank about his dreams, about the things that stir his passion for life. To my surprise, his eyes lit up and he immediately began talking about baseball. Ever since he played sandlot ball with a secondhand glove, playing major league baseball had been Frank's dream.

But the ministry had always been his father's dream. A successful church planter and senior pastor, Frank's dad had been careful to sound open and neutral when the two of them had discussed Frank's future.

"I want whatever's best for you, Son," his father had said, "whatever God wants for you." But it was always clear from

59

the stories his father told of the successful churches he had planted and the people he'd reached with the gospel that the ultimate calling anyone could aspire to was the ministry. And if there'd been any doubt in Frank's mind, it was forever dispelled by the slogan his father loved to repeat when he spoke to church youth groups. "Young people," his father would say, his face alight with fervor, "if God calls you to be a preacher, don't stoop to be a king!"

For Frank, it was a no-brainer. He loved and respected his dad a great deal. So when it came time to choose a career, he knew there was only one choice: He buried his dream to play major league ball and went to seminary.

But seven years later Frank realized he didn't love the ministry as his father did. Nor did Frank's family, who resented his long hours and low pay. Frank didn't want to disappoint his father, and he certainly didn't want to disappoint God. But he knew that if he didn't make some changes soon, he might be risking more than just his career.

That was four years ago. I still see Frank from time to time. He's still in the ministry, and his family is still with him. I don't presume to know what choice Frank should make; that's between him and God. But I do know that he continues to feel torn over this issue and that his father's approval means much to him.

It's relatively easy to identify the harm that comes from an Abusive or Absent Father. But how can we determine if the father wound we received was from a Controlling Father?

The standard for determining healthiness is, once again, the model of the Father Blessing given by God the Father in Matthew 3. Flowing out of that passage are three questions to ask yourself:

1. Did my father communicate to me that I was "beloved"?

2. Did he let me know that he was "well-pleased" with who I am?
3. Was the blessing unconditional?

If your father required you to live out his game plan for your life in order to secure his approval, the result is an increase in your shame core. The message we receive from a Controlling Father is that who we are is not good enough; we have to become someone else to be acceptable. Ultimately, in our pursuit of approval we'll develop a false self and suppress the natural gifts and calling God has put within us. Inevitably we'll find that the life we based on a false self fits us poorly.

There are obvious lessons in this for our own parenting styles as well. As fathers we can give a priceless gift to our sons and daughters if we affirm their uniqueness, rather than requiring them to be carbon copies of us. I've always thought it ironic that God gifted my son, David, with mechanical ability, an intuitive sense of how things work, while his dad has trouble operating a toaster. The Father Blessing requires us to throw away our molds for our children and to recognize and affirm the unique design their heavenly Father has crafted in them.

But there is a tougher question we must ask ourselves about this particular father wound. For every Controlling Father, there is a son who decides as an adult to perpetuate that unhealthy dynamic. If that's true—although it takes a great deal of honesty—we must ask ourselves what the payback is for us. We may be getting something out of being passive. Perhaps we're afraid to strike out on our own and be our own persons.

We may find, as Craig did in the previous chapter, that several generations of fear confine us to a narrow world that was never God's destiny for us.

61

Perhaps the cruelest abuse of all occurs whenever a father deliberately tries to emasculate his son—scorning and belittling his masculinity. The very area in which God intended a father to build up his son—his masculine self-esteem—is torn down by him instead. This father wound cripples a son with the message that he simply doesn't measure up as a man.

For this reason, most men experience the wound left by their father as a deeper and more painful wound than the wound left by their mother. This was graphically illustrated in a true story told by Richard Rohr. A friend of his, a nun, was working in a men's prison. One spring an inmate asked the nun to buy him a Mother's Day card to send home. She agreed. But word traveled fast in the prison; soon hundreds of inmates were asking for cards. So the nun contacted a greeting card manufacturer, who happily sent crates of Mother's Day cards to the prison. All of the cards were passed out.

Soon afterward the nun realized that Father's Day was approaching and, thinking ahead, once again called the card manufacturer, who responded quickly with crates of Father's Day cards. Years later, the nun told Rohr, she still had every one of them. Not one prisoner requested a card for his father.[4]

Steps to Healthiness

As deep and painful as our father wounds may be, the good news is that there is hope and healing for men. There are at least three important steps we can take.

1. Seek to Reconcile with Your Father

I've known for a long time that I need to do what I can to tear down the wall between my father and me. In the last couple of years I've made a few stumbling attempts to open up a more vulnerable level of communication between us. But each attempt seemed to sputter and die. We were both uncomfortable moving our relationship into unfamiliar territory. We'd developed a habit of superficial dialogue around activities. Talking about events relieved us of the need to wade into the scarier swamp of hidden feelings. But I still felt some hurt in the relationship, and in my more honest moments I didn't know if I was ready to release that hurt and move toward true reconciliation.

A few months ago a phone call changed all that. My mother called to say that Dad had just been told he needed emergency eye surgery, and the surgery would take place at a hospital near my home. He would be coming into town by bus in two days and would probably stay five days. It was to be an outpatient procedure, so he needed a place to stay. And he was coming alone. I insisted that he stay with us.

When I got off the phone, I knew without a doubt that God was engineering these circumstances to give Dad and me a chance to heal our relationship. I hadn't spent five days alone with Dad, without my mother present, since I was ten. And the timing was eerie. I was in the middle of writing this book; I had just finished working on the material about the father wound; and as part of that process I had told God that I was finally ready to move toward true reconciliation with my father.

Before Dad arrived I was filled with strong feelings. I was intrigued, wondering what God was going to do, but I was also scared. I was afraid of Dad's reaction, afraid of his anger, his rejection, or who knows what. Just little-boy scared. When I'm around Dad, I feel like I'm eight years old.

For the first several days, Dad and I were together almost constantly. I took him to all his appointments and waited with him before his surgery. He looked old and frail, and for the first time I'd ever seen—afraid. Just before he went into surgery, for the first time in his life he asked me to pray for him.

Half blind, unable to walk fifty yards without exhaustion, my father's aging had softened his hard edges and made him more approachable. Or maybe the softness was always there, and I didn't have eyes to see it. Whichever, I felt a rush of compassion and tenderness, even of protectiveness, toward my father in his weakened condition. It was a completely new experience for me, like walking on the surface of the moon. Dad had always been the strong one, and I the weak one.

The day before my father was to leave, I suggested we take a drive together. I knew this was probably my last chance to talk to him alone. We drove in silence for a while as I thought about what I wanted to say. Finally I took a deep breath, swallowed my fear, and said, "Dad, you know how all little boys want their dads to be proud of them?"

"Yeah," he said, looking startled.

"Well, I don't feel like I've ever gotten that from you. At least I don't know if I have." With the floodgate finally open, forty years of pent-up words tumbled out. "I've never felt like I was big enough or strong enough or mechanical enough to make you feel like I was a man, or that you were proud of who I am. And I didn't want to take over the farm, and I know that was a disappointment to you."

There. I'd finally done it. What I was afraid to do for all those years.

"Well," he said, shifting uneasily, "I never blamed you, as far as that goes. It was always your ma who was pushing you toward the books."

We drove in silence for a few moments.

"But," he went on, "you don't need to worry about me not being proud of you. I'm very proud of you."

"Really, Dad?"

"Yes," he said. "That doesn't mean there aren't things I wished had gone another way when you were growing up. But I've always been proud of you."

I digested that for a few moments, searching inside myself to see if I was getting what I needed out of the conversation. Finally I said, "It would be meaningful to me, Dad, if I could hear what you're proud of me for."

"Well," he said, "I'm proud of your education—how far you've taken it. I had to leave home after the tenth grade to get away from the Old Man." He paused. "And I'm proud of Marsha, and I'm proud of your two fine kids."

I savored that for a while and then said, "Thanks, Dad. I appreciate hearing that. And you know, it may be a little late, but now I'd be proud to have you teach me some of the things you're good at—like fishing."

"That'd be just fine and dandy," Dad said. He was quiet for a minute. "But . . . you're gonna have to be my whole strength, Son. I just don't have any left."

"I'd be proud to be, Dad," I replied. I felt touched and deeply happy. I'd found out that Dad does love me and is proud of me in his own way. But more than that, he asked me to be his strength—a vulnerable request that demonstrated a lot of trust. This from a man who's always been tough and independent.

Since that exchange I feel as though a locked door has been thrown open in my relationship with my father. He's been tender with me, his tone gentle, telling me he loved me when I saw him off at the bus station the next day, waving from the window as the bus pulled out. And for the first time that I can remember, I had tears in my eyes and a hollow feeling in my heart because he was leaving. It feels for all the world like I have my father back for the first time in thirty-five years.

Because there's a kind of affirmation for us as men that can only be given by our fathers, few things we do will bring greater satisfaction and peace of mind than to reconcile with an estranged father.

In a prophetic passage in the Old Testament book of Malachi, we see the importance God places on healing the father-son wound. There God proclaims, "Behold, I am going to send you Elijah the prophet before the coming of the great and terrible day of the LORD. And he will restore the hearts of the fathers to their children, and the hearts of the children to their fathers, lest I come and smite the land with a curse."[5]

Where there are restored relationships between fathers and sons, there is blessing; where there are broken relationships, there is a curse.

The apostle Peter in his first epistle echoes a similar theme of blessing. Peter encourages us to humble ourselves and seek reconciliation in any relationship in which we have been wronged. "Let all be harmonious . . . ," he says, "not returning evil for evil, or insult for insult, but giving a blessing instead." The result of such a reconciliation, Peter promises, is that we "inherit a blessing."[6]

How do we effect reconciliation? I suggest thoughtfully working through exercises 1 and 2.

We need to look not only at the possible negatives in the father-son relationship but also at the positives. After work-

---

Exercise 1

The first step in any movement toward reconciliation is to understand the nature of the wound itself. It might be helpful for you to journal your answers to the following questions. Or you might want to talk out your feelings with a trusted friend or support person.

- Was your father absent, physically or emotionally, while you were growing up?
- Was he highly critical or controlling? (Be specific.)
- Was he abusive, verbally or physically? In what ways?
- In your opinion, what effect did your relationship with your father have on your masculine self-image?

Exercise 2

Below are validating messages men say they have received from their fathers or have wanted to hear from their fathers. Check yes or no beside each one to indicate whether your father said these words to you.

yes *no*

☐ ☐ I'm proud of you.

☐ ☐ I think you've grown into a fine man.

☐ ☐ I forgive you.

☐ ☐ Please forgive me.

☐ ☐ I love you.

☐ ☐ You've been a good son to me.

☐ ☐ Thanks, Son.

Others (write them in)

☐ ☐ _____

☐ ☐ _____

☐ ☐ _____

---

ing through exercise 1, spend a few moments reflecting on exercise 2 suggested by Dr. Ken Druck.[7]

If you mark "no" more than "yes," consider talking to your father about it. You could begin by saying something like, "Dad, I've been thinking a lot lately about our relationship. It would mean a lot to me if we could talk about it."

Druck advises: "Remember—do not accuse, blame, judge, criticize, or attack him. You do not want a confrontation. But, on the other hand, do not beat around the bush with him. Go straight to the point."

During your conversation, tell your dad about the list of validating messages from the previous exercise. Consider asking him how he would have liked to have been validated by his own father.

Before you end the conversation, ask your dad to tell you the positive qualities he sees in you, as a father to his son, so you can know how he feels about you. Listen attentively without interrupting. Pray beforehand that God will make this a healing exchange.

Record your father's answers in your journal. Remember that the most you can expect from this exchange is whatever your father can authentically give you, even if that is less than you would want.

If you are unable to effect a direct reconciliation with your father, either because he is no longer living, or is living at some distance from you, consider writing him a letter in which you honestly address your feelings about the kind of relationship the two of you had or have. Talk about the impact—both positive and negative—his fathering style had on your adult life and behavior, or about the affirming statements you would most like to hear from him (as identified in exercise 2 on the previous page).

Again, this exercise is not about blaming someone else for our wrong choices or sinful behavior. It is about finally being able to tell the truth. And the truth is, every human father has fallen short in some way. Only God the Father has all the qualities we need in a father. But dragging our feelings out into the light helps them lose their toxic power and can be the first step toward experiencing authentic forgiveness toward our fathers.

Hebrews chapter twelve encourages us to "pursue peace with all men." If we don't, the writer says, we run the danger of a "root of bitterness" springing up inside us that "causes trouble" and "defiles many." When we carry bitterness and resentment inside us, it spreads toxin through all our other relationships.

But even if your father is no longer living, it is important for you to do what work you can on the father wound. I recently spoke to a men's group in a local church. After the presentation a man in his twenties introduced himself.

"I was at the men's retreat where you spoke last month," he said. "I especially appreciated what you said about the father wound. I lost my dad when I was fourteen, and I'd never stopped to probe the extent of that loss, or to think through how to make up for that loss in other ways. I'm now working through all that with the help of my men's group."

Other men have found they are able to bring closure to painful father memories by visiting the areas where they grew up. Author and therapist Daryl Quick tells the story of one man's pilgrimage to healing: "One of my clients had been abused numerous times by his alcoholic father at the restaurant his father had owned. His father was dead now, but every time this man drove by that restaurant he felt the old fear and rage.

"One day he drove 300 miles to visit that restaurant in order to put to rest the old ghosts. He told me later, 'After I came out of the restaurant, I felt a door to my past finally close inside me.'"[8]

What each man does to bring healing to his father wound will differ. What is important is that we summon the courage to face our old demons and attempt to make peace with our past.

2. Make Deeper Friendships with Other Men

We tend not to establish deep friendships with men, partially out of homophobia and partially because we've been trained to view other men as enemies and competitors. We're most comfortable with a superficial, semi-rowdy kind of relationship with other men formed around activities.

But as Proverbs 27:17 says, men sharpen each other when they're together, "as iron sharpens iron." Other mature men

69

who have healthy self-esteem can provide a model for us as we seek to rebuild our own masculine self-image.

In the wilderness period in my life following my divorce, an old college friend got in touch. Roy and I had been fraternity buddies in college, and God had used our friendship to help draw Roy to the Lord. He had gone on to seminary, and then to a successful career as a publisher and book editor. But we had not kept in close touch for most of the twenty years since then.

So I was surprised and delighted to receive a note from him. Roy said he'd heard about the divorce and expressed his concern about me. He graciously offered to be a good listener if I needed to talk about what I was feeling and going through.

I remember writing back with a mixture of gratitude and fear. "I really want and need a friend right now," I replied, "but I have a lot of fear even in writing back to you because I've never shared deep feelings with another man before. I've only shared deeply with women."

In the years since then, God has enriched my life with several deep friendships with other men, including the five men I meet with regularly in my men's group. The six of us have laughed together, cried together, shared our defeats with each other, and celebrated one another's successes. I'm sorry I had to wait until midlife to discover the extraordinary blessing of man-to-man friendship. But I'm grateful to have found it when I did. I now count it as an absolutely essential resource in my life.

Most men, unfortunately, are squarely where I was when I first responded to my friend's letter—no deep male friendships and afraid to develop any. In the Men's Confidential Survey taken in our Manhood Without Models seminars, we ask, "How many men in your life right now would you consider to be close friends or confidants (i.e., men who know you extremely well—your secrets, your weaknesses, your fears, your dreams)?"

More than a third of the men indicate they have no one playing that role in their lives. And of the remainder who say they do have close male friends, a large percentage identify men from their past—from college days or the military—or they mention men who live on the other side of the country. Less than 25 percent of the Christian men I've surveyed have a close male friend actively involved in their lives right now. And for pastors the percentage is even smaller—less than 5 percent.

I met Frank after speaking at a conference in California three years ago. When we first talked, Frank was just getting in touch with his father wound and its impact on his adult life and relationships. Frank's father had always been cold and distant, and Frank had compensated by establishing a close, overly dependent relationship with his mother. One of the results was that ever since he was a teenager Frank had struggled with homosexual feelings.

Now married with a family of his own, Frank was frustrated on several fronts. He found himself confused and insecure about his own masculinity. His relationship with his wife had become suffocating, just as his relationship with his mother had been. And he had no close male friends.

I'm not a trained therapist, and I encouraged Frank to seek help from a professional. But we talked for some hours and agreed to keep in touch.

Several months later I received a wonderful phone call from Frank. He had decided to take responsibility for pursuing healing on several fronts. He had been working with a counselor and had seen a lot of progress. He had also decided to deepen his relationships with several men in his church. He had gotten together with different ones for coffee, organized a couple of fishing trips, and gone on several motorcycle outings. The result was deeper sharing and several solid friendships.

"The more time I spend with these men," Frank told me, "the healthier I feel about myself and my masculinity. For a long time I didn't have any conception of what it meant to be a man. That's no longer a mystery to me. And it feels good for the first time in my adult life to have other close friends besides my wife."

One of the greatest benefits of developing close male friendships is an increase in spiritual and emotional healthiness. James 5:16 says healing happens as we confess our sins to one another and pray for one another. As they say in recovery circles, we're only as sick as our secrets, and finding another man or group of men with whom to share our deepest struggles is both freeing and life-giving.

But we should be selective in our self-disclosure. Not everyone is a safe or appropriate person to share our deepest secrets with. A healthy person generally develops relationships over the entire relational spectrum from superficial to intimate. The diagram below captures that relational spectrum. In reality, each of us has a public, a personal, and a private self.

Public (acquaintances)	Personal (friends)	Private (confidants)	SECRET

Your acquaintances only see your public self. They know what you look like (at your best), perhaps where you work or go to church, your wife's name, and so on. Your friends know your personal self: whether you golf or fish, what you're good at, some of your most glaring character weaknesses, how you get along with your wife in social situations.

Your confidants, on the other hand, know you *very* well. They know your private self: your secrets (including your most shameful ones), the issues and behaviors you currently struggle with most, what your relationship with your wife is *really* like, as well as your innermost dreams and fears. If there are areas or behaviors in your life that not even your confidant knows about, then there is a compartment in your life marked secret.

Exercise 3

List the names of the ten to twenty people who know you best, under the category below that reflects how well they know you.

Public (acquaintances)	Personal (friends)	Private (confidants)

If you are journaling, reflect on exercise 3 and jot down your insights. What does the exercise reveal about the overall relational balance in your life? How do you feel about the number of confidants in your life? Do you have any other man who knows *everything* going on in your life right now? Did you list your wife as a confidant?

Deep friendship—being known completely and still loved and accepted—is not possible without sharing our innermost selves with another person. But relational health cannot be measured in black-and-white terms. It's more important to reflect on whether we are moving toward greater openness with those closest to us, or whether we are stuck in self-protective fear.

Deep friendships don't happen all at once. Both work and risk are involved. It is certainly appropriate to test a relationship by initially sharing only certain parts of yourself. If what you share is received respectfully, confidentially, and without judging, you'll probably feel it is safe to share other aspects of your private self as well.

If you have a male confidant or are beginning a men's group, I suggest you discuss important ground rules for your times together that will create a safe place for each to share his deepest struggles and burdens.

- *No advice.* Consider it out of bounds to attempt to fix or correct each other. When we listen attentively and supportively, without trying to think of solutions for the other person, we create a safe, nonjudging atmosphere. Giving advice almost always destroys an atmosphere of vulnerable sharing, because its net impact is often shaming. "What you should do is . . . ," or "What you should have done was. . . ."
- *Avoid spiritualizing problems.* Be as honest as you can about your feelings whether or not you can figure out how it all fits together spiritually or even logically.

The result of that kind of more critical and cognitive analysis is often the conclusion "I shouldn't be feeling this." But it's extremely important to be able to feel all your feelings and express them in a safe environment so that you can understand what's going on inside you.

3. Let God Give You the Father Blessing

The third step toward healing your father wounds separates Christian men from those in the secular men's movement. Christian counselors Rick Koepcke and E. James Wilder capture the difference clearly.

"The secular men's movement does not make the mistake of minimizing pain; however, perhaps the reason the father wound is displayed so glaringly in secular writings is that leaders of the secular movement are not connected to the source of healing for that wound. They are unwilling to take the last, courageous step, the 'leap of faith' to connect to God as Father. They are quite aware of, and willing to face, the damage done by sin in their fathers' lives and [in] their own. Unable to find a remedy for the damage, however, they settle for suffering together, crying together, beating out their rage together on drums that echo into empty skies. They have not realized that the blessing of the Father is stronger than the curse of the father."[9]

God has promised to be "a father to the fatherless."[10] To those men who have not received the blessing from their earthly fathers, God stands ready to give it.

For example, the patriarch Jacob's father, Isaac, favored Esau over Jacob. Esau was a "man's man," a skilled hunter and outdoorsman. Jacob, on the other hand, "was a peaceful man, living in tents." The result? "Now Isaac loved Esau, because he had a taste for game; but Rebekah loved Jacob."[11] Because of his father's favoritism toward Esau, Jacob never received a Father Blessing.

At that point Jacob decided to use deceit and manipulation to gain the blessing of his father he so desperately wanted. He got what he wanted, but as happens when we try to meet our legitimate needs in illegitimate ways, the fruit of his manipulation soon rotted, and he was forced to flee to a far-off country to escape Esau's wrath.

But God wasn't finished with Jacob. Some twenty years later as Jacob was returning home finally to face the music with his elder brother, God met Jacob by the river Jabbok. The encounter turned into an all-night wrestling match between Jacob and the Lord.

By daybreak the next morning Jacob was exhausted, his thigh was dislocated, but he wouldn't let go of the Lord. "I will not let you go," Jacob said, "unless you bless me."

So the Lord did bless Jacob. But it was not a blessing that had to do with Jacob's circumstances or external signs of success. This blessing had to do with Jacob's identity—who he was.

"What is your name?" the Lord asked. When Jacob told him, the Lord said, "Your name shall no longer be Jacob, but Israel; for you have striven with God and with men and have prevailed."[12]

So Jacob received from the Lord what he had been unable to receive from his father: a new identity and a legitimate blessing. God's new blessing, however, was not without its price. Jacob had to give up his old identity, with its deceit and manipulation. And he had to experience true brokenness. God dislocated his thigh as they wrestled, and Jacob limped to his rendezvous with Esau. But the benefits were great. By allowing God to break and bless him, Jacob made peace with his past and was reconciled with his estranged brother.

If you have not received the Father Blessing from your earthly father, and doubt that you ever will, set aside a special time and place to seek your heavenly Father for his blessing.

I took such a time three years ago midway through a vacation with my wife in the state of Baja California in Mexico. Interestingly, like Jacob's experience at the river Jabbok, it also involved a painful tussle with God and a need for brokenness.

Partway through our vacation, my wife caught me staring at a pretty Mexican girl. Marsha was hurt and angry. When she confronted me with my behavior, I became defensive and lied. "I'm just people-watching," I said. "There's nothing wrong with that." We exchanged more angry words. Finally, realizing I couldn't bluff my way out, I relented. I acknowledged that, yes, I had been staring at the girl; lust was involved; and I was truly sorry for the hurt I'd caused. The incident caused turmoil in our relationship and spoiled a lovely vacation, but it did plow the ground for new growth in me. When Marsha returned home, I decided to stay on alone for a few days for some inner spiritual work.

After my moral failure and loss of my family years before, I had spent time examining my heart and life, asking God to show me where the walls had crumbled and needed to be rebuilt. At that time I adopted several new standards for my behavior in relating to women, steps I hoped would prevent inappropriate behavior before it started. I determined I would never again counsel women alone. And I would be extremely careful with demonstrations of affection with women and with touching women in general. Other inner work had gone on, too.

But now I realized that God, by way of the mirror held up to me by my wife, was revealing deeper levels of work he needed to do. I had assumed I'd been through enough of God's discipline for me—my woodshed experience— that I was "fixed" in my relationships with women. But the Christian life is like peeling back the layers of an onion; you no sooner get one stripped away than you discover another layer underneath to work on. The vacation incident had pointed me to another layer.

As I spent time with the Lord there in Baja, I probed what was going on inside me that prompted my behavior. The picture wasn't pretty, and it wasn't complex. I made flirtatious eye contact with women, hoping for some silent signal of approval in return. Enough positive signals, and I'd feel good about myself as a man.

It was clear to me that the underlying problem was a wound in my masculine soul, an insecurity about my manhood. But I would never get the reassurance I needed from flirting. I was causing pain to the woman I loved, and God wanted me to give it up. The heart of my work that week was to confess to God that my behavior was sin, to accept his forgiveness, and to ask him to heal the wounded place underneath that was prompting the wrong behavior. And that, quite unexpectedly, led to an experience of the Father Blessing from God himself.

I knew I needed to somehow apply God's view of me to that wound in my masculine soul. So following my time of confession and introspection, I searched the Scriptures for words that reassured me of God's love and of the high value he placed on me. I also let him impress on me the specific masculine character traits he had formed in me over the years, in keeping with his assurance in Psalm 139 that we are "fearfully and wonderfully made." As I listened to the Lord's view of me, I recorded the insights in a journal. In the process I felt a new confidence in the authentic manhood God had created in me. And with that I realized I didn't need to get something from any woman to complete my manhood. That next layer of the onion, an unhealthy dependence on women's approval, was being peeled off by the Lord, and I felt freer than I had in years.

God may lead you to spend time alone with him in this way. As with Jacob, you may find that a wrestling match with the Lord is part of the experience. Ask him to show you how the wound in your masculine soul manifests itself. Ask him to heal that wound.

Let him also affirm your manhood. Think through the ways you have demonstrated courage, for instance, or sensitivity or quiet confidence. Write these down. These are the fruit of God's work in your life as a man. As God reminds you of these qualities and reassures you of his unconditional love and esteem for you, you too may experience a powerful form of the Father Blessing.

Other men have shared with me their own creative ways of structuring a time in which God can give them the Father Blessing. Some have taken a weekend apart with a small group of men. In times of affirmation, these trusted friends have mirrored the admirable qualities they see in each other.

Even for those who haven't had good masculine role models, we can count on God's promise to be a father to the fatherless. He wants to model for us the qualities of a Father who is perfectly loving, perfectly caring, always consistent, always reliable, always trustworthy. Over time as we get to know our heavenly Father better, the old father wounds will be healed. On the other side of that healing we'll find the freedom to love our dads in ways we never could before and to pass on the Father Blessing to our own children—and to the generations that follow.

You Can't Heal
What You Don't Feel

Pain, Grief, and Anger

Rage blooms in the deep soil of unresolved loss.
David Damico, *The Faces of Rage*

G. Gordon Liddy, asked if it hurts when he holds his
hand over an open flame to show how tough he is: "Of
course it hurts. The trick is not to let yourself feel it."

Jack McGinnis spent a lifetime trying to outrun the pain of his father loss. Ultimately he found the only way out was through.

Born the son of a well-to-do orthodontist in Beaumont, Texas, Jack's world changed forever when he was only five. His parents divorced and his mother moved away, leaving him with his father, a chronic alcoholic. Jack soon became his primary caretaker. Even as a small boy he would help his father drive the car home from the beer joints at night and then tuck him into bed. "I became completely consumed with my father's safety and welfare," Jack recalls.

One night when Jack was ten years old, his father drank late into the night. Jack stayed up to watch him but fell asleep on the sofa. Jack's dad went to bed and continued to smoke. That night the bed caught on fire, and Jack's father

80

sustained third-degree burns over 90 percent of his body. He died the next day.

"Needless to say," Jack says, "when my father died, I felt totally alone and abandoned. My mother never returned or requested to care for my older brother or me." Jack went to live with his aunt and uncle, loving people who tried to surround Jack with support. "But they had their own emotional issues and stress," Jack says. "In that home, no one was ever allowed to openly express their feelings. So there were many nights when I grieved alone, crying for hours in my pillow. I thought if I cried hard enough, my dad would come back."

When he was thirteen years old, Jack took his first drink of whiskey and discovered that alcohol would alleviate his inner pain temporarily. "I never drank a little from then on," he recalls. "I was an alcoholic from the first moment."

When he was eighteen years old, Jack entered seminary to study for the Roman Catholic priesthood. Eight years later, assigned to parish ministry in Houston, Jack became overwhelmed with the pressures of caretaking. "People were coming to me with the pain of their lives, and I had no way to respond to it," Jack says. "So I just drank more."

By 1969 Jack was drinking, smoking marijuana, and taking tranquilizers, all to short-circuit the intense pain of his father loss. "At times," Jack says, "I would drive around Houston all night, at thirty years of age, drinking and crying for my father. I'd cry, 'Why did you leave me?' In some ways the pain was worse then than twenty years before when my father died."

Jack could find nothing to touch that pain. "I tried encounter weekends where we'd scream at each other for twenty-four hours and never sleep. That didn't work. The chemicals didn't work. I was a professional caretaker, but my work didn't work."

On July 14, 1970, while driving home drunk, he heard a voice. "I believe it was God's voice," Jack says. "The words were 'You don't have to do this anymore. It's all over.'"

He immediately drove to a friend's house—an old drinking buddy—and rang his doorbell at 3:30 in the morning. When his friend came to the door, Jack said, "Johnny, I can't go on this way anymore. I need some help." Johnny smiled and said, "You came to the right place, pardner." He'd been in Alcoholics Anonymous for a year, and so he took Jack to his first A.A. meeting the next night. Jack's been sober ever since.

At about the same time, Jack had been visiting a charismatic church in Houston. There he discovered that God was a God of love, that he loved him personally. "My A.A. friends were encouraging me to turn my life and my will over to God," Jack recalls. "And my church friends were encouraging me to accept Jesus Christ as my Lord and Savior. To both groups I said, 'Wait a minute! I'm a priest, for Pete's sake! Don't you think I've done this already?' And they said, 'You must have left something out of the transaction, because you're dying.'"

So he did both. Jack accepted Jesus Christ as his Lord and Savior and gave his life to God. "It was an embarrassing thing to do for someone who's been a priest for eight years, but my life has been so different since."

Although Jack's addiction to alcohol was lifted and he saw many changes in his life, he still felt a deep core of pain inside.

"In A.A.," Jack says, "I'd been told, 'Read the Big Book, work the Twelve Steps, go to meetings, and you're going to be okay,' but I wasn't. The Christians told me, 'Read the Bible and do all the other things you're supposed to do, and you'll be fine.' I was doing all those things, but I was still dying inside."

In desperation Jack checked himself into a treatment center. During eight weeks there, he came to see that unidentified losses and unresolved grief were at the core of his anguish. "I had to learn to finish my grieving to go on living. As I've learned to grieve, I've experienced extensive freedom from addictive behavior. I see now that rather than grieving in a healthy way, I'd been stuck in grief for thirty years. I couldn't bring it to closure, and it was killing me! My inner space was stuffed with frozen feelings about my losses, and I didn't have room for joy."[1]

It took him thirty years, but Jack McGinnis finally found healing through grieving his losses. But first he had to find the courage to feel his painful feelings. Emotional healing is invariably linked to emotional honesty.

This has been true in my own life as well. I'll never forget my first experience in a recovery support group. I stumbled into the group shell-shocked from having just blown apart twenty years of adult life and ministry through my own bad behavior. Though I don't remember all that went on, I do remember being amazed by the honesty of the group—honesty about their failures, and honesty about their feelings. They weren't fixed yet, and they openly admitted it.

Stepping into that first recovery group felt like stepping outside into the fresh air and sunlight after having lived for two decades in a dark, stuffy room. It's been an exhilarating experience in the years since then to begin giving myself the freedom to be truly honest—honest about my feelings even when they're negative, and honest about my brokenness on those days when I feel anything but healthy, let alone "victorious."

But learning how to identify and express my feelings has been a difficult task after spending more than forty years living out of my head. By and large, the inner landscape of my emotions remained an uncharted, frozen territory. I had even traveled around the country in my previous ministry speaking on The Feelings Fallacy. I warned Christians not to trust their feelings, that their feelings would surely lead them down a primrose path toward disaster.

But it was I who was pulled into disaster. I see now that if I had paid better attention to my feelings, to the alarm bells that were going off, perhaps some of my own pain could have been avoided. God gives us our emotions for a number of reasons, one of which is to alert us when something is wrong. If we don't listen to our pain and address its causes, we'll be tempted to simply "stuff" the pain. But stuffing our negative feelings almost always sets up a blowout of one kind or another: an outburst of rage, an onset of depression, or compulsive behavior.

Being honest about our feelings—especially our pain, grief, and anger—is the first and most important step in interrupting that downward slide. But achieving emotional honesty is not an easy task for men in our society. If we are to succeed, we must confront several myths about what it means to be a man.

The Myths of Manhood

Myth 1: "Real Men" Are from Marlboro Country

Men are taught from boyhood that "real men" don't cry, aren't sensitive, don't show softness, sadness, or anything that could be construed as weakness. In our society men are basically allowed to express just two emotions: anger and happiness. With the darker emotions flowing from hurt or grief, men are expected to slip into the Marlboro Man mode: the rugged individualist who's so tough he doesn't even acknowledge pain, who wears a No Fear tee shirt under his cowboy duds. This perpetuates the myth that it's unmanly to be emotional.

Barry and I had developed a deep friendship over several months working through our Mentor Leadership

Training course. The material on emotional wholeness was especially helpful to Barry, a talented young engineer at the Boeing Company in Seattle.

"My father's favorite phrase when I was a kid was, 'That doesn't hurt,'" Barry told me. "When I fell and broke my arm, he said, 'That doesn't hurt.' When I was injured playing football in high school, he'd hold me by the shoulder, look me straight in the eyes, and say, 'That doesn't hurt.'

"My dad was the original Marlboro Man. He never acknowledged pain, never admitted to being sick. In forty-five years of working life from high school to retirement, he only missed one week of work—and that was following a severe heart attack."

The message to Barry was clear: Disregard your negative feelings; act as if they don't exist.

The Marlboro Man may be the norm for North America, but he shouldn't be the norm for a follower of Christ. Jesus grieved and wept and showed tenderness to sinners and small children. He sweat great drops of blood as he agonized in the Garden before the cross. "My Father, if it is possible," he prayed, "let this cup pass from me."[2] But he also had a sense of humor, went to parties, and experienced the heights of joy. In short, Jesus experienced and expressed the full range of normal human emotions, from deep indigo to bright yellow.

Myth 2: God Made Men Logical and Women Emotional

Bill was another man I met at one of our Manhood seminars. A committed Christian, he had revealed a secret drug habit to his wife and his employer two years earlier and had been faithfully working a recovery program ever since.

"What's been the most encouraging result of your recovery work so far?" I asked. Bill's face lit up.

"Without a doubt," he said, "it's becoming emotionally whole for the first time. If emotions were crayons, when I

85

first got into recovery I only had two—a black one and a white one. I was either angry or happy. Those were the only two feelings I was in touch with. Now, two years later, since I've stopped numbing my feelings with drugs, I've gotten back a whole bunch more. It's as if I've graduated to the eight pack box, you know, red and yellow and green, the main ones.

"But it's not going to end here," he said, still smiling. "I shared my crayon story the other night in my support group. There was an older man there. He said, 'It only gets better, son. I started with only two crayons like you eight years ago, and now I've got the jumbo sixty-four crayon set with the built-in sharpener!' We all laughed. It feels so good to be getting healthier."

For more than a thousand years our society has encouraged men to carry only two crayons. Unlike the biblical Hebrews, the ancient Greeks exalted reason over emotion and intuition. This Hellenistic influence was passed down to us in North America from our European forebears. Especially among men, reason is viewed as vastly superior to emotion or intuition in decision making and problem solving. While that may be appropriate when it comes to mathematics or certain kinds of scientific experiments, it is extremely limiting in relationships and the inner realities of the spirit and psyche.

Still, our culture continues to paint women as emotional and men as logical. True, recent research has shown that men's and women's brains do function differently when emotions are communicated. One result, evidently, is that men have more difficulty than women in expressing their feelings. But these differences in the ways our brains function don't lessen our responsibility as men to develop our full potential as emotional beings.

Besides Jesus himself, the Bible overflows with examples of men who were comfortable with a breadth of emotions.

King David was both a warrior and a poet. His psalms are filled with rage and tenderness. There were other times when he sang and danced before the Lord in ecstasy. The biblical material is clear: God intends for both women and men to fully develop their capacity for feeling as well as their capacity for thinking and reasoning.

Myth 3: Successful Men Are Always Positive

The "power of positive thinking" philosophy has influenced several generations of North American men, especially businessmen, to distance themselves from all "negative" emotions and to strive always to be optimistic, upbeat, and enthusiastic. I practiced a Christian version of this philosophy for years. Instead of facing my pain and dealing with it, I tried to envelop myself in a wraparound "happy" environment. So I listened nonstop to Christian music and inspirational tapes, I read positive-thinking books, and I discouraged my coworkers and family from "polluting" my environment with "negative nuggets."

Several years after beginning my journey back toward spiritual and emotional health, I was talking with my two teenagers about the importance of being honest about our feelings. "I want you to know," I said, "that you always have the freedom to tell me what you're feeling, even if those feelings are negative."

Their eyes widened, and they both grinned. "Boy, Dad," they laughed, "you have changed! Do you remember what you used to make us say whenever we complained about anything?"

I didn't remember, and I was pretty sure I didn't want to know. "No, what?" I mumbled.

With smirks on their faces they both broke into a loud, unison chant: "Boy—am—I—en—thu—si—as—tic!" Then they laughed some more.

"Remember *now?*" my daughter, Sarah, asked. "You'd heard it from one of your inspirational speakers, and you drilled us to say it whenever we felt like complaining or being grumpy!"

Our sins do come back to haunt us. But it was true. I couldn't stand to hear other people's pain or negativity because it reminded me too much of my own. So instead of dealing with it, I sought to keep the lid screwed down tight on my pain bottle, and the atmosphere around me relentlessly cheery. It was, of course, just one more version of the "Don't talk" rule of dysfunctional homes.

The truth is, truly successful men don't repress or ignore their negative feelings. They face them and deal with their causes. Repressed emotions only migrate to a different sector of our inner landscape, erupting as a peptic ulcer, migraine, or outburst of rage.

Myth 4: It's Unspiritual to Show Negative Emotions

Among some Christians today, if you admit to feeling anger or sadness, and especially depression, you run the risk of being labeled unspiritual. In those circles, the unfortunate impression is given that deliverance from all negative feelings is only a prayer away. My wife and I sat through a healing service in a church not long ago in which the minister entreated people to come forward and be delivered from, among others, the "demon of loneliness." Spiritual warfare is certainly a reality. But it would be sad if we encouraged others to believe we don't have to go through all the hard work of making friends and nurturing relationships to cure loneliness; we can simply go forward and be delivered.

One article I read a while back was written by a well-known Christian leader and carried the title "Every Day Like Easter!" That's simply not true. Nor is it biblical. Every day is not like Easter. There are bad days as well as good days. Jesus went through nothing less than the crucifixion to get to Easter, and he warned us that we too must take up our cross daily if we're truly to follow him.

We do others a disservice when we imply that they can skip over the pain and sadness and anger and grief work that is essential to true change, and can cut straight to the triumph and the lilies.

The prophet Jeremiah faced a similar ecclesiastical situation in Judah in the seventh century B.C. False priests tried to paper over the brokenness of the people with a superficial healing. God condemns the ministry of these false priests: "Everyone deals falsely. And they have healed the brokenness of My people superficially, saying, 'Peace, peace,' but there is no peace."[3]

True healing is a process that involves feeling our feelings. If we're feeling anger, we heal by owning our anger and dealing with its source. The only way out is through.

The Masculine Mask

Most men respond to these masculine myths by hiding their true feelings behind a mask. Some men hide their feelings so completely, they themselves are not aware their feelings exist until they experience some life-damaging blowout. Being cut off from their feelings consigns men to a life of isolation, loneliness, and superficiality.

But not all men experience blockage because they believe their emotions are unmanly. For some the issue is raw fear. These men have never been trained to deal with distressing emotions. They are terrified to let their feelings out, lest they find them to be too big and too strong to handle, like some evil genie loosed from a bottle. They fear they will ultimately be destroyed by them. The truth is, our negative feelings are even more destructive when they are repressed, and they are much more likely to blindside us when we least expect it.

89

How can we more intentionally move toward healthiness in this area? We begin by embracing several key principles from Scripture.

Feelings Signal That Something Is Wrong

Psalm 139:23–24 says, "Search me, O God, and know my heart; try me and know my anxious thoughts; and see if there be any hurtful way in me."

David asks God to help him plumb the depths of his heart, to identify any anxious thoughts or hurtful ways that may be lurking inside him. When we get in touch with our anxieties or anger or other negative feelings, we're one step closer to determining what is causing those feelings and to dealing with it. If we refuse to search our hearts in this way, we will continue to be blind to the hurtful ways that may be poisoning us and our relationships. Remember, you can't heal what you don't feel.

Sadness and Anger Are Not Wrong

In Ephesians 4:26 Paul exhorts, "Be angry, and yet do not sin; do not let the sun go down on your anger."

The implication of the passage is clear: It is possible to be angry and not sin; it is also possible to possess a kind of anger that is sinful. The sinful kind, verse 31 goes on to explain, is the kind characterized by "bitterness and wrath . . . and slander . . . along with all malice." It's the kind of anger that turns to deep, smoldering hatred, that wishes ill for another. But anger that is not wrathful or bitter, anger that is the normal, healthy response to an offense or a violation of some kind, is not sin.

My wife and I have heard many heartrending stories of childhood sexual abuse from both women and men in our seminars in the last few years. Many of these men and women responded to their abuse by trying to bury their feelings. The act of burying those feelings helped them survive as children. But without exception, the act that saved their sanity as children ultimately caused incalculable damage in their adult lives. The healthy response to a violation such as they experienced is anger—anger that says, "This was an offense; this was extremely hurtful and unfair, and I'm angry that it was done."

To remain healthy, we can't get stuck in our anger or let it develop into hatred. That only releases the acid of bitterness throughout our system, causing us even greater inner pain. But to deny that we have experienced anger in the first place, or to stuff it and pretend that it's gone, only traps the toxic waste inside, out of reach of God's healing. Honesty in our emotional life is hard work, but it's essential for personal healthiness.

For years I believed all anger was sinful. I expended a lot of energy trying to convince myself and others that I wasn't angry. All that achieved was a stockpile of bottled resentment. Every so often one of my bottles of resentment would spring a leak, and passive-aggressive behavior would ooze out.

It's been freeing for me as part of my growth toward healthiness to honestly own my anger, while taking full responsibility for not expressing it abusively. Just last week I became angry over something my wife did. I told Marsha I was angry, but I also assured her that I was committed to communicating in a healthy, respectful way. We discussed the issue relatively calmly.

When we finished, Marsha said, "I'd appreciate it if you'd let me know when you're over being angry." I told her I would and returned to my study.

Twenty minutes later I realized I was no longer angry. Talking openly and calmly about my feelings had taken care of the frustration. "I'm not mad anymore," I called out to Marsha from the study.

She came to the doorway. "I love you," she said with a chuckle, and walked over and gave me a kiss. It's been freeing to be in the kind of relationship in which it's okay to acknowledge negative emotions without either person trying to punish the other for their feelings.

Emotional honesty is also essential when it comes to sadness and grief. Romans 12:15 says, "Rejoice with those who rejoice, and weep with those who weep." In contrast to the admonition of this Scripture, many of us are uncomfortable with sadness—our own or anybody else's.

I recently conducted a men's retreat for a local church here in the Pacific Northwest. God worked in a significant way during the retreat in a number of men's lives. We ended the weekend by arranging our chairs in a large circle, and each man shared something he had gotten from the time together. One man in particular seemed overcome with emotion. When his time came to share, Steve's eyes filled with tears and his lips began to tremble; he looked toward the ceiling in an attempt to regain control.

Immediately one of the other men jumped up from his chair and ran over to Steve. He put his arm around him and hugged him tightly and said, "That's okay, Steve, that's okay. You don't have to say anything." Steve nodded silently, his eyes full of tears, and the sharing passed on to the next man in the circle.

As Christians, our first impulse when we see others who are sad is to try to fix them, cheer them up, or talk them out of their sad feelings. But sadness, like anger, has a healing purpose in our lives. It is our emotional system's response to loss, just as anger is our system's response to violation or offense. Sadness signals that we have come to one of life's endings. That ending must be grieved before we can authentically make a new beginning.

God Can Heal Us If We Acknowledge Our Pain

"Blessed are those who mourn, for they shall be comforted," says Jesus.[4] "[God] heals the brokenhearted, and binds up their wounds," says the psalmist.[5] Over and over the Bible makes it clear that mourning precedes comfort, and brokenheartedness must precede healing.

With his own sorrow and grieving, Jesus again sets the standard for authentic manhood. In Luke 19:41 he weeps over the spiritual bankruptcy of Jerusalem. Isaiah 53:3 describes Jesus as "a man of sorrows, and acquainted with grief."

In Matthew 14:12–13 we have a poignant picture of how Jesus responded to personal loss. John the Baptist, whom Jesus loved, had just been beheaded by the wicked King Herod. "Then John's disciples came for his body and buried it, and came to tell Jesus what had happened. As soon as Jesus heard the news, he went off by himself in a boat to a remote area to be alone" (LB).

Losses hurt, whether it's the loss of a loved one or the loss of a dream. Jesus models the healthy response to loss. He immediately stopped his busy ministry, found a place to be alone, and took time to grieve. Grieving helps bring closure to our losses and prepares us for a new beginning.

It's often hard for men to admit we hurt. But when we overcome the false masculine stereotypes imposed on us by society and give ourselves permission to grieve, we open the floodgate of God's comfort.

Steps to Healthiness

How can we as men build greater emotional and spiritual healthiness into our lives? Four steps are essential.

1. Learn How to Identify Your Feelings

Consider setting aside fifteen minutes every day this week to do some inner work with your journal. Find a quiet place

and get in touch with what's going on inside. The following Life Rating Scale by Joe Dominguez and Vicki Robin[6]
may help you identify your feelings more specifically. Reflect
on the five lists, then select the column of adjectives that
most closely applies to your life right now.

Life Rating Scale

1	2	3	4	5
Uncomfortable	Dissatisfied	Content	Happy	Joyous
Tired	Seeking	Doing OK	Growing	Enthusiastic
Incomplete	Not enough	Average	Satisfied	Fulfilled
Frustrated	Relationships could be better	Acceptable	Productive	Overflowing
Fearful		Sometimes happy, sometimes blue	Relaxed	Ecstatic
Frequently lonely	Coping		Free of tension	Powerful
Angry	Getting better	Stable	Efficient	Making a difference
Need love	Not very productive	Normal	Time available	
Insecure	Need reassurance	Few risks	Fun	
		Fitting in	Secure	

As men (and as Christians), we have been so conditioned
to never acknowledge negative feelings, this exercise may
be difficult to do at first. Ten years ago if I had tried to identify which column represented my life, I would have picked
number four or five without hesitation: happy, growing, sat-
isfied, or joyous, enthusiastic, fulfilled. I would have picked
those adjectives to describe myself because I believed them
to be the qualities a victorious Christian leader should be
experiencing. In reality I was experiencing the feelings represented in lists one and two but was not honest enough to
admit it, even to myself.

That emotional dishonesty meant that my pain kept increasing, and I went on trying to numb it with addictive behavior. The blowout that finally resulted was much more damaging for many people than if I had owned my discontent up front and dealt with it honestly.

2. Learn to Communicate Your Feelings

Those of us raised in families with "Don't talk" and "Don't feel" rules find it extremely difficult to talk about our feelings in a healthy way. We often go to one extreme, stuffing them and pretending they're not there, or to the other extreme, blaming someone else for them. But we always have choices in what we do with our feelings, and as we become healthier, we are able to acknowledge that.

Once again, the first step in this process is being honest about what we're feeling. If, for instance, I feel anger or irritation because of something my wife did, and it's interfering with our relationship, I need to bring it out into the open and talk with her about it.

The second step involves learning to communicate those feelings in a healthy way. Instead of blaming and using "you" statements such as "You make me so mad!" use "I" statements like "I feel angry."

The "I" statement is healthier because we're taking personal responsibility for our feelings, instead of claiming the other person made us feel a certain way.

Barry, the Boeing engineer with the Marlboro Man father, was never allowed to feel hurt or even acknowledge being sick growing up. "The message I got," Barry explains, "is 'Your feelings don't matter.' So I learned to deal with my feelings by pretending they weren't there."

Later, in his marriage, relational problems began to crop up. He realized during the course of our mentoring experience together that the problems were based on a fear of intimacy. Intimacy, of course, is based on vulnerably opening up and sharing feelings. Because he'd never been allowed to express anything negative growing up, it was especially difficult for Barry to say to his wife, "That comment hurt me," or even, "I feel frustrated."

So Barry began by rewriting the old childhood rules. "I had to start by telling myself, 'Barry, your feelings do matter. Dad was wrong.'" Several times a week he would write in his journal, trying to identify the shape and texture of his feelings.

At first this was very difficult. He often said that all he felt was numbness when he looked inside. But eventually it got easier, not only to identify his feelings but to talk to his wife about them. A recent letter from Barry indicates that God is using all his hard work to ignite a wonderful new level of closeness with his wife. Change for the better is possible one small step at a time.

A word of caution: When we first get in touch with our feelings, all the emotions we detect may not be based in reality. Phil is another graduate of our mentoring program. He's a recovering alcoholic and the leader of a church based Twelve Steps group.

"I began numbing my feelings with alcohol and pot at age nine," Phil told me. "So I never gave my emotional life a chance to mature much past the twelve-year-old level. To a twelve-year-old, feelings are gigantic. I was stunned to realize that a lot of my inner reactions today are the reactions of a little boy. When somebody says I'm bad, I'm destroyed.

"So I've needed to approach this area with balance. I need to give myself the freedom to feel. But I also have to realize that, at least at first, those are going to be the feelings of a twelve-year-old. In many cases they won't be reality-based."

For many men like Phil, taking their feelings out of cold storage is a lot like thawing your fingers after frostbite. It feels unpleasant at first, but you have to go through it for your fingers to feel normal again. The only other option is to leave them frozen and risk permanent damage.

3. Allow Others to Express Negative Feelings

A few years ago I read about a listening service in a major midwestern city. People paid "professional listeners" up to forty dollars an hour just to listen to them talk about their problems. These listeners were not therapists; no advice was given. These were just ordinary people who recognized a need and stepped in with a service to meet that need. At last report their business was booming. There's a desperate need in our culture for people who will listen.

Compassionate listening is a healing ministry. People are burdened with hurt and pain and fear, and they don't want to carry those feelings alone. But many Christians fear they will be judged or preached to if they share their negative feelings. The truth is, unsolicited advice-giving almost always shuts down true communication. The key is learning to become an active listener: affirming, supporting, never trying to talk someone out of his feelings.

Karen Dockrey and her husband, Bill, have two school-age daughters—one who suffers from leukemia, the other with severe hearing loss. Karen wrote *When a Hug Won't Fix the Hurt* to help other parents deal with crises in their children's lives. In one especially helpful section she describes the many ways people responded to their pain as a family. There were two extremes. Some Christians, Dockrey writes, ". . . make heroes out of those who suffer. Or they pretend it's not really suffering at all but an opportunity to be joyful." Neither of these responses were helpful. Her counsel: "Hear the pain, feel along with your friends, and give them the love they need to make it through the journey unscarred." Dockrey encourages us to replace any

of our old responses that shut down communication with
new ones that open it up.

Rather than say . . .	Let's say . . .
I admire you.	I'm so sorry.
Have faith!	I'm glad God is walking through this with you. I'll come along too if you want.
This will bring you a blessing.	It's hard, isn't it?
All things work together for good.	I'm sure God is as sad about this as we are.
Don't be angry!	Tell me what makes you maddest.
It could be worse.	This is terrible. Tell me what hurts the most.
Your son will make it.	It's a long, hard road, isn't it? [7]

Emotional healthiness involves more than just honestly
expressing our own feelings; it also involves a willingness to
"weep with those who weep" as they share their pain with us.

4. Grieve Your Losses

Sean is a heavy-equipment operator for a construction
company in Portland, Oregon. He is also a lay leader in the
men's ministry at his local church and another of the men
I worked with in our Leadership Training course. For Sean
the concept of grieving childhood losses was new, and not
altogether comfortable. "I used to think 'What's done is
done,'" Sean explained. "Why go back and rehash the past?"

But the reality is, the wounds from the past will continue
to haunt us until we face them in a healthy way. Throughout his adult life Sean became depressed at Christmas and
on his birthday. He never knew why, but every year without fail a heaviness descended on him before those two days
and gradually lifted afterward.

As Sean and I worked together through the steps of the grieving process, a number of long-locked doors swung open and a series of memories drifted out.

In particular Sean recalled that Christmas and birthdays were always a disappointment to him growing up. His father was never involved in the celebrations and never bought gifts for Sean or his brothers and sisters. Sean realized that his adult episodes of depression were a form of grieving his loss of never having a close relationship with his father.

One vivid memory from Sean's childhood was especially painful. When Sean was twelve years old, his Boy Scout troop scheduled a father-son banquet as the climax of the year. Merit badges and awards would be given out, and all the boys were encouraged to bring their dads. Sean eagerly approached his dad about coming to the banquet, but his father quickly brushed him off. "I'm too busy," was all he said. So Sean's mother intervened and pestered her husband about it until he finally agreed to go.

The night of the banquet arrived. Sean dressed in his uniform and got ready to go, but his father still had not arrived home from work. Almost an hour late, his dad came in, changed clothes, and they left for the banquet. When they arrived, everyone else had finished eating. Sean and his dad walked in, followed by every eye in the room. They found their places, ate their plates of cold food, and left soon after. The two of them drove home in silence, with Sean slumped in disappointment in the front seat.

Thirty years later Sean's voice is low as he talks about the feelings surrounding that experience. "I desperately wanted my friends to know I had a dad, just like them. Their dads were always involved with them in the activities, and mine never was. But the way the evening turned out, I wished we hadn't come at all. I felt like even more of an outsider than before. And I felt ashamed."

But as Sean began to work through the grieving process, he identified specifically what he had lost through this event and others involving his father. He was able to get back in touch with the pain, and as we talked it through, he felt the weight on his heart lighten some.

"I think I'll always wish my dad and I could truly be friends," Sean says wistfully. "But I've accepted that it will probably never happen in this life, at least in a deep way. It still hurts some, but I've made my peace with it, which is more than I could have said before doing the grief work. It's helped."

Recovery author Jack McGinnis, whose story we heard at the beginning of this chapter, developed the following powerful, ten-step exercise to help us grieve our losses and experience inner healing from our hurts.[8]

Phil, the recovering alcoholic we met earlier, had a father who was a hard-driving perfectionist. He would beat Phil

---

Grieving Exercise

1. On separate paper, write down in detail an event in which you experienced loss in childhood, or at some other time in your life.
2. What were your feelings when it happened?
3. After the event, how did you cope with your feelings, or deny them?
4. Clearly identify what you lost when this happened.
5. What are your feelings now about the loss from the event?
6. If your original response to the event was denial, what have been the consequences of your denial?
7. Who do you consider, in your perception, to be responsible for your loss? (Yourself? Another person? God?)
8. Where are you in the process of forgiving whomever you consider responsible?
9. Is there a risk in forgiving this person? If so, what is the risk to you?
10. Are you willing, with the help of God and your friends, to take the risk of finally forgiving the person responsible for your loss?

---

when he brought home a poor report card. "You'll never amount to anything!" his father would shout at him.

Phil's response was to overachieve and retreat into chemical comfort. When Phil was thirty, his father committed suicide. Suddenly waves of anger toward his father compounded Phil's feelings of loss.

Phil worked through the grieving exercise outlined above, sobbing through much of it. He worked hard to identify what in particular he had lost because of his father wounds. As he probed his heart, Phil realized he'd lost the ability to deal with failure and criticism in a healthy way. This led to the reaction of feeling destroyed when someone criticized him.

Phil also worked through his rage until he was finally able to release it, leaving only a feeling of profound sadness. As part of bringing closure to his grieving, Phil wrote his deceased father a letter, and then burned it. Afterward he talked about the fruit of his grief work.

"All my life I have allowed my father to be the judge of my worth," Phil said. "I did that even though it was obvious he had a lot of problems of his own. Grieving the losses helped me put it all in perspective. I see now that I need to take back my father's judgment of me and put it in the hands of a loving God."

As healing as grieving can be, however, it's not something we can necessarily "get over with" in one sitting. Like so many parts of the journey through life, grieving may well be an ongoing process. Jack McGinnis illustrates this from his own experience:

"Not long ago," Jack said, "my brother and I shared a deep experience of talking through all the childhood losses we both sustained. With a burst of resolve I decided I would go out that weekend and bring closure to all my grieving by forgiving everyone who had ever hurt me. I drove up into the hills, put some soothing music on the car stereo, and as the sun was setting I had a time alone with the Lord,

forgiving everyone I could think of who had ever hurt me—
my mother, my father, my aunt and uncle—everyone. It
was an emotional time, an incredible spiritual bath, and as
I drove back down the mountain, I assumed that I had completed all my grief and forgiveness work involving these
people from my past.

"Two weeks later," Jack went on, "I was leading a retreat,
role-playing the exercise of going back into our past and visu-
alizing scenes where we'd been hurt. Much to my surprise,
right in the middle of this exercise I was flooded with the
memory of a Christmas Day scene in which my uncle had
hurt me deeply when I was twelve. I was filled with anger
that I hadn't felt in forty years! I thought I had forgiven everyone who had ever hurt me—including my uncle—two weeks
before. Now I realize that I will have to deal with those hidden hurts one at a time as they come up in life."[9]

Pain, grief, and anger are all feelings we men tend to minimize or repress. And yet, we have to walk through the darkness to get to the light. Note David's use of the word
"through" in Psalm 23:4. "Even though I walk through the
valley of the shadow of death, I fear no evil; for Thou art
with me. Thy rod and Thy staff, they comfort me."

God doesn't promise to deliver us from the dark experiences of life. He promises to walk with us through them—
to the healing on the other side.

When the Hits Don't Keep On Coming

Adrenaline Addiction

> The content of [any] addiction, whether it be an inges-
> tive addiction or an activity addiction (like work, buy-
> ing or gambling) is an attempt at an intimate relation-
> ship. The workaholic with his work and the alcoholic
> with his booze are having a love affair. Each one [numbs
> his pain] to avoid the feeling of loneliness and hurt in
> the underbelly of shame.
> John Bradshaw, *Healing the Shame That Binds You*

> How many people on their deathbed wish they'd spent
> more time at the office?
> Stephen Covey, *First Things First*

In his book *Showstopper*, G. Pascal Zachary provides a behind-the-scenes view of the grueling five-year drive to make Microsoft the dominant force in the global software market. The book paints a clear picture of the value system held by corporate America in the nineties—a value system that encourages men to sacrifice marriage, family, and personal life to achieve the goals of the company. In one particularly poignant vignette, Zachary describes how the seven-year-old son of an overworked employee promised to throw away all his toys if only his

103

father would stay for a Saturday morning soccer game. To his credit, the father took the morning off.

And to their credit, thousands of Christian men are cutting back on their work and outside commitments to nurture their marriages and family relationships. But many other men today continue to struggle in the grip of what has been called the invisible addiction. The external symptoms of this addiction manifest themselves in a variety of ways: overworking, a continual crisis orientation, overspending habits, or excessive ministry activities or athletic endeavors. But the core addiction underneath all these behaviors is an addiction to adrenaline—to that hit that delivers a feel-good signal to our brain and body.

There is nothing wrong per se with work, ministry, or a satisfying purchase. But for an adrenaline addict, it's not that simple or innocent. He continually calls on his adrenal glands to kick in with a turbocharged hormone injection that makes his heart beat faster, his skin perspire, and—not incidentally—a euphoric high to follow. That is, until the postadrenaline low kicks in. Then he feels fatigue and a darkness that can easily turn into depression. Which leads him to look for another activity that will give an adrenaline hit, whether that involves finding one more crisis to solve (his or someone else's) or impulsively treating himself to a purchase at the local computer store. The result is always the same: The high is followed by the low is followed by another high—until finally his adrenal glands and nerves wear out. I know from my own experience as a recovering adrenaline junkie.

Three years ago, I was rereading Keith Miller's excellent book *A Hunger for Healing* in preparation for leading a Twelve Step group in a local church. In his chapter on Step One of the Twelve Steps, Miller describes symptoms that might indicate one's life has become unmanageable. After listing symptoms such as irritation and blaming; uncontrollable, exaggerated feelings; and forgetting to do the things that nurture our relationships, Miller summarizes: "We're frantic all the time. We've got more to do than we can handle. But we're not really conscious of how hectic and confused our lives are; we think it's temporary and 'normal.' When it becomes clear that it isn't temporary, we become depressed about our lack of ability to 'get straightened out.' . . . This frustration and confusion are common symptoms of powerlessness and unmanageability."[1]

A tingle of shock ran through me as I read Miller's description. I recognized all of those symptoms as being my own. Yes, I had already dealt with some major issues in my life. But there was no denying it: He was describing *my* frantic, stress-filled, out-of-control life! I had brushed aside the symptoms as temporary or the fault of someone else. But somehow my own denial had cracked, and I saw that I was responsible for the chaos. What had started as preparation to lead others became a humbling spiritual breakthrough for me.

When I first became involved in the recovery process, I had an immediate, negative reaction to the pull-no-punches language of the Twelve Steps. I especially disliked the part that says we need God "to restore us to sanity." I knew I had problems, but I was pretty sure I wasn't *insane*. But then I heard one recovery veteran define insanity. "Insanity," he said, "is repeating the same unhealthy behavior over and over and each time expecting different results." That got through to me. I'd certainly done a lot of that.

As I looked at the symptoms of insanity in my own life, I began to see a pattern of self-defeating behavior emerge. I saw that I regularly go through a cycle of overcommitting to some gargantuan project—something far beyond the margins or limitations of my human resources—and crash and burn on the other side.

Six years ago I crammed a new marriage, a new job, and building a new house into one year, followed by collapse. Five years ago I volunteered to plan and organize a major regional conference for Christians while simultaneously upgrading and expanding the magazine I served as editor, followed by another collapse. And four years ago I topped it all off with a major move to another city! Marsha had tried to point out the obviously dysfunctional pattern to me before, but I had always said the emergency we happened to be in at that time was temporary. "This is an exception," I'd say. "We'll have smooth sailing once this event is behind us." But it just so happened that one or two of these "exceptions" showed up every year, year after year.

It was a sobering moment when I acknowledged that the stress and insanity in my life were *not* the result of special circumstances. I had brought these situations on myself and on my family. So for the last three years, like a toddler learning to walk, I've begun to learn how to "do life" in a more balanced way.

In his excellent book *Margin* Richard Swenson describes the chemical reaction between salt and water to illustrate how overload can strike a person without warning. You can dissolve large amounts of salt in warm water, until the water reaches the saturation point. At that point if you add even one more teaspoon of salt, the saturated water won't hold it, and the extra teaspoon will precipitate out.

But you can add more salt through a process called supersaturation. Supersaturation occurs when you turn up the heat under the solution. The hotter the water, the more salt it can hold. Eventually, though, you "hit the wall." Even with the heat turned up, the solution can only hold so much salt. If you add even one more grain to the solution at that point, the saturation goes into overload, and virtually all of the suspended salt drops out.

We men do the same thing. We reach our physical and emotional limit but feel as if we have to cram more in somehow. So we turn up the heat, kick in the adrenaline, cut back on sleep—whatever we have to do to make it all fit. And then we hit the supersaturation wall, the absolute outer limits of our bodies and minds. Turning the heat up a notch worked before; it won't work here. At this point, we squeeze in one more thing, and the whole system crashes.

Many of us have lived through such a crash. The *Annals of Internal Medicine* recently reported that 24 percent of Americans complain of experiencing burnout and exhaustion that has sidelined them for two weeks or more. Fatigue is now among the top five reasons people call the doctor.[2]

Fuel of the Adrenaline Addiction

For me, the journey toward healthiness started with an honest look at what fueled my adrenaline addiction. I found at least three major contributors.

1. Emphasis on Doing, Achieving, and Producing

Society does not encourage the simple life. Society encourages busy-ness, rewards productivity, and excuses consumption. It is not an exaggeration to say that our society is *based* on unhealthy behavior, with compulsive behavior of one kind or another considered the norm. Those who seek to live within their limitations are looked down on and viewed as strange. They need to be prepared to swim upstream, with no encouragement or understanding from the community at large.

Harvard economist Juliet Schor documents our nation's three-hundred-year-long love affair with work in her book *The Overworked American: The Unexpected Decline of Leisure.* The Pilgrims, believing that idle hands are the devil's workshop, eliminated fifty annual holidays traditionally celebrated by the English. Sunday was the only work-free day.

The Pilgrims' tough work ethic became the norm during the Industrial Revolution, says Schor. Labor unions had to work for more than a century just to secure eight-hour workdays and a day off a week. But World War II saw the gradual erosion of these leisure safeguards.

That erosion became an avalanche during the recession of the '80s. Downsizing became official corporate policy across America; nearly half of the country's businesses reduced their work force in the last decade, according to the Department of Labor. Today it's not uncommon for a company to ask one employee to do the work of 1.3 people—for the same pay and with less time off. Overtime is at a record high level, an average of 4.7 hours a week, says Schor. And during this same ten-year period the average yearly vacation and other paid absences decreased by 3.5 days.[3]

Many men responded to the pressure by asking more from their bodies and minds, and relying on adrenaline to fuel it.

2. The Need to Medicate Emotional Pain

Many of us who would be offended to be labeled as alcoholic are just as drug dependent as any wino or cocaine addict. The only difference is that our drug of choice is manufactured within our own bodies. We use the drug for basically the same reason that an alcoholic uses booze—to stay ahead of our pain, to numb the feelings we can't stand to feel: the hurt, anger, feelings of rejection or resentment. But the reality of course is, as with any addiction, our problems only get worse, not better.

We can also monitor certain physical symptoms to determine if we're hooked on adrenaline. In his book *Adrenalin and Stress* Dr. Archibald Hart explains the body's adrenaline process. Our bodies produce adrenaline to help us cope with stressful or demanding situations. In effect, our brain dials 911, and our adrenal glands dump the hormone into our bloodstream. Our heart rate goes up, extra glucose is pumped into our blood, and extra oxygen is sent speeding to our muscles.

But what goes up must come down. As time passes, the level of adrenaline in our blood drops, and the body begins repairing itself from the wear and tear of stress. Without this time of healthy R and R between emergencies, the adrenal glands become exhausted and damaged. The outer layer of the adrenal gland becomes enlarged, lymph nodes (which ward off infection) shrink, and the stomach and intestines become irritated. The adrenaline system eventually crashes, leaving the person in a state of prolonged and severe fatigue.[4]

Just like any drug addiction, adrenaline addiction brings on withdrawal symptoms whenever the body is deprived of the adrenaline. My withdrawal symptoms inevitably showed up the first few days of a vacation. I would be restless and fidgety and irritable because of the absence of the workaholic behavior I was using to numb my pain.

3. A False, Workaholic Theology

I remember one internationally known Christian speaker at a conference I attended telling us that rest and leisure activities had no place in a Christian's life here on earth. "We'll have plenty of time for fun and rest in heaven," he said. "Our time here on earth is to be taken up in saving souls; that's the only reason God left us here."

Yet we all know that any machine, whether it's an automobile or the human body, will break down when not properly maintained.

God *has* called us to serve others, to reach out to others. But he also wants us to be in touch with our needs and take responsibility for meeting them.

I remember the first time I was exposed to the philosophy that taking care of your legitimate needs is sinful. I was ten years old. I was at vacation Bible school, and there amid the clutter of Kool-Aid and plaster plaques of praying hands, Mrs. Kleinsapper was explaining the JOY principle.

"Children," she intoned, "always remember that joy is spelled J-O-Y. The only way to be happy in life, the only way to please God, is to put Jesus first, others second, and yourself last."

It's true that we must constantly be on the lookout for self-indulgence and self-centered thinking within ourselves. Those attitudes block our relationship with God and ruin our relationships with our loved ones. But there must also be space in our theology for taking care of our legitimate physical, emotional, and spiritual needs. If taken to an extreme, Mrs. Kleinsapper's JOY principle will encourage us to ignore our human limitations and meet our needs by meeting others' needs.

I received a letter from a gifted young couple a few years ago describing their own struggle with these issues. Bill and Ann were Sunday school superintendents and youth group sponsors in their church. But they were also the parents of young children, and when their involvement in Bible studies and other church activities reached four nights a week, they went to their pastor and his wife.

"We need to cut back on our responsibilities," they shared. "We feel it's harming our family life."

At this point the pastor's wife burst into tears. "How can you possibly say that three or four nights a week is too rough for you," she sobbed, "when five nights is a *good* week for us?"

Thoroughly shamed, Bill and Ann resumed their pace for several more months until serious cracks developed in their marriage and family. That's when they finally went to their pastor and told him they were cutting back.

"We want to love the things we do for God," they told him. "But at the current pace we will soon hate everything we are doing. And we don't want to risk hating him as well."

We all have limitations and needs that are ignored only at our own peril. When Elijah fled from Jezebel in 1 Kings 19 and sank into suicidal depression, the Lord didn't rebuke him for his lack of faith or his lack of dedication. In fact, God didn't attempt to treat his depression with a spiritual solution at all. He sent an angel with food and told Elijah to eat and sleep—and when he woke up, to eat and sleep again.

Jesus often took time out from serving others to rest and be alone. He knew the value of having boundaries, that if you give until the cup is dry, you'll soon have nothing left to give at all.

The JOY principle is based on a faulty model—the model of Christians without cracks, superbeings who have no needs of their own and thus are free to give unstintingly of themselves to others.

But that's not God's view of us. While loving us and believing in us, he knows we have needs. Hebrews 4 says Jesus our high priest sympathizes with our weaknesses because he too lived in a human body. Psalm 103 eloquently sums up God's view: "Just as a father has compassion on his children, so the Lord has compassion on those who fear him. For he himself knows our frame; he is mindful that we are but dust."[5]

At its heart the JOY principle is not only based on a faulty view of what it means to be a Christian. It's based on a faulty view of God as well. Although he has tasks for us to do, our God is not a demanding taskmaster who resents our taking the time we need for rest and rejuvenation. He's also a compassionate father who wants us to learn to live our lives in balance.

Steps to Healthiness

I still struggle with the effects of stress and adrenaline addiction, as well as the issue of lifestyle balance. And what is balance for one man won't necessarily be balance for another. But whatever our situations, we can restore a measure of sanity and rest to our lives.

In Matthew 11:28–30 Jesus gives a promise that is startling—almost incomprehensible—from our frenetic vantage point in the 1990s.

> Come to Me, all who are weary and heavy-laden, and I will give you rest. Take My yoke upon you, and learn from Me, for I am gentle and humble in heart; and you shall find rest for your souls. For My yoke is easy, and My load is light.

Jesus makes an offer that almost sounds like a con to our jaded ears: He will exchange our heavy-laden lifestyles, characterized by weariness, for his gentle and humble lifestyle, characterized by rest. The key, he says, is to learn gentleness and humility. Gentleness will woo us away from our drivenness and competitiveness, and humility will teach us to accept our limitations.

It starts with humility. Humility urges us to identify and accept our resources and limitations in four key areas:

- Emotional energy
- Physical energy
- Time
- Finances

With my pattern of overcommitment, I consistently overspent my "account balance" in all four areas—emotional and physical energy, time, and finances.

I describe the boundaries that define my emotional, physical, temporal, and financial limitations as the Box. When

I stay within the boundaries of the Box God has given me, when I don't overspend in any of the four key areas, I'm living inside my human limitations. I don't strain my resources to the breaking point. I don't have to rely on high-octane adrenaline to make it through the day. In short, I'm living a sane, healthy, balanced life.

The diagram below illustrates what your lifestyle might look like when you're in an unhealthy, overcommitted mode. Instead of living inside your Box, you make commitments outside your resources, as indicated by the *X*s scattered outside the perimeter of the Box. You commit to projects that you do not have the time, emotional strength, physical energy, or finances to pull off without a breakdown somewhere along the way. Wisdom is to know our God-given limits and stay within them.

This is the same gritty wisdom that Jesus recommends to the multitudes in Luke 14:28–30. "For which one of you,

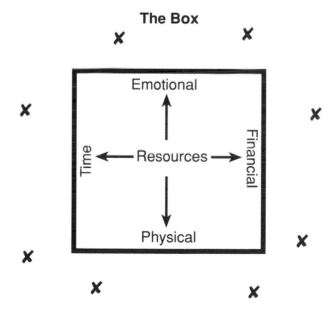

when he wants to build a tower, does not first sit down and calculate the cost, to see if he has enough to complete it? Otherwise, when he has laid a foundation, and is not able to finish, all who observe it begin to ridicule him, saying, 'This man began to build and was not able to finish.'"

I don't know about you, but I've started a lot of towers in my adult life that I haven't been able to finish. And there have been other towers that I have finished, but by the time they were done, the construction sites were littered with the bodies of the workmen I'd pressed into service (often my loved ones and friends).

Basically we have two commodities to work with in constructing a life: time and money. These are the two resources I most frequently overspend, which puts pressure on all the other areas of life: my emotional, spiritual, and physical well-being. And I've found the same to be true for the men I minister to. The Men's Confidential Survey I take in our seminars documents the scope of the problem among Christian men: More than one-third indicate that some of their families' basic needs are going unmet because of a lack of money, and a staggering 85 percent say they do not have enough time to adequately fulfill their various responsibilities.

But there is hope. I've seen my own out-of-control life turn around. And I've worked with a number of men in mentoring relationships who have also reduced stress and restored balance to their lives. In every case, the key lay in learning how to be better stewards of time and money. Following is an overview of what these men discovered, including their top suggestions for dealing with time and money resources.

Spend Your Time Wisely

A recent Harris survey has confirmed the sobering trends we discussed earlier in this chapter. The amount of leisure time enjoyed by the average American has decreased 37 percent since 1973. During those same two decades, the average work week, including commuting, has jumped from less than forty-one hours to nearly forty-seven hours.[6]

And of course, more than the loss of leisure time is at stake here. The demands of our work are squeezing out time for family as well as for personal and spiritual growth. Recent surveys show that the average husband and wife spend four minutes a day in meaningful conversation. The amount of time spent by parents with their children is between thirty-seven seconds and five minutes a day (depending on the study).[7] "The inevitable loser from this life in the fast lane," says psychologist James Dobson, "is the little guy who is leaning against the wall with his hands in the pockets of his blue jeans."[8]

The result, even for most Christian families today, is a fundamental reversal of biblical priorities. Our activities outside the home—our work and church meetings or ministry activities—take up virtually all the hours of the week, forcing us to squeeze our family and personal growth into the tiny amount of remaining discretionary time.

In *When I Relax I Feel Guilty* author Tim Hansel talks about a crossroads he came to early in his ministry with Young Life. He was busy around the clock with ministry activities, helping others find the Lord, but rarely taking time to let God minister to his own inner needs. He realized he had become "a tired, driven salesman of the abundant life," and that if anyone were to peep through the windows of his house and see the way he truly lived his life, that person would never want to become a Christian. His "doing" outstripped his "being," and he realized he needed to nurture his personal life, or he had no right to be in ministry at all.

God does, indeed, expect us to work hard and to be involved in ministry to others. But it is his clear intention that our "core" be healthy *first*—that we take whatever time is needed to continue growing in our personal lives and in

115

our primary relationships as husbands and fathers. The diagram below illustrates God's priorities for us.

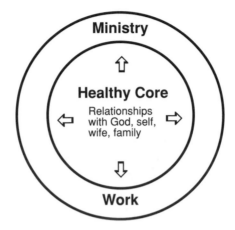

We are to minister out of a healthy core—which means working on crucial issues of personal and character growth, taking whatever time is necessary to nurture our relationships with our wives and children. Our work and outside activities, including our ministry activities, are a lower priority.

In my first ministry and marriage, I was a classic example of someone who put ministry first and spent little time working on my personal growth and character. I was ministering out of an *unhealthy* core, and I lived to deeply regret it.

I have heard other Christian leaders spiritualize the imbalance between ministry and family life by teaching that God would supernaturally bless and protect our primary relationships if we "put God first" by serving him with what amounted to all of our available time. But in my twenty years of supervising others involved in unbalanced ministry, I saw little evidence of divine blessing. Just the opposite. I met outwardly successful ministry leaders with painfully conflicted marriages and estranged children.

Much of the rest of this book will focus on the activities that will help us develop a healthy core: mentoring relationships with other men; time to communicate with our wives, to listen to them, to be tender and passionate with them; time to be fathers; time alone with God for reflection and direction; time to play and relax. Without solid chunks of time set aside for these endeavors, our core will soon be unhealthy, our lives will be filled with low-priority busy-ness, and we will once again be fueling our lifestyles with adrenaline.

The challenge for us as men, of course, is to find the time to develop these important areas. For every new, nurturing activity we say yes to, we have to say no to something else. We have to release some of our present activities and replace them with others we feel are more important. Following are the five most frequent suggestions for time-savers made by the men in our mentoring workshops.

1. Kill your TV. This may be one of those pieces of bumper sticker wisdom that may be on target. You may not be ready to terminate your tube entirely, but consider giving it a mortal wound by turning it off several evenings a week. For the average adult, pulling the plug entirely would give them back more than thirty hours a week.[9]

2. Evaluate your hobbies and athletic activities. Are extracurricular activities eating large amounts of time in your weekly schedule? We all need the freedom to relax and have fun in meaningful ways, but if our outside activity starts to look more like a career than a hobby, it's probably time to cut back.

A number of years ago I trained for and competed in several marathons. At its peak, this hobby of mine required around two hours of training time per day, six days a week. That's a lot of time that had to come from somewhere. It couldn't come out of my work schedule, so it came out of my family time. In retrospect, there was no way I could jus-

117

tify the amount of time I spent pounding the pavement in the name of "health," especially considering the people I was robbing the time from.

3. Consider un*volunteering.* If you have determined there are needy areas in your personal or family life that urgently need attention, it may be appropriate to cut back for a time on volunteer responsibilities with committees, boards, and other outside commitments.

4. Cut the commute. The average North American spends forty-five minutes a day commuting to and from work.[10] For many men the long commute by itself eliminates the possibility of time for healthy-core activities in the evening. Consider finding a job closer to home or a home nearer your job, and thereby buy back all your evenings.

5. Reduce the hours you work. Several of the men I have worked with faced a tough dilemma. It wasn't their TV watching or hobbies that robbed them of their healthy-core time; it was their jobs. Some men in management were told before they assumed their positions that the job would involve long hours (read, sixty to ninety). Other hourly employees were pressured to work a significant amount of overtime each week.

Different men responded to these challenges in different ways. One manager talked to his supervisor and worked out an understanding on shorter hours. He reasoned with his boss that an employee with a stable family and personal life was a more effective employee. It worked, and my friend got most of his evenings back. It might work for you.

Other men decided to begin turning down overtime requests. One man quit his job entirely and found a new one with shorter hours. All of these men took a cut in pay as a result. But as Joe Dominguez and Vicki Robin point out in *Your Money or Your Life,* we all exchange one of the most precious things we have—the hours of our lives—for money. There is nothing more basic to give away. If we give too many hours away—even in exchange for money—we no longer have a life. This may be an option for you and your wife and family to consider. Because a shift in standard of living will probably be involved, everyone should give their input.

You might think of other ways to buy back the hours of your life. But whatever you do, keep your compass firmly in view: a healthy core is job one.

Spend Your Money Wisely

The second major area of stress for men today is finances. An increasing number of Christian men in our Manhood seminars have gone through the scarring experience of bankruptcy. Bankruptcies today are at record levels, nearly one million each year in the United States.[11] In addition, the cost of buying a home has skyrocketed. The average mortgage today requires over one hundred hours of factory labor a month to pay, compared to only forty hours twenty years ago.[12] The tough economic times in the '90s are obviously putting the squeeze on all of us and our families. How can we approach the issue of money more wisely?

In one of the most comprehensive teachings on money in Scripture, Paul advises:

> Godliness actually is a means of great gain, when accompanied by contentment. For we have brought nothing into the world, so we cannot take anything out of it either. And if we have food and covering, with these we shall be content. But those who want to get rich fall into temptation and a snare and many foolish and harmful desires which plunge men into ruin and destruction. For the love of money is a root of all sorts of evil, and some by longing for it have wandered away from the faith, and pierced themselves with many a pang. But flee from these things, you man of God; and pursue righteousness, godliness, faith, love, perseverance and gentleness.[13]

119

In addition, Paul says this about debt: "Let no debt remain outstanding, except the continuing debt to love one another."[14]

I justified violating many of these principles for years, until God finally broke through my denial. I've now come to see that I've lived out a pattern of overspending all my adult life. That was a part of my larger character flaw of grandiosity and overcommitting. Here are some of the lessons I've had to learn the hard way in recent years.

1. Live within your limits. This comes down to a simple rule of thumb: Don't spend more each month than you earn each month. Though it's simple, many of us have found it difficult to do. Credit card offers come through the mail to us weekly; advertising creates an artificial need for all kinds of goods we can't afford. I've found that nothing less than a sacred commitment to stay within your means, no matter how great the temptation, is what it takes to live debt free in our society. For me, that has meant questioning the standard of living I have always taken for granted and beginning to simplify my life. We have discovered there is a "simplify your life" movement growing in America today. It's made up of individuals who are downsizing and finding creative ways to live on less but enjoy life more. (Numerous resources are available through your local library for those interested in investigating this further.)

2. Make a budget and stick to it. There is probably no other area related to money matters that I have resisted more than making a budget. I rationalized my negativity about budgeting many different ways, but in hindsight I see I was simply afraid of being controlled in my spending (which is just another way of saying *I* wanted to stay in control in that area). Because of all this internal drama, submitting to a budget has been a deeply spiritual act for me. It has involved putting things on the altar I've never been able to put there before and trusting God with a host of irrational fears about deprivation and want.

This may be a spiritual discipline for you, too. Or it may simply function as a necessary enforcement mechanism for living within your limits.

3. Discard the cards. Researchers tell us the average North American carries seven to ten credit cards with him at all times (Don't leave home without it!). When I finally acknowledged the need to cut up all my cards, I hedged. I insisted on holding on to one like a security blanket. I even went to the trouble to freeze the card in a pan of water in our freezer so it would not be available for impulse buying. But after several months I found I had not really needed the card, so I melted the block of ice with a blow dryer and cut up the last one. (My wife danced a jig.)

For most of us, credit cards are dangerous. We tell ourselves we will only use them to make purchases we can fully pay off in a month—but then run up balances that will take years to get rid of.

4. Minimize your housing costs. The single biggest expenditure for most families is housing. Financial counselors recommend that we not spend more than 40 percent of our *net* (take home) income on housing. That 40 percent includes real estate taxes, insurance, maintenance, and utilities. For our family, the need to shrink our mortgage payment has led us to move from a custom home in the mountains to a condo in the city. It's taken some adjusting (and some selling of the accumulated stuff of over two decades of adult life), but I can honestly say we're enjoying our new home a great deal—and our new mortgage payment. And learning to live within our limits has produced a sense of freedom we never knew was possible.

Your friends and relatives may not applaud or even understand your decision to downsize. It is the opposite of trading up, and trading up is what our society encourages. In the end, only you can decide what is best for your family.

In the movie *Mr. Jones* Richard Gere plays the role of a manic-depressive. During his manic highs, Gere is super-confident, optimistic, and charming. Unfortunately he also thinks he can jump off tall buildings and fly. During his depressive cycles, Gere is intensely despondent and suicidal. When he finally seeks help at a hospital, the doctors put him on medication that flattens out both the highs and lows of his illness. But Gere ultimately walks away from treatment, even though it's saving his life, because it is too painful to live without the fix of his manic highs. Life is just too drab, too boring.

The same choice faces many of us today: Can we live without the temporary hit in order to achieve long-term healthiness?

Personal Assessment:

Lifestyle Symptoms

Because our society applauds adrenaline addiction and the activities that promote it, it is more difficult to recognize its hold on our lives. The following personal assessment may help you identify areas of potential concern. Check yes or no for each question.

Work		
yes	no	
□	□	Does your family complain about the long hours you work?
□	□	Do you rarely have time to be involved in school or social activities with your family?
□	□	Do you have to keep constantly busy on various projects at home, even in the evenings and on weekends?
□	□	Do you have trouble sleeping because your mind is preoccupied with your work?

Spending

yes   no

☐   ☐   Have you intentionally gone shopping to lift your spirits or to help deal with depression, rather than because you needed something?

☐   ☐   Do you sometimes use one line of credit to pay off another?

☐   ☐   Have you sometimes hidden your purchases or lied about them so your family wouldn't know you had been shopping?

☐   ☐   Have you felt guilty, remorseful, or anxious after a shopping spree?

A yes answer to any of the questions above may indicate you are using the activities listed to produce the adrenaline rush that keeps us ahead of our emotional pain.

Stress Test:

Personal Factors

Rosalind Forbes, author of *Corporate Stress and Life Stress*, has formulated a stress test to help you evaluate the amount of stress you are carrying on the job.[15] To take the test, read the question, check the box which reflects your answer, total the points, and read the comments associated with your score.

never	*seldom*	*sometimes*	*often*	*always*	
(1 pt.)	(2 pts.)	(3 pts.)	(4 pts.)	(5 pts.)	
☐	☐	☐	☐	☐	Do you try to do as much as possible in the least amount of time?
☐	☐	☐	☐	☐	Are you impatient with delays, interruptions?
☐	☐	☐	☐	☐	Do you have to win at games to enjoy yourself?
☐	☐	☐	☐	☐	Are you unlikely to ask for help with a problem?

123

When the Hits Don't Keep On Coming

never	seldom	sometimes	often	always	
(1 pt.)	(2 pts.)	(3 pts.)	(4 pts.)	(5 pts.)	
☐	☐	☐	☐	☐	Do you constantly strive to better your position or achievements?
☐	☐	☐	☐	☐	Do you constantly seek the respect and admiration of others?
☐	☐	☐	☐	☐	Are you overly critical of the way others do their work?
☐	☐	☐	☐	☐	Do you have the habit of looking at your watch?
☐	☐	☐	☐	☐	Do you spread yourself too thin in terms of time?
☐	☐	☐	☐	☐	Do you have the habit of doing more than one thing at a time?
☐	☐	☐	☐	☐	Are you angry or irritable?
☐	☐	☐	☐	☐	Do you have a tendency to talk quickly or hasten conversation?
☐	☐	☐	☐	☐	Do you consider yourself hard-driving?
☐	☐	☐	☐	☐	Do your friends or relatives consider you hard-driving?
☐	☐	☐	☐	☐	Do you tend to get involved in multiple projects?
☐	☐	☐	☐	☐	Do you have deadlines in your work?
☐	☐	☐	☐	☐	Do you feel vaguely guilty if you relax or leave the office at lunchtime?
☐	☐	☐	☐	☐	Do you take on too many responsibilities?

Total your points and write your score here: _____

124

Score	Interpretation
18–30	You probably work best in nonstressful, noncompetitive situations, like to set your own pace, and concentrate on one task at a time. Interruptions drive you crazy. Stress is likely to hinder your performance rather than enhance it.
31–60	You can handle a bit of stress and probably enjoy it as long as it doesn't happen during more than 20 percent of your working hours.
61–90	Look out! The people who work with you better look out, too. You need constant pressure to perform. You tend to stay up all night to finish reports, or you expand tasks to increase pressure when deadlines or the job's demands aren't stressful enough. You probably grind your teeth. Your situation is dangerous if not handled properly. The human body and mind were not designed to hold such extreme pressures. Something has to give.

The Search for the Magic Wand

Women and Sex

> At the heart of the problem of [men with wounded masculinity] is our society's bizarre attempt to raise sons without fathers. . . . So our boy marches forth to find a female whose magic wand will turn him into a man. The quest is fraught with doubts and dangers.
>
> Frank Pittman, "The Masculine Mystique"

> Is there beauty in Sodom? Believe me, that for the immense mass of mankind beauty is found in Sodom. . . . God and the devil are fighting there, and the battlefield is the heart of man.
>
> Feodor Dostoevski, *The Brothers Karamazov*

Ron and I had been meeting in a mentoring relationship for several months. A shift supervisor at the giant Georgia Pacific lumber mill, Ron had remained clean and sober for more than a year. He now felt he was ready to work on relationship issues. As we moved into course material dealing with sexuality and relationships with women, Ron became agitated.

"Women run my emotions," he said angrily. "It's been that way all my life."

Ron's father had been a lifelong alcoholic. A brooding, verbally abusive man, he went unemployed for long periods while Ron was growing up. Ron learned to avoid him whenever possible and sought refuge in his relationship with his mother.

"Mom and I were especially close," Ron recalled. "She'd protect me from Dad when he was drunk, and she'd tell me secrets—things she didn't tell Dad."

Ron's mother often talked to him about her unhappiness in the marriage and about the pain she carried. Ron soon learned to comfort and reassure her. He shook his head in embarrassment as he described dozens of scenes where a dry-eyed, twelve-year-old boy held his mother while she cried.

"I became her emotional caretaker," Ron said. "I could walk into the room and instantly know what mood she was in. If she was happy, I was happy. If she was down, I knew it was my job to make her happy again. It's like I didn't have an emotional life of my own.

"It's scary," Ron went on, "but I see the same thing happening in my adult relationships. I'd rather talk to a woman than a man, and I always seem to end up being a friend and counselor to some emotionally needy woman."

More than once at the office where he worked, Ron found himself strongly drawn to female coworkers. He found excuses to spend time talking to them, and his joking and lighthearted banter often progressed to flirting. In a couple of instances, the office relationships spilled over into long one-on-one lunches where both Ron and the female coworker shared intimately about their frustrations in their own marriages. Ron kept those luncheon meetings secret from his wife.

"I told myself, 'As long as it isn't a physical affair, it's okay. You can look, but don't touch. You're not doing anything wrong.'"

Eventually, however, a red light began flashing in Ron's conscience. "It wasn't fair to my wife," Ron said. "I knew those relationships violated my spiritual and emotional bond with my wife, even if they didn't violate our physical bond."

His eyes narrowed and a hard look crossed his face. "Besides," he said, "I've been living off women's emotions for thirty-eight years, and I'm tired of it. I figure it's time I got an emotional life of my own."

Many men carry a father wound *and* a mother wound into adult life. Like Ron, these men were both underfathered and overmothered. Their mothers, with good intentions, tried to step into the gap left by an absent father. The unnaturally close relationship that develops between mother and son in these circumstances is a kind of surrogate spouse relationship. The son becomes the mother's confidant and emotional caretaker, and never bonds with his father. These men graduate to manhood not only with a wounded masculinity but also with an unhealthy dependency on women's approval.

This dependency on women's approval can add a dangerous undertow to a man's relationship with all women. Often a man who needs women's approval unconsciously looks for a positive signal from the women he meets, as Ron did, and reacts in an unhealthy way if he doesn't receive it.

The Subconscious Consequences of Seeking Women's Approval

A couple of years ago my wife and I were hiking on the majestic flanks of Mount Rainier in Washington. It was a gorgeous, sun-splashed day, and I had brought our camera to take pictures. Partway up, we heard the peculiar, shrill whistle of a marmot, that furry little groundhog-type creature whose tunnels honeycomb the mountainside.

We soon spotted the little guy standing up on hind legs not more than thirty feet away. Unsnapping the camera case, I stepped a couple of paces off the path in the direction of the marmot to get a better picture.

Suddenly I heard a shout behind me, "Hey, what do you think you're doing?"

Turning around, I saw a matronly tourist in her mid-fifties stalking angrily up the trail behind us. "Can't you read?" she shouted in a voice loud enough to be heard in Montana. "The signs say 'Stay on the trail.' That means *you*."

In a nanosecond, a wave of molten rage swept over me. Without a word I slapped the cover back on the camera, whirled on my heel, and took off up the trail at double speed. My wife watched in amazement as I disappeared around the next bend.

It took Marsha twenty minutes to catch up, and when she did she said, "For Pete's sake, what happened back there? Why'd you take off like that?"

We sat down and talked it through. Eventually we laughed about my overreaction, which more or less reflected the emotional maturity of an eight-year-old. Like my friend Ron, I too had bonded with my mother while growing up, but not with my father. I had entered adulthood with an unhealthy dependency on women's approval and a reaction of volcanic anger toward women's anger. The rage response that fueled my flight up the mountain was instinctive, perhaps even primal. The little boy in me had developed a set of survival instincts growing up. One of those instincts warned him that angry women were dangerous, and my system kicked in with an irrational fight or flight response.

This same response, I see in retrospect, had kicked in numerous times in my marriage. During each of those conflicts it had felt as if my wife were at fault, as if my anger reaction was justified by the circumstances. But what was really going on was a little boy's outmoded survival skills. I'm learning to take responsibility for my reaction patterns. Now when I happen to run into an angry or critical woman and the alarm bells go off inside me, rather than reacting instinctively, I do a reality check. About eight times out of ten I decide a fight or flight response is not appropriate. (I'm not healthy enough yet to come to that conclusion every time.)

The Personal Assessment exercise at the end of this chapter may help you detect whether or not you have an unhealthy dependency on women's approval.

The need for approval from women can be so great that when a man experiences the inevitable conflicts that come with marriage, he looks for another woman who will approve and affirm him. Even if this outside relationship never becomes sexual, it can easily become an emotional affair, draining time, energy, and intimacy from the marriage. Of the married men responding to our Men's Confidential Survey at our seminars, 19 percent—almost one in five—acknowledge having had an emotional affair with another woman since they've become Christians.

There are early warning signs that a relationship may be developing into an emotional affair. Here are three questions for personal reflection:

- Are you currently developing a relationship with any woman other than your wife that raises a red flag in your conscience?
- Do you have meetings with other women (even if they are not of a romantic nature) that you deliberately hide from your wife?
- Are there women in your life right now, other than your wife, whom you often think about, are excited by, and find yourself looking forward to being with?

A yes answer to any of these questions suggests that you may be sailing into dangerous waters.

Of course, when we give women this kind of power over our emotions, when we make them the arbiters of our worth as men, the resulting dynamic is not only unhealthy, it is another form of idolatry. Solomon's seven hundred wives and three hundred concubines "turned his heart away after other gods; and his heart was not wholly devoted to the Lord his God."[1] Just as those playing a Hero role substitute society's approval for God's approval, men with a masculine wound substitute women's approval for God's approval.

The process of renouncing our dependency on women's approval and moving toward something healthier is every bit as challenging as the process an alcoholic goes through giving up alcohol. Old behaviors and habit patterns need to be given up; we need to invite God the Father to heal our masculine wound and to take his rightful place in our hearts; and we need to begin the tough, daily work required to reprogram our thought life and self-talk.

Not all men who wrestle with sexual temptation are looking for women's approval. Some are afraid of women and simply watch them from a distance. For these men, depersonalizing women as sex objects gives them a feeling of power over women to compensate for their fear.

A young man approached me during a break at a recent Manhood seminar I gave at a university campus. We had just finished discussing the material about dependency on women's approval, and Ray came up to give feedback.

"You talked about how some men make eye contact with women in public and look for some positive response from them. I'm definitely not looking for women's approval," Ray said. "I'm too scared to approach women that closely, and I avoid eye contact at all costs!"

Ray went on to say that although he wasn't trying to win women's approval, he knew he had a problem.

"I have what I suppose you'd call a watching addiction," Ray said. "I watch women everywhere I go. And that starts

131

the sexual fantasizing." He explained that his habit started when he was nine years old. An older neighbor girl used to take him out in the woods, and they'd both disrobe. Eroticized at an early age, he agonized with his watching addiction all his life.

"I know it's dishonoring to God," Ray said earnestly. "I've prayed and prayed about it and asked God to take it away, but it doesn't seem to do any good."

For many men, like Ray, the issue is not female approval. The issue is the seductive appeal of sexual addiction.

Sexual Addiction

The unhealthiness that comes from a man's wounded masculinity is often heated as hot as a supernova by a society saturated with sex. The resulting sexual addiction creates a tidal wave of pain—personal, marital, and familial—that continues to sweep through the ranks of Christian men and their families. Headlines trumpet stories of church leaders caught in sexual sin. And for each headline involving a Christian leader, there are thousands of unannounced stories about sincere Christian laymen whose secret sexual lives have erupted into the open, causing untold hurt and damage.

The Men's Confidential Survey referred to previously polled 350 men from more than a dozen evangelical denominations. Ten percent of the respondents are pastors. Of the 90 percent who are laymen, the majority hold leadership responsibilities in their churches—deacons, elders, and men's ministry leaders. The survey results reveal the extent to which Christian men, even church leaders, struggle with their sexuality:

- 64 percent struggle with sexual addiction or sexual compulsion, including but not limited to use of por-

nography, compulsive masturbation, or other secret
sexual activity.
• 25 percent admit to having had sexual intercourse
with someone other than their wife, while married,
since becoming a Christian.
• Another 14 percent acknowledge having had sexual
contact short of intercourse outside of their marriage
since becoming a Christian.

When the figures for those having had sexual intercourse
outside marriage, sexual contact short of intercourse, and
emotional affairs are combined, it reveals that more than
half of our most committed laymen and pastors have had
some kind of inappropriate involvement with women outside marriage. These findings are generally confirmed by
other recent national surveys.[2]

Many other men who have never acted out sexually tell
me of their constant struggle with sexual fantasizing or compulsive masturbation and the cycle of guilt these behaviors
produce. All of this makes it clear that illicit sexuality is not
just an issue "out there" in the world; it is a painful reality
for a majority of Christian men as well, a reality we need
to address directly and honestly.

In *Godric* Frederick Buechner expresses the cry of anguish
that most men feel regarding lust:

> Lust is the ape that gibbers in our loins. Tame him as we will
> by day, he rages all the wilder in our dreams by night. Just
> when we think we're safe from him, he raises up his ugly head
> and smirks, and there's no river in the world flows cold and
> strong enough to strike him down. Almighty God, why dost
> thou deck men out with such a loathsome toy?[3]

Of course, illicit sexual behavior is sin, and the Bible
doesn't mince words in describing the consequences: "Can
a man take fire in his bosom, and his clothes not be burned?

133

Or can a man walk on hot coals, and his feet not be scorched? So is the one who goes in to his neighbor's wife."[4]

But from my own painful experience and from my work with scores of men in the last five years, it is not enough to simply label these behaviors sin. If that were true, Gordon MacDonald and David Hocking and thousands of other mature Christian men would not have succumbed to adultery or other sexual sin. In addition to the label, we must understand what's going on beneath the behavior. The journey that ultimately ends in adultery or addiction to pornography most often began long ago. Understanding that painful journey and how to avoid it is where our investigation must begin.

Reverend Stephen Smith's story illustrates that process clearly. A pastor and personal growth coach, Stephen's story begins in his childhood. Stephen grew up in a rigidly religious home where sex was not mentioned, and true feelings were rarely expressed. He cannot remember seeing his parents touch or kiss, and he developed a longing for love and affection that went largely unmet. When Stephen was four, and again when he was nine, he was sexually abused by someone outside his family.

When Stephen reached puberty, his love needs were eroticized when he discovered his older brother's pornography. A pattern quickly developed. He would escape the rigid, nonfeeling family dynamic through pornography and masturbation. Throughout college, dating, and marriage, Stephen's obsession with pornography grew in scope and energy.

In spite of his sexual addiction, or perhaps because of it, Stephen became aggressive in his search for significance. He had been active in youth leadership in his church and eventually sensed God calling him into the ministry. Seminary followed, then foreign mission service and college chaplaincy. Ultimately he accepted a staff position at a large southern church, where his work in evangelism, renewal, and healing consumed seventy to eighty hours a week.

Stephen said later of this period: "I was Spirit-filled and knew all the renewal songs, but the size of my heart was shrinking. My private thoughts, the roaming of adult bookstores, and masturbation all increased. . . . My sexual behaviors had become riskier and more extreme in order to give the same level of momentary thrill."[5]

One Sunday night Stephen realized his life was out of control. As he prepared to conduct the service, he began to obsess about visiting an adult bookstore. All through the evening, even during the prayer time, fantasy danced on the edge of his consciousness. After the service he changed clothes and drove to the bookstore. He felt intense fear that someone might see and recognize him. Afterward, as always, he was flooded with shame and self-loathing. He knew what he was doing was wrong but didn't know how to break its hold.

Prior to this, Stephen's wife had developed her own substance addiction. When the church discovered her addiction (his own was still a secret), Stephen was told to fix his wife's problem or leave the church. Ultimately a friend suggested Stephen go to a treatment center to work on codependency issues related to his wife's addiction.

"I panicked inside," Stephen recounts. "'What if they find out about my secret life?' I asked myself. 'They'd tell my church and I'd lose my job. And then what would I do?'"

But the increasing pain in Stephen's life finally forced him to action. Not long afterward, he checked into a treatment center. Soon after arriving, his counselor handed him a stack of books on sexual addiction, codependency, anger, and shame. But none of the books had anything to do with his wife's issues.

"As I took the books from the counselor," Stephen remembers, "I smiled my best pastoral smile and said, 'Thank you. I'll be sure to read these when I get home. But I'm here to learn how I can help my wife with her problem.'

"My counselor looked at me and said, 'Just read the books, Stephen.'

"'No, really,' I replied. 'I appreciate them, but I'm only here a short time, and I really do need to focus on how to help my wife with her problem.'

"At that point, with several other patients looking on, my counselor made exaggerated movements of looking all around me and behind me. Then she looked at me and said with mock surprise, 'Well, gosh, Stephen, I don't see your wife here, do you? So why don't we take a look at you?'

"I was immediately both enraged and terrified. I went to my room and broke down crying. 'Now they know, and I'm going to die,' I sobbed. I knew then that God had brought me there because of the insanity in my own life, and not my wife's."

Stephen was at the treatment center for six weeks. During that time he completed a sexual history inventory that forced him to face the destructive patterns in his life. As the levels of his denial fell away, Stephen was shocked to realize how he'd been willing to use anyone and anything, including the church, to foster his addiction. After a lifetime of struggle, he had finally reached a turning point. His denial was broken, and he turned his life and will over to God in a new and deeper way.

Wisdom from the Word

Motivated by love, God gave us our sexuality, knowing it contains powerful potential for both pleasure and pain; with love, his gift included an instruction book. One of its clearest passages on this subject is found in Proverbs 4:23–27:

Watch over your heart with all diligence,
For from it flow the springs of life.
Put away from you a deceitful mouth,
And put devious lips far from you.
Let your eyes look directly ahead,
And let your gaze be fixed straight in front of you.
Watch the path of your feet,
And all your ways will be established.
Do not turn to the right nor to the left;
Turn your foot from evil.

Using the analogy of the body, Solomon gives solid, streetwise advice here in four key areas: the heart, the mouth, the eyes, and the feet.

Heart

The most powerful sex organ given to man is the mind, and Solomon starts right at the top. (The Hebrews used the words *heart* and *mind* as roughly analogous.) We are to "watch over" our hearts as men, Solomon says, which means monitoring our minds. This includes watching over our thought lives, our sexual fantasizing, our preoccupation with women and their responsiveness to or approval of us. The battle over lust, Solomon says, is won or lost here, in the mind.

There are two steps in this confrontation with lust. The first step, according to 2 Corinthians 10:5, is to "take captive" the offending thoughts. That means not tolerating them, pushing them forcibly out of our minds. The second step is to replace the unhealthy thoughts with healthy ones. The apostle Paul exhorts us in Philippians 4:8 to "let your mind dwell" on things that are pure and honorable and right. Some men find it helpful to meditate on Scripture as a thought-stopper; others find it more effective to simply wrench their focus back onto their work or whatever activity was interrupted by the fantasizing.

137

Whatever method you use, avoid the temptation to be simplistic. Lust is a tough, wily foe, and needs to be fought on several levels at once. Just memorizing Scripture won't deliver us from the clutches of our dark sides. That's magical thinking. If the devil and his henchmen can persuade us to put all our eggs in that basket, then he has most likely already won the battle.

Mouth

The second area Solomon exhorts us to work on is our mouth. Put away "a deceitful mouth" and "devious lips." Because of the shame associated with sexual sin or sexual compulsivity, deceit is often an integral part of our pattern. We lie to ourselves, telling ourselves we don't really have a problem, and we hide the truth from others, fearing their reaction.

Being honest about our struggle—first with ourselves and then with another person—is one of the keys to victory. James puts it plainly: "Confess your sins to one another, and pray for one another, so that you may be healed."[6]

It is important, however, that the person you choose as a confidant be someone you trust. If no one else seems safe enough, meet with a counselor or therapist. Unless the abuse of a minor is involved, these professionals are sworn to confidentiality.

Eyes

Solomon next tackles the age-old issue of what we look at. Our eyes, he wisely says, are to "look directly ahead," and our gaze is to be "fixed straight in front" of us.

My inner work in this particular area had to begin with my built-in "antenna" toward women. I have had to literally retrain my senses, to turn down the strength of my antenna when it comes to noticing women in public. When the signal comes to my brain now, telling me that a woman is in my vicinity, I make a conscious attempt not to respond to the signal, but instead to look directly ahead.

One of the men I work with told me about accompanying his son on a recent third-grade field trip. An attractive woman in her thirties was also along on the trip, and as my friend put it, "Her antenna was constantly sending out signals that said, 'I'm here. I'm attractive.'" He found he had to rudely ignore this woman all afternoon just to draw the appropriate boundary around himself.

The way we relate to women in social situations is worth evaluating, too. I try to relate to women in exactly the same way I relate to men—no more charm, warmth, or "niceness" with women than with men. I've come to see that for me *charm* is just another word for flirting.

We probably can't improve on the commitment Job made nearly four thousand years ago: "I made a covenant with my eyes not to look lustfully at a girl."[7]

That kind of commitment may involve the kinds of magazines we allow in our homes, as well. One friend of mine who is recovering from an addiction to pornography has asked his wife not to bring lingerie catalogs into the home because they present a temptation.

Feet

Last, Solomon warns us about our feet—where we go, the places and situations we choose to put ourselves in. Some men know they simply are not free to go to certain parts of town where the adult bookstores are. Others know that certain women at the office are out of bounds for them to socialize with.

Each of us has our own "fault lines"—the cracks and weaknesses in our foundation. It is wise to know where those weaknesses lie and to draw a firm boundary around them.

But above all, realize there are no quick fixes in re-programming old mental habit patterns. If you have worn a groove in your mind in an unhealthy direction, it will take time to build new habits. Commit to this as a long, ongoing process, and give yourself grace along the way. At first you may fail as often as you succeed. The important thing is to pick yourself up and keep heading in the right direction.

Philip, a good friend of mine, pastors a large church in Canada. We worked together in a mentoring relationship for over a year. During one particularly helpful exchange about men and lust, Philip related a true story from his past. It perfectly illustrates the danger of magical thinking when it comes to combatting lust.

"One summer during seminary," Philip told me, "I had a job in downtown Vancouver at a seafood plant. The place where I worked was only a few doors away from an adult bookstore. I'd had an on-again, off-again problem with pornography ever since I was a teenager, and I was deter-mined not to give in to the temptation to go into that book-store. So I claimed Psalm 119:11, "Thy Word have I hid in mine heart, that I might not sin against thee." I decided I would use my noon hours to memorize the entire 119th Psalm that summer to keep me from temptation.

"Every lunch break, I'd dive into Psalm 119, memoriz-ing like crazy. But every day, before the lunch break was over, I'd find myself walking into the porno shop, some-times carrying my Bible verse cards!

"By the time the summer was over, I had committed to memory all one hundred and seventy-six verses of Psalm 119, but had consistently succumbed to the temptation every day anyway. I found out the hard way that memoriz-ing Scripture by itself doesn't work."

I asked Philip what does work for him in his battle with pornography.

"A combination of several things," he replied. "First, I admit to God I can't overcome this problem in my own strength. Second, I tell another person about my struggle. I can't whip this alone, and I don't think any man can. Third, I ask myself, 'What are the patterns? What triggers the behavior?' I've learned, for instance, that I am visually stimulated. So I don't even go into the big video superstores that have whole sections of videos with sexy covers. I can only go into grocery store video departments.

"And fourth, I've found it helpful to discover what the unhealthiness is underneath my struggle with pornography. With a therapist's help, I've discovered I have a fear of intimacy that fuels the addiction. That fear of intimacy supercharges anything sexual and creates a "forbidden fruit" dynamic. Now, I consciously work on sharing vulnerably with my wife in order to break that fear of intimacy. It's made my relationship with her and with all women healthier.

"And," he chuckled, "I do still memorize Scripture."

Steps to Healthiness

I've worked personally with a number of men in the last few years who have experienced consistent victory in their struggle with sexual addiction. Without exception, each of these men has emphasized the following three elements in his personal recovery program.

1. Replace Your Faulty Belief System

Dr. Patrick Carnes is one of the most respected authorities on treatment for sexual addiction and sexual compulsion. His research has identified four core beliefs that encourage addictive behavior for all sex addicts. Those old beliefs and the new beliefs that must replace them are listed on the following page.[8]

Old core beliefs	New beliefs
I am basically a bad, unworthy person.	I am a worthwhile person, with positive self-esteem.
No one would love me as I am.	I am loved and accepted by people who know me as I am.
My needs are never going to be met if I have to depend on someone else (my wife).	My needs can be met by others if I let them know what I need.
Sex is my most important need (or the most important sign of love).	Sex is but one expression of my need and care for others. The nurturing that I long for can come from a variety of experiences.

Men caught in the cycle of sexual addiction isolate themselves from others because they believe they will not be loved and accepted if people know them as they really are. Compulsive sexual behavior becomes a way to medicate the loneliness they carry and to create a counterfeit intimacy.

The cycle is fundamentally broken when we confront the falseness and destructiveness of our old belief systems, and replace them with the grace-full, life-affirming belief system found in the Bible (such as the passages of Scripture at the end of chapter 2).

2. Eliminate Stress from Your Life

Stress is a killer in more ways than one. In the last chapter we saw the way stress leads to adrenaline addiction, workaholism, and other socially acceptable but destructive habits. Unmanaged stress is also one of the biggest factors leading to destructive sexual habits because it builds inside us until we seek release in the pseudocomfort of illicit sex. Dr. Carnes summarizes several situations that can trigger unhealthy behavior:

Addicts often point to the connection between their addiction and the stress of high performance demands. . . . The stress of proving one's self in an arena where every inadequacy is evaluated is a potent flashpoint for the ignition of sexual addiction. [This may include] new jobs, promotions, and solo business ventures. Unstructured time, a heavy responsibility for self-direction, and high demands for excellence seem to be the common elements in these situations which are easy triggers for addictive behaviors.[9]

The men I've worked with who have suffered the fewest relapses are the men who have made fundamental changes in the stress, pace, and busy-ness of their lives. The result was a new sense of personal integrity as they found victory in an area they'd grappled with for much of their lives.

3. Join a Support Group

If you have identified sexual addiction in your life, you may find the personal help you need in a Twelve Step support group focused on sexual addiction issues. These groups are confidential and anonymous, and led by individuals experienced in recovery from sexual addiction. To obtain the address of the nearest Twelve Step group specializing in sexual addiction, write to one of the groups listed at the end of this chapter.

Earlier we heard a portion of Stephen Smith's story and of the corner he turned at the treatment center. Eight years later Stephen's involvement in a Twelve Step support group and a daily dependence on God have given him a new freedom from his addictive behavior.

"For me," Stephen continues, "personal health in the sexual area comes down to a daily decision to live in broken dependence on God. The psalmist says, 'You do not delight in sacrifice. . . . The sacrifices of God are a broken spirit; a

143

broken and contrite heart, O God, you will not despise.'[10] I now know that there is help and healing for any man struggling with his sexuality. It all starts with a willingness to leave the shadows and reach out for help from another brother in Christ."

Personal Assessment:

Dependency on Women's Approval

yes   no

☐ ☐ Do you react strongly (with rage, depression, or harsh blaming) when a woman is critical of you?

☐ ☐ Do you tend to mirror your wife's or girlfriend's emotions (for example, when she's happy, you're happy; when she's upset or irritable, so are you)?

☐ ☐ When your wife or other women around you are unhappy, do you feel it's your responsibility to make them happy again?

☐ ☐ Do you react more strongly to criticism from a woman than from a man?

☐ ☐ In public, at social gatherings, or while driving, do you tend to notice the women more than the men?

☐ ☐ When you dress or groom in the morning, do you think about how women will perceive you that day?

☐ ☐ Do you worry about looking older, heavier, or balder because of how women will perceive you?

☐ ☐ Do you make deliberate eye contact with women in public?

☐ ☐ If yes, do you look for some positive signal or response from women through their eye contact with you?

☐ ☐ At social gatherings do you find it more enjoyable to talk to women than to men?

☐ ☐ At social gatherings do you act differently around women than around men?
If yes, how would you describe the difference?

☐ ☐ Have you ever been accused by your wife or others of flirtatious behavior?
If yes, what has been your response?

Support Groups

The following is a directory of national organizations offering Twelve Step support groups for sexual addicts and their families. Those seeking help should make their own determination of the appropriateness of any particular group. This information is provided as a service to the reader and does not constitute an endorsement of any particular group by the author or the publisher.

COSA—Co-Dependents of Sex-Addicts Anonymous
P.O. Box 14537
Minneapolis, MN 55414

National Council on Sexual Addiction
P.O. Box 3006
Boulder, CO 80307

SA—Sexaholics Anonymous
P.O. Box 300
Simi Valley, CA 93062

SLAA—Sex and Love Addicts Anonymous
P.O. Box 119
Booton, MA 02258

For further information for pastors recovering from a variety of addictions, contact:

The National Clergy Network
National Association for Christian Recovery
P.O. Box 922
Yorba Linda, CA 92885
(714) 528-6227

Rev. Stephen Smith can be reached in care of:

Sacred Space
1690 Buck Street
West Linn, OR 97068
(503) 557-2282

When Your Happily Ever After Isn't

Relationship Styles

And the man and his wife were both naked and were
not ashamed.

Genesis 2:25

Intimacy is a difficult art.
Virginia Woolf

Tears welled up in Karen's eyes, blurring the hurt and frustration mirrored there. "Why can't you open up to me?" she pleaded.

Her husband, Don, sat a few feet away on the sofa, staring uncomfortably at the floor.

"We've been married eight years, Don, but I don't feel like I know you at all." She pushed a tissue across each cheek. "We never talk," Karen went on. "Not really. You come home from work, we eat dinner, and you go straight to your workshop until it's time for bed. I ask you about your day, and you say, 'Fine.'

"You're a good, moral person, Don, and a hard worker. But I feel like I'm married to a stranger. And I just don't think that's enough for me anymore."

Don watched helplessly as Karen began to cry in earnest, rivulets of mascara running down her cheeks.

The best-kept secret about men is our deep longing for intimacy. Women think we're afraid of intimacy, and they're right. We've been socialized to look strong, and we're afraid to look weak. But what most women don't know is that we hunger for emotional intimacy as much as they do, that we want to lower the drawbridge of our lives and invite them inside where our fears and dreams and deepest feelings live. But it is scary, and in most cases we don't know how because we've never seen it modeled.

Though these aren't their real names, Don and Karen are a real couple. Don told me about their painful conversation during a weekend men's retreat where I spoke a few months ago.

"I feel like everything you've said this weekend was directed right at me," Don said, "especially the part about workaholism and not making time for relationships. I know I'm a workaholic, and I'm afraid my marriage is in trouble. Karen and I never communicate; I want to, but I just don't know how."

I encouraged Don to go home and start fresh with Karen, to open up and share his heart. I told him that he didn't have to be a communications expert; he could just be himself and let Karen inside in ways he never had before.

Several weeks later I was back at Don's home church speaking once again to their men's group. Afterward Don came up, beaming. His words came tumbling out.

"It's been so great!" Don said. "I went home from the retreat determined to start over. That very Sunday afternoon I sat down with Karen and told her I wanted to change. We talked and talked. I've never shared deeply or vulnerably with her. In fact, she didn't even know I was a Christian—she thought I was an atheist! But this has taken our relationship to a whole new level. It's more satisfying than I ever would have dreamed! I know if Karen were here, she'd give you a big hug. All I can say, Pat, is thanks."

God's norm for marriage is relational intimacy. That kind of intimacy can be defined as a committed relationship in which it is safe to share your body, soul, feelings, fears, and dreams, knowing that you will be accepted as you are.

Adam and Eve experienced relational intimacy in Genesis 2. They were completely exposed to one another—fully known—yet without shame. When we can fully disclose ourselves to another person, and are loved and not shamed, deep healing takes place. God intended for marriage and other committed relationships to be catalysts for that kind of deep healing within us.

Unfortunately we all enter marriage and other adult relationships burdened with baggage from our past. That baggage may take the form of relationship styles we've seen modeled in our childhood families. Or it may result from father wounds and mother wounds we carry inside. Whatever the source, we have to jettison the baggage if we want to keep growing toward the "happily ever after."

There are a handful of genuine heroes whose pictures hang in my mental hall of fame. One is an eighty-four-year-old man named Wilbur, who attended a men's retreat where I spoke last year. At the closing session, a number of the men reflected on what they had gained from the weekend. After several men had shared, Wilbur spoke up.

"I'm taking home an appreciation for my wife," he said, his voice strong. "Some of you men have said that your wife is not your confidant, and I'm sad about that. Esther has been my lifelong love and my confidant. We've been married for fifty-four years, and we went together for five years before we got married. So we've been in love for almost sixty years. For all that time she has been my best friend. When I left home yesterday to come to the retreat, we said goodbye at the door. Esther held my face with both her hands and kissed me. 'Drive carefully, Dear,' she said. 'You're all I've got.'" Wilbur's eyes were filled with tears, and so were the eyes of most of the men in the room.

I don't believe in a fairy-tale approach to relationships. But as far as I'm concerned, relationships like that of Wilbur and Esther come as close to happily ever after as we'll find among human couples. Two people, doing the hard work required to nurture intimacy through the seasons of life, still in love after almost sixty years.

We *can* get there from here—but not with the baggage.

In the next few pages we're going to look at several of the heaviest pieces of baggage as we explore three common relationship styles adopted by men. You may find your own among them. Each of these relationship styles creates an atmosphere in which intimacy dies. Then we'll highlight three powerful principles which when applied create an environment where intimacy thrives. Finally, we'll examine a unique approach to reducing conflict and resentment in marriage—even if your mate chooses not to participate in the process.

Three Toxic Relationship Styles

Each of the following relationship styles is a product of our past. The underfathered and overmothered male often adopts either the Controller, the Caretaker, or the Isolator relationship style in adult life.

The Controller

The Controller will seek to "manage" his wife (and other women) as he was managed and controlled by his own mother. The primary emotion underlying the Controller's relationship with women is rage.

Several years ago Marsha and I conducted a class on relationships at a local church. A young woman named Gwen came every week and sat near the back. We both noticed that Gwen seemed extremely shy and almost never made eye contact with us when we spoke.

But one evening after the class, Gwen stayed behind. "Could I ask you a question?" she asked nervously. "Do you believe the man should make all the decisions in a marriage?"

My wife and I looked at each other, then back at Gwen.

"No," Marsha replied. "We don't believe it's much of a partnership if only one person makes all the decisions. But tell us what's behind your question."

"Well," she said, twisting her hands and looking at the floor, "my husband says the Bible teaches that the man should make all the decisions, so he does. He decided whether or not I can work outside the home; I'm not allowed to use the checkbook; he tells me what I should and shouldn't buy at the grocery store; and he's decided I should home-school our kids, even though I don't feel up to it."

Gwen glanced up quickly. "We get in arguments all the time, but he just says I'm being disobedient and sinning. I've begged him to come with me to a marriage counselor, but he refuses. He says it's fine with him if I go, because I'm the one with the problem. I just don't know how I can go on."

Gwen's husband, quite obviously, is a Controller. Controllers often come from highly conflicted relationships with domineering mothers. In their most extreme form, Controllers can become wife-abusing misogynists. But in any case, the Controller is afraid to share decision-making with his wife. His attempts to regulate all aspects of his environment are his way of protecting himself from ever again being powerless around a woman. As we'll see later, despite the protestations of some Controllers, this relationship style is unbiblical and spells death to intimacy.

The Caretaker

The Caretaker, on the other hand, is a typical approval junkie in his relationships with women. In marriage he seeks an unhealthy kind of enmeshment with his wife. The primary emotion underlying his relationship with women is fear—fear of disapproval and abandonment. The Caretaker often takes the role of the passive male.

I met Arthur during another of our men's seminars. After the session on relationship styles, he asked if we could talk. Over lunch Arthur sketched the outline of an impending crisis in his marriage.

Growing up, Arthur was his mother's favorite among her four children. She not only doted on him, she jealously guarded the gates to his social life. From the seventh grade on, his mother vetoed every girl Arthur suggested as a potential date—with one exception. She finally relented and allowed Arthur to take a date to his senior prom after making it clear that she in no way approved of the young woman.

As might be expected, his mother strongly disapproved of his wife, Shirley, when Arthur married at age twenty-one. For the next twelve years Arthur's marriage was a war zone. His mother sent birthday and Christmas cards to Arthur and his son. But she never sent cards to Shirley on her birthday, nor to Arthur's stepchildren, Shirley's children from her first marriage. His mother often criticized Shirley as well. Arthur tried to placate both the women in his life, but with little success. The weekend before our conversation, Shirley had told him she'd had enough; Arthur would have to choose between his mother and his wife.

Arthur saw himself as a victim, the innocent man in the middle. But passivity is a choice. We can't drag our mothers or our caretaking habits into our marriages without destroying intimacy.

Psychologist Robert A. Johnson says:

> No son ever develops into manhood without being disloyal to his mother in some way. If he remains with his mother to comfort her and console her, then he never gets out of his mother complex. Often a mother will do all she can to keep her son with

her. One of the most subtle ways is to encourage in him the idea of being loyal to mother, but if he gives in to her completely on this score, then she often winds up with a son who has a severely injured masculinity. The son must ride off and leave his mother, even if it seems to mean disloyalty, and the mother must bear this pain. Later, like Parsifal [the legendary seeker of the Holy Grail], the son may then come back to the mother and they may find a new relationship on a new level, but this can only be done after the son has first achieved his independence and transferred his affections to a woman of his own age.[1]

Women married to both Controllers and Caretakers eventually feel smothered and resentful. The resulting marital conflict invariably leads to decreased intimacy and may also prompt a man to search for emotional closeness with other women.

The Isolator

Fear is also the fuel that drives the Isolator. The Isolator fears failure in relationships. More specifically he fears intimacy—being known. The Isolator believes that if he was fully known, he'd be rejected. Usually the Isolator feels like he doesn't know how to "do relationships" or to communicate vulnerably about feelings. So to avoid these intimidating experiences, he isolates himself, usually through overworking or involvement in other activities that take him away from home.

Both Controllers and Caretakers are overinvolved in their wives' lives—one in a boss-subordinate role, the other in a parent-child role ("I know what's best for you, dear"). In reality, our wives are full adults, and more than that, fellow children of our heavenly Father.

In contrast to the Controller, who seeks to run his wife's life, and the Caretaker, who smothers his wife with his "helping," the Isolating Husband has little or no involvement with his wife.

Ironically the Isolating Husband often has the polar opposite profile in his work or ministry: He generally shows great initiative, energy, and leadership in those spheres. But his fear of failure blocks his ability to focus that same energy on his marriage.

Most men find that they practice some elements from all three styles, depending on the circumstances. After completing the relationship styles exercises at the end of this chapter, one of the men I mentored was struck by the information he received about himself.

"It was really humbling," he said. "I saw that I was both a Controller and an Isolator. I make most of the major decisions involving money. For instance, I chose the last car we bought without getting any input at all from my wife. But the Personal Assessment exercise you had me do showed me I spend only ten to thirty minutes a week, on average, communicating with my wife. I just make the decisions and leave."

Steps to Healthiness

It's often hard to see ourselves clearly, no matter how humble our intentions. Use the three exercises at the end of this chapter to help you determine if you practice any elements of the relationship styles we've discussed. Ask God to give you eyes to see as you work through the questions.

Whatever patterns you identify, the next step is to pinpoint the behaviors you would most like to see changed, and to apply biblical insights to those behaviors. The following three principles can dramatically enhance intimacy in a marriage or other committed relationship.

Intimacy Enhancer 1: Focus on Your Own Faults

Other than heaven and hell, Jesus had more to say about relational health than any other topic. The Sermon on the

Mount, his parables, his teachings on love—all are rich with God's insights on relationships. In one such passage in Matthew 7, Jesus does a CAT scan of the human heart— and we wince as we recognize ourselves in his words.

> Do not judge lest you be judged. . . . And why do you look at the speck that is in your brother's eye, but do not notice the log that is in your own eye? Or how can you say to your brother, "Let me take the speck out of your eye," and behold, the log is in your own eye? You hypocrite, first take the log out of your own eye, and then you will see clearly to take the speck out of your brother's eye.[2]

When we overfocus on fixing our wives, either through controlling or caretaking behaviors, we inevitably underfocus on ourselves. Jesus establishes the principle here that our primary concern should be working on our own weaknesses and personal growth. Jesus uses strong language— "You hypocrite"—to address those who are overinvolved in others' growth issues and underinvolved in their own. Intimacy is enhanced when I accept the truth of the statement "The only person I can change is me."

Several years ago Marsha and I were asked to conduct several weeks of training sessions in a local church. One of our sessions dealt with intergenerational sin, the ways one generation leaves its imprint on the next. After the session, a young man approached, seemingly quite agitated. He said his name was Jose and asked if we could talk.

"This was all really great," Jose said. "I just wish my wife could have been here today. I saw her in everything you said—the sexual abuse as a child, the acting out as an adult, the addictions—all of it was her to a *T!* In fact, I took three pages of notes today for my wife.

"It's been frustrating, though," he said. "I can't seem to get her interested in working on any of this. So my question is, How can I break through my wife's denial?"

If Jesus had been the one listening to this young man's question, I think he would have quietly but firmly said, "Jose, your wife's problems are not your concern. She answers to me, and I am speaking to her about all these things. You can do more for your wife and your marriage by taking care of the log in your own eye."

Intimacy is enhanced in an atmosphere of love and acceptance. It is diminished in an atmosphere of criticism.

Intimacy Enhancer 2: Practice Servant Leadership

In Mark 10:41–45 Jesus reminds his disciples that the leadership style of the "great men" in the world's system is to "lord it over" those they ruled. Jesus told the Twelve that it was not to be so among them, but that "whoever wishes to become great among you shall be your servant; and whoever wishes to be first among you shall be slave of all." Jesus' leadership style was humble and gracious, never forcing himself on anyone. He exhorts us as men to practice servant leadership, not authoritarian leadership. By inference that also applies to our leadership in the home.

Earlier we read about Gwen and her take-charge husband. Gwen's husband practiced the kind of authoritarian leadership that Jesus denounced. Her husband lorded it over Gwen and would undoubtedly have struggled with Jesus' concept of being a servant to her.

Jesus also honored an individual's right to make his or her own decisions. He believed the right to free choice is so important that Jesus extended it to include his or her choice of eternal destiny. Revelation 3:20, John 3:16, and countless other verses show that despite the potentially tragic results of a wrong decision, Jesus so honors individual autonomy that he allows people to make their own choices and to live with the consequences. This is not the instinct of the man who practices the Controller or the Caretaker relationship style. If Jesus, who knew better than any human what is good for someone else, still allowed others to make their own choices, how can we do otherwise?

Intimacy is enhanced when we practice servant leadership. Intimacy is diminished when we disrespect our partner's volition.

Intimacy Enhancer 3: Respect Your Partner's Feelings, Thoughts, and Opinions

Romans 14 presents a strong defense of the right of each child of God to hold her or his own opinions, without being judged or condemned.

The focus of Paul's comments in this well-known passage is on the hundreds of minor, daily issues about which we humans have opinions—for example, whether to be a red-blooded American meat eater or to be a vegetarian, whether to drink wine or to abstain. Paul's goal is to promote tolerance and mutual acceptance in the body of Christ, and like a lawyer arguing his case in a courtroom, he slams home his points relentlessly, one after another.

- Don't judge other people. They have a right to their opinions (v. 1).
- Don't regard others with contempt because they believe differently than you (v. 3).
- Your brothers and sisters don't answer to you; they answer to the Lord (v. 4).
- You too will stand before the judgment seat of God, so there's no room for self-righteousness (v. 10).

Then Paul comes to the climax of his argument in verses 15–19. It all comes down to the law of love. Don't take such harsh stands on minor issues that you end up hurting your brother or sister in Christ. Instead "pursue the things which make for peace and the building up of one another."

At a recent Manhood seminar, a man in his thirties approached me at the break. "You were talking about your own struggle with anger, Pat. I've got the same problem. I didn't even recognize it as a problem until my wife called me on it when we first got married. I learned it from my father. I saw Dad use anger to get what he wanted. So I always thought anger was just a manly thing—it's what men use to get their way. I honestly never realized it could be abusive."

I was struck with the same thought after reading Harriet Lerner's book *The Dance of Anger*. Lerner says much of the anger expressed in relationships is at best wasted energy and at worst abusive. Such anger tries to forcibly change our partner's mind on some issue. Most people resent being told what to believe or feel and quite naturally resist our attempts to control them. If we do "win" the argument, it is usually at the expense of our partner's feelings. Instead Lerner suggests we follow this life-affirming principle: Make space for your partner's feelings and opinions without trying to change them.

As I reflected on what I'd read, I realized that I often spend huge amounts of energy in my marriage trying to get my wife to see reality from my perspective. More than once, Marsha has said that in these discussions I remind her of a bulldog with a death grip on a bone.

In my childhood home, just about everyone except the cat was strongly opinionated. I went on to refine my case-building ability by romping through high school debate tournaments, decimating opponents.

Without realizing it I brought a wheelbarrow full of bad communication habits into the marriage. If we had a decision to make, I saw my role as being an advocate for my side of the issue, and my objective was to persuade my wife to see things my way. The only problem was, this wasn't a high school debate tournament anymore; it was a marriage. And debate tournaments are lousy environments for fostering intimacy. So I'm trying to genuinely listen more, and to make space for my wife's perspective.

The foundation underneath my desire to change is my late-dawning recognition that my insights on life are no more valid than my wife's. My brain is not the only one allotted to this marriage. My wife has a perfectly functional one, too, with her unique perspectives as well as her own direct connection to God. We are both fallible human beings who, as the apostle Paul says, "see through a glass, darkly."[3] We need each other.

Intimacy is enhanced when we seek to understand more than persuade. Intimacy is diminished when winning becomes more important to us than nourishing the relationship.

Taking Responsibility for Our Own Happiness

"But let each one examine his own work, and then he will have reason for boasting in regard to himself alone, and not in regard to another. For each one shall bear his own load."[4]

The application of this powerful principle would *prevent* many marital hurts from ever occurring. This principle is simple: We are each responsible, with God's help, for our own happiness—for taking the steps that will meet our needs in a healthy way. It is not our wives' responsibility to make us happy.

Marriage counselors tell us that most of us marry a particular person to meet some fundamental need. In many cases the need is one that went unmet in childhood, or perhaps was met in an unhealthy way.

The Hole in Our Hearts

For instance, a man whose masculinity was wounded in childhood may unconsciously marry a woman he believes will make him feel like a man—a woman who will respond to him, adore him, be passionate with him. Others who were emotionally or physically abused as children carry a high need for respect and affirmation and may unconsciously search for wives who will fill the aching hole in their hearts by constantly building up their damaged self-esteem.

But it's not our wives' responsibility to complete the unfinished business of our childhoods; it is *our* responsibility, under the direction of God's Spirit, to work on healing those wounded places. We set ourselves up for marital conflict when we put an unrealistic demand on our wives. When they fail, as all humans do, we become blaming and resentful. Generally when a man takes personal responsibility for his own needs, the level of marriage conflict is greatly reduced.

The diagram below illustrates the negative dynamic that often results when we drag these unspoken expectations into marriage. The husband wants and expects to get something back from his wife (respect, approval, or some other "feel good" response). There is nothing wrong with *wanting* these responses; it is the unrealistic *level of demand* that is counterproductive. Initially the husband does not express his feelings out loud to his wife; he expects her to automatically know his need and take action to meet it. When his wife fails to meet his unspoken need, he becomes angry and *demands* to have his need met.

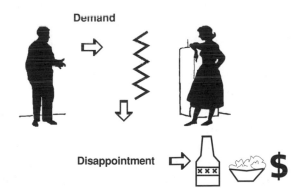

159

Reacting out of his hurt and disappointment, the husband seeks to numb his hurt in unhealthy ways—through alcohol abuse, overeating, overspending, unhealthy relationships with other women, or workaholism (including religious workaholism). The wall of resentment only grows between the husband and wife.

The Triple-R Response

I suggest a healthier alternative to this all-too-common scenario: the Triple-R Response. Triple-R stands for request, release, respond. It's rooted in the principle that we each take personal responsibility for our needs.

Instead of silently expecting or angrily demanding that our wives meet our need in a certain area, we make a request. We vulnerably make our need known to our wives and *ask* if they can meet it. We don't pressure or attempt to use guilt to shame them into responding. Ideally, we also reassure them that we will not react with anger or with isolating behaviors if they decide they are not able to meet the need we've expressed.

Sometimes we can authentically give up part of our need if our wives can't meet it all—we release them from our expectation that they'll meet it. At other times we can't give it up. It is then that we need to use the third *R*—respond. We respond proactively by taking personal responsibility for finding a *healthy* way to get that part of our need met that our wives cannot meet.

For instance, in the figure on the next page, the wife indicates she cannot meet her husband's need, or perhaps she can only meet part of his need. Rather than getting angry and resentful, the husband then takes responsibility for meeting that need in other *legitimate* ways.

As I shared in chapter 6, I graduated to manhood with a skewed sense of masculinity and an unhealthy need for approval from women. This is not a need I should expect

my wife to meet. I must take personal responsibility before the Lord for pursuing healing in that wounded area.

I've begun to do that in the ways I described in chapter 3: forming deeper friendships with a network of other men, finding older men as mentors, and doing a lot of inner healing work directly with God in the area of the Father Blessing. As a result I am more contented and much more secure in my masculinity than I was ten years ago—and I'm no longer expecting my wife to reassure me of my manhood.

On the lighter side, I occasionally enjoy watching shoot-em-up action movies. My wife Marsha hates blood and violence and would rather have her fingernails pulled out with pliers than be forced to sit through such a movie. So sometimes I'll attend a movie alone or with a male friend, or I'll check out a spy novel from the library and spend the evening reading.

I've decided that when Marsha says she'd rather not see a particular movie, it's out of bounds for me to attempt to pressure her to change her mind. But I've also come to see that it's not healthy for me to sit at home feeling resentful either.

That's how the Triple-R Response works: We request that our wives help us meet a certain need, we release them from responsibility for the part of our need they cannot meet, and we respond proactively to meet our need ourselves in a healthy, legitimate way. That produces another of those paradoxes of life: Separateness produces closeness. When we give each other the freedom to be our own person, conflict is greatly reduced. In that kind of mutually respectful atmosphere, true intimacy flourishes.

Personal Assessment:

The Controller

Answer the questions to determine if you tend to be a Controller in relationships or in your marriage. (If you are not married, answer the questions as they apply to your relationships with your closest friends and loved ones.)

yes	no	
☐	☐	Do you tend to make decisions that affect your wife without first getting her input?
☐	☐	Are you a perfectionist? Do others find you hard to please?
☐	☐	Do you find it difficult to listen to your wife talk about her needs, feelings, or opinions?
☐	☐	Do you often interrupt or impatiently cut her off during discussions?
☐	☐	Do you have difficulty admitting your mistakes or faults?
☐	☐	Do you alone make the decisions on what's spent and not spent in your family?
☐	☐	Do you not allow certain topics to be discussed between you and your wife?
☐	☐	Do you often feel strong waves of jealousy or anger toward your wife as a result of choices she's made or things she's done?
☐	☐	Are you highly competitive? Is it difficult for you to lose?
☐	☐	Do you simply announce your decisions to your wife and expect her to fit in and support them?
☐	☐	Do you tend to use guilt or manipulation to convince your wife to go along with your preferences? Do you ever spiritualize your arguments with her, implying that your choice is the only godly or spiritual one?

yes   no

☐ ☐ Do you ever shout when communicating with your wife?

☐ ☐ Might others find your language abusive, degrading, or sarcastic in tone?

_____ Score (total yes responses)

Score	Interpretation
1–2	*Low control.* Control is not your dominant style (if you answered the questions honestly) and presents little problem for you.
3–4	*Medium control.* You have a tendency toward controlling behaviors under certain circumstances. Look at the questions you answered yes and reflect on the situations represented in each.
5 or more	*High control.* Your marriage relationship is currently in trouble. You must give immediate attention to your controlling behaviors before your marriage suffers irreparable harm. That attention should include seeking the help of a trained marriage counselor.

Personal Assessment:

The Caretaker

Answer the questions to determine if you tend to be a Caretaker in your marriage. (If you are not married, answer the questions as they apply to your relationships with your closest friends and loved ones.)

yes   no

☐ ☐ When others around you indicate they have a problem or are unhappy, is your first impulse to fix them?

☐ ☐ If you are unable to solve another person's problem or to make that person happy, do you feel personally responsible?

☐ ☐ In your marriage, do you assume it is your responsibility to make your wife happy?

163

yes	no	
☐	☐	Do you assume it is your wife's responsibility to make you happy?
☐	☐	Are you constantly monitoring the moods of those around you, especially of your wife?
☐	☐	Do you sometimes find it easier to determine what your spouse is feeling than what you yourself are feeling?
☐	☐	Do you experience anxiety when your wife's mood seems to become negative?
☐	☐	Are you uncomfortable talking about your needs to others?
☐	☐	Do you often find yourself making suggestions to the people around you out of a sincere desire to help them?
☐	☐	Do you try to shield your wife from experiencing negative reality or from hearing news that might upset her?
☐	☐	Do you assume you know your wife's needs better than she herself does?
☐	☐	Do you often feel underappreciated by your wife for all the things you do for her?
☐	☐	Do you find you are frequently on an emotional roller coaster in your marriage?
☐	☐	Do you tend to justify decisions within the marriage on the basis of what you feel is good for your mate rather than letting her represent her own feelings and needs?

_____ Score (total yes responses)

Score	Interpretation
1–3	*Low tendency.* Caretaking shows up occasionally in your relationships but is not a pronounced pattern.
4–5	*Medium tendency.* You have some tendency toward caretaking. This could become destructive if not dealt with. Analyze your yes answers and reflect on the situations you visualized when you answered those questions.
6 or more	*High tendency to caretake.* There is not enough separateness in your marriage and too much parent-child dynamic. These behaviors threaten to smother your marriage and should be addressed with professional help.

Personal Assessment:

The Isolator

Answer the questions to determine if you tend to be an Isolator in your relationships and in your marriage.

yes	no	
☐	☐	Do you tend to isolate yourself from your wife through over-work?
☐	☐	Do you avoid deep or serious conversations with your wife?
☐	☐	Are you uncomfortable being involved in decision-making with your wife over family matters? Do you leave most family decisions to be made by your wife alone?
☐	☐	Do you leave the house or isolate yourself in another part of the house when you sense your wife is angry or in a bad mood?
☐	☐	For fathers whose children are still in the home: Are you rarely involved with your family on outings, or in school or extracurricular activities?

How much time have you spent talking with your wife in the last week? (Time spent in the same room without talking doesn't count!)

☐ 0–10 minutes   ☐ 10–30 minutes   ☐ 30–60 minutes
☐ 60–90 minutes   ☐ More than 90 minutes. Specify: _____

_____ Score (total yes responses)

Score	Interpretation
1–5	Because of the scope of each of the questions, a yes answer to any one question indicates a significant problem in your marriage and/or family relationships. If you answered yes to more than one question or if your time totals were ninety minutes or less, your marriage is almost certainly starving to death. If you want to save your marriage, begin by sitting down with your wife and expressing your desire to change. Begin working with a trained marriage counselor. *Soon.* And remember—nothing changes if nothing changes.

The Long, Dark Trek into a Secret Life

The Secret Life Syndrome

> No man, for any considerable period, can wear one face to himself, and another to the multitude, without finally getting bewildered as to which may be the true.
> Nathaniel Hawthorne, *The Scarlet Letter*

> We need to face the plain fact that about an inch beneath our Christian skins is a barbarian . . . who desperately wants to get out and express himself.
> Gordon MacDonald, *Pastors at Risk*

By now it was a familiar story. Bill sat across from me at the restaurant, his eyes unmoving and unfocused, the steam gone from his coffee cup. He'd been careful to use only his first name when he'd called last night to ask if we could meet. He said only that he was a pastor and that someone had given him my name.

"It all started so innocently," he said. "She was a first-time visitor at our church six months ago. I called on her the following Thursday, as I do with all our visitors. She told me about her recent divorce, how hard life was. She cried a bit, and when I left I gave her a comforting hug. I told her if she needed to talk again, to just call my office for an appointment.

"I mean, we *pride* ourselves on being a caring church," he said defensively. His eyes locked on mine for a moment and then dropped.

When he started again, his voice was low, almost inaudible. "She called that next week but said she worked days and only had evenings free. She said she was desperate. I agreed to come.

"That started a pattern of my visiting her a couple of evenings a week at her apartment. She told me what a help and encouragement I was, how she'd never met a man like me before, so sensitive and caring."

He glanced up. "It's been a *long* time since I've gotten those kinds of strokes at home. It felt good—I admit it. There *are* a lot of times I feel underappreciated—by the church and by my wife. Always too much to do and not enough of me to go around, always on somebody's blacklist.

"Anyway, I knew I was motivated by more than pastoral sympathy when I began making up stories to tell my wife about where I was spending all those nights out. But I still never intended to get involved physically.

"But pretty soon the hugs I gave her progressed to caressing and kissing, until one night about six weeks after my first visit we ended up in bed together. I knew it was wrong, but it was like a drug. When I was with her, I felt like a different person. I felt like a *man* for the first time in a long time."

The light in Bill's eyes flared briefly, then died.

"That went on for six months until just last week when the whole thing was discovered. The board has asked me to resign, and my wife and family are going through hell." His eyes were full of pain. "I'm really scared, Pat. I never in a million years thought this would happen to me."

Early Warning Signs

Bill's story is repeated every week in towns all across North America. In the last three years I've worked with scores of sincere Christian men with some form of secret life. Some of the secret lives revolved around sex. Others involved alcohol and drug abuse. And yet others had to do with overspending and secret purchases. The variety of secret lives is limited only by the imagination of man. Basically, any activity that causes our conscience to raise a red flag, that we deliberately keep hidden from our spouses or best friends, qualifies as secret life activity. The result is a break in our relationship with God and with those from whom we're hiding the habit. And ultimately the consequence is enslavement.

We've already looked at the results of our Men's Confidential Survey. More than half have had some kind of affair, either emotional or physical; more than 60 percent admit to struggling with sexual addiction; 20 percent have abused alcohol or drugs since they've been Christians. But the statistic that saddens me the most is the one that reveals that, of the men who admit to participating in a secret life, almost a third say they have not reached out to anyone for help—not a counselor, a pastor, or a support group. The reasons most often given are "embarrassment" or "no one safe to tell." And so as Keith Miller says, our internal shame voices continue to use our secrets to keep us in bondage.

But after my work with many pastors and Christian laymen in the last few years, I believe more strongly than ever that men don't have to fall prey to the secret life syndrome.

Prevention begins by identifying the at-risk factors that precede the development of a secret life. Long before the first liquor bottle is hidden in the garage or the extramarital affair is initiated, several early warning signs appear. We have touched on each of these factors previously; now we will examine how four of them work together to make a man more vulnerable to crisis.

Factor 1: The False Self

Children raised in dysfunctional homes—whether those homes are alcoholic or rigidly religious—learn that who they are simply isn't enough. As we saw in the chapter dealing with the hero subculture in America, men learn to play a role in our society and to erect a facade to garner the approval of others. The result, we saw, is the creation of a carefully designed image. This image is our false self and includes only those parts of us that we choose to reveal.

Society actively encourages the creation of a false self; it's called putting your best foot forward. The problem, of course, is that to maintain our sanitized image we must keep our dark side hidden, along with its potential for sin and destructive behavior. In fact, we humans are capable of playing a role so effectively that we even fool ourselves. This is what the Bible calls being "hardened by the deceitfulness of sin"[1] and what twelve steppers call denial.

As a teenager I tried to hide the fact that I was a Christian from my friends in high school in order to be popular. A kind of double life developed in which I had one set of friends and activities at church and an entirely different set of friends and activities at school—and I expended great energy in trying to insure one world never intersected with the other. The nonreligious persona I adopted at school was a false self.

I also developed a secret life of sexual fantasizing as a teenager. All during this time I never talked to anyone about my secret fantasy life, and I cultivated a squeaky-clean image at church as a young Christian leader. We all have dozens of ways we hide parts of ourselves in the shadows and prop other parts out in the light. The more discrepancy there is between our hidden self and our public self, the greater the danger of becoming entrenched in the secret life syndrome.

One of the greatest dangers in the development of a false self is the potential for what Chuck Colson calls the Pedestal

Complex. In an article in *Christianity Today* Colson decried the tendency among Christians today to exalt our stars and leaders and put them on pedestals. He quite properly labeled the tendency as idolatry.[2]

But I hate pedestals for a different reason. I hate them for what they do to the people occupying them. Pedestals have their perks, but ultimately they're just another kind of prison. In a tragic catch-22, the leader on a pedestal can't admit to struggling with anything in his personal life, or according to the unspoken rules of the game, he loses his perch. At that point, for many leaders it's a relatively short walk from the pedestal to the closet.

In my own case, I was so obsessed with my image as a Christian leader that I didn't want to let anyone see my weaknesses. So as my first marriage became increasingly conflicted, I refused to go to a marriage counselor. I was afraid someone might see me, and then my reputation would be harmed. By the time I did finally agree to go, I was already involved in the sexual sin that ultimately damaged so many.

By contrast, a few years ago a good friend of mine found himself overwhelmingly attracted to the wife of his business partner. She, in turn, expressed a similar attraction to him. They didn't know if they were "falling in love" or not, but they knew that if they acted on their feelings, it would be wrong. So they did something courageous. They immediately went to their spouses and told them about their feelings, as well as their commitment to remain faithful to their marriage vows. The four of them discussed the issue calmly and openly. And a fascinating thing happened. By dragging their feelings out into the light rather than leaving them hidden, they found that their feelings lost their power. In fact, it all turned out so positively that the two of them actually went on to share about their healthy experience with the entire adult Sunday school class at their church.

It was a wonderful model for how to handle impulses from our dark side.

Dr. Ken Druck, in his book *The Secrets Men Keep,* lists five benefits of acknowledging our secrets and living transparently:

1. Our whole world changes when we tell the truth.
2. We fulfill our human need to be known and accepted.
3. We simplify our lives.
4. We improve our relationships.
5. We become more secure.[3]

And to those five benefits I would add a sixth: We restore our relationship with God.

Factor 2: Untreated Pain

The second major factor that sets a man up for the development of a secret life is the presence of unacknowledged, untreated pain from childhood.

My wife went to a sports medicine clinic for a few months last year for treatment of a back injury. After she'd gone there for several weeks, she noticed that most of the people coming for treatment were women. So she asked her physical therapist whether the preponderance of women indicated that relatively few men incurred sports-related injuries.

"No, not at all," he said, laughing. "There are a lot more men out there with injuries than women. But most men are too macho to admit they're injured and come in for treatment."

What's true of physical pain is doubly true of emotional pain. Men are strongly conditioned in our society not to acknowledge or seek treatment for their inner pain.

Denial, however, only pushes the pain down into the subterranean caverns below our conscious level, where it brews and builds and eventually bursts out in some other form. The

171

form it takes may be drivenness in our work or periodic out-bursts of rage or an overwhelming desire to numb our pain with alcohol or drugs or sex. How it shows up will be different for every man, but the most important principle to remember is this: Pain that is unacknowledged and untreated does not go away. "Time heals all wounds" may look nice on a wall plaque, but in most cases it simply doesn't work.

Men who have developed a false self and who also carry within them unresolved issues from childhood are walking time bombs. The question is not *will* they blow their lives apart in some destructive behavior; the question is *when*. I've seen it happen in my life and in scores of other Christian men.

Factor 3: Nonintimate Marriage

The third factor that sets up a secret life is the presence of a highly conflicted, nonintimate marriage. (For singles, the absence of a confidant—a true best friend with whom you can share your struggles—provides the same negative dynamic.)

All deep relationships experience conflict, and all marriages, no matter how good, can benefit from outside counsel from time to time. But in some marriages the level of conflict and resentment is so high that needs and deep feelings such as fear are no longer shared with one another. Physical intimacy may still be present, but it no longer feels safe to be emotionally vulnerable. Those marriages are in danger.

For most men, a nonintimate marriage creates a classic checkmate situation: The husband feels it isn't safe to talk about his pain to his wife; he has no close male friends, so he ends up talking to no one at all. If a man in this instance is taking the first steps toward substance abuse or sexual temptation, he is condemned to fight his secret war alone. Few men win that lonely battle.

Factor 4: Out-of-Control Lifestyle

The final factor that accelerates the slide downward toward a secret life is an out-of-control, fast-lane lifestyle. The '90s-style, nonstop life has at least three lethal results: greater stress, less time for reflection, and an increased tendency to control those around us in the name of getting more done.

Under these conditions the first victims to fall are usually our healthiest habits: nurturing important relationships and taking the time to deal with our own spiritual needs and broken places.

Eventually the open throttle lifestyle itself becomes a drug even as it burns out our bodies and minds and imperfectly masks our pain.

The Stages of the Syndrome

In this profile of the man most likely to develop a secret life of destructive behavior, you may find conspicuously absent such factors as a lack of Bible study and prayer. I don't wish to be misunderstood here. As important as Bible study and prayer are to our spiritual health, my experience is that these spiritual activities by themselves do not prevent the slide into a secret life.

When I was a young boy, my pastor wrote in the front page of a gift Bible I was given: "Pat, this Book will keep you from sin, or sin will keep you from this Book." Like so many cliches, that aphorism contains a kernel of truth but is decidedly unhelpful if applied simplistically. I had a masters degree in biblical studies and participated in a discipline of regular Bible study and prayer *well into* the period of my secret life of sinful behavior. So did many other Christian leaders who have had what Gordon MacDonald calls a "broken world experience."

173

Bible study, prayer, fellowship with other Christians, and the other traditional spiritual disciplines *do* make a difference in one's life. But if the person who is doing the studying and praying is operating out of a false self, as I was, and is carrying a pool of unacknowledged emotional pain, is in a conflicted, nonintimate marriage, and is living an out-of-control lifestyle, then that person—*despite* his Bible reading and prayer—is vulnerable to the secret life syndrome. Let's look more closely at how the secret life actually develops.

The Secret Life Syndrome

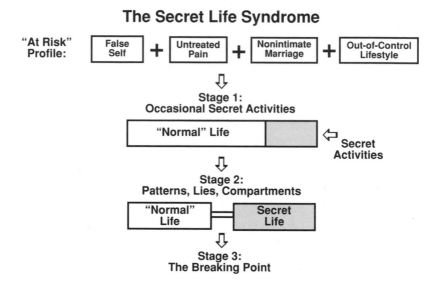

Stage 1: The First Step over the Line

Stage 1 occurs when we take the first step over the line and knowingly violate our conscience.

One Christian man I met in a Twelve Step group talked about his addiction to hard-core pornography and prostitutes. He grew up in a good Christian home where he had no contact with pornography or illicit sexuality. In fact, his wife was the first person he'd ever had sexual relations with.

But one day in his midthirties while on a business trip, he picked up a *Playboy* magazine in the airport gift shop and spent a pulse-pounding five minutes browsing through it. "It was just an impulse, and I acted on it," he said. "I knew it was wrong, but I did it anyway."

He never told anyone about the incident, and in the absence of any accountability, he soon found himself buying and devouring pornographic magazines on all his trips. This eventually led to a consuming addiction. He took hours away from his work, even in his home town, to cruise adult book stores and red light districts. After each episode he was filled with shame and begged for God's forgiveness. Although he swore each time he would never do it again, he would feel the tension build in him and inevitably found himself in his car headed toward the wrong side of town.

He didn't seek help until he was arrested for soliciting a prostitute, who was actually an undercover police officer. His name was published in the paper along with all the other johns arrested that week, and his wife gave him the choice of getting help or getting a divorce. To paraphrase recovery veteran Earnie Larsen, no one ever truly deals with his secret sins unless he is about to lose something he's not prepared to live without.

But in the early stage of the secret life, most of a man's life goes on as usual. To others, and even to himself, his life looks normal. The transgressions across the line are relatively infrequent and are repented of immediately. In fact, the infrequency of the stage 1 transgressions, combined with his own fervent repentance, convinces the man that his actions are aberrations that won't ever happen again.

But the capacity for self-deception within each of us is enormous. "The heart is more deceitful than all else and is desperately sick," Jeremiah mourns. "Who can understand it?"[4]

Paul warns in Ephesians that our old sinful nature is constantly being corrupted by "the lusts of deceit."[5] Lust, in

175

fact, is almost always accompanied by deceit, for when we want something badly enough, we'll deceive whomever we have to in order to get it. And the first person we have to deceive is ourselves. In stage 1 we accomplish the self-deceit by telling ourselves two lies: (1) I don't really have a problem, and (2) I can handle this alone.

Stage 2: Patterns, Lies, Compartments

The decision not to seek help in the early stage of the secret life is only the first indication of self-deceit at work. At least at this point we still believe our action is wrong. But as our secret activity increases in frequency and risk and becomes a regular pattern, so too do the lies we tell ourselves. Here are some of the self-justifying messages our minds conceive to silence our clanging conscience:

- This (the secret activity) is helping me be a better husband (or father or worker). It relaxes me and makes me happier, so I'm easier to be around.
- As long as I'm not hurting anyone else—and I'm not, as long as no one finds out—this activity is all right.
- I'm an exception. This activity is *normally* wrong, but circumstances are so extreme (my marriage is so bad, my job is so stressful) that this activity is okay for me.

Or a man can simply redefine in his own mind where the line is between right and wrong: "Well, technically alcoholism (adultery, overspending, whatever) doesn't take place until you do such and such—and I'd never go *that* far!"

Many affairs begin with nothing more than a heart-to-heart sharing between a man and a woman, an experience of self-disclosure that produces a form of relational bonding. But when our conscience warns us that we're in dangerous territory, the rationalizing and relabeling often kick in: "This isn't really an affair (though I look for excuses to be with her and I find myself thinking about her all the time) because we haven't been involved physically." When these rationalizations no longer still our conscience, we may have to move on to the next level of denial: compartmentalization of our behavior.

One of the primary defining qualities of sin is self-deception; that is, we can do bad things yet convince ourselves we are doing nothing wrong. Compartmentalization is one of the most sophisticated mechanisms our mind uses to accomplish self-deception.

At the beginning of this chapter we talked about Bill's affair with the woman from his church. Every time Bill left the woman's apartment, he felt overwhelming guilt and shame. But he developed a ritual that helped him cope with his feelings. He prayed and acknowledged his behavior as sinful before God and tearfully begged God to forgive him. He told God that, unlike previous times, this time he was truly repentant, and he would never do it again. Then he would firmly close the door to that compartment of his life and act as if it didn't exist. After all, hadn't he just told the Lord that he would never do it again? Compartmentalizing his bad behavior in this way allowed him to step back into his other world and pick up his roles as pastor and husband and father with his conscience muted.

In reality, the exercise of "repentance" Bill went through two nights a week was false repentance, with no deep-down commitment to change his behavior. But his desire to be with the woman would again build to a fever pitch, and despite his tears of repentance three days earlier, he soon found himself knocking on the door to her apartment once again.

When it comes to giving up a secret life, I believe there is a simple test to help us know whether we're experiencing true or false repentance. If I'm willing to tell someone else what I'm struggling with and ask for help, then it's true

177

repentance. If I'm not willing to tell anyone else, I'm only fooling myself.

Stage 3: The Breaking Point

By the time a man is involved in maintaining a secret life of this scope, he is burning huge amounts of energy deceiving others and keeping the denial mechanisms operating within himself. Because all this takes a toll, his behavior is increasingly characterized by irritability, nervous tension, mood swings, insomnia, and other stress symptoms. And because more and more of the addictive substance or behavior becomes necessary to deliver the same high, in this final stage of the secret life syndrome a man's work will probably be suffering, as well as his relationships with family and friends. This is the dynamic the writer of Proverbs describes when he says, "Bread of deceit is sweet to a man; but afterwards his mouth shall be filled with gravel."[6]

No one can bear up under this strain forever. Either a man will voluntarily reach out for help to end his bondage, or he will take one too many risks and be discovered. (Some experts feel that many men in this final stage of the secret life take increasing risks because on an unconscious level they are weary of their shame burden and *want* to be found out.)

Jay was a Christian pharmacist I met through one of our seminars in California. A leading layman in his church, he taught an adult Christian education class and was highly respected by all who knew him. But unknown to anyone— even his wife—Jay had been diverting drugs for his own use from the pharmacy where he worked. This had been going on undetected for more than ten years. Every night, Jay would use illegally obtained downers to help him make it through the evening, and then uppers the next morning to help him make it through the day.

But inevitably, as his tolerance for the drugs increased, his body required higher and higher doses to experience the same effect. That meant taking greater risks to forge the false prescriptions he used to obtain the drugs. Then one day about a year ago, Jay got sloppy and made a mistake as he forged a prescription. An alert coworker caught the mistake and investigated the incident, and later that day Jay was escorted from the pharmacy in handcuffs by sheriff's deputies. Today Jay is clean and sober with a revitalized walk with the Lord, and with a felony conviction on his record.

Gary is another man I've worked with in a mentoring relationship. Gary too had a substance abuse problem, but his drug of choice was alcohol. His secret habit had gone on for more than twenty years, undiscovered by family or friends. Gary's alcoholism had never reached the down-in-the-gutter stage, but he knew it was taking a toll on his health and his marriage.

One day at work about two years ago, a coworker who knew him well looked him in the eye and said, "If you could get help for your problem, and no one here would know anything about it, would you be interested?" Gary was ready, and he voluntarily ended his secret life and stepped into a recovery program. Gary is honest about the fact that he still has a plate full of issues to deal with, but he's enjoying the first freedom from alcohol he has experienced since he was a teenager.

No secret life can be kept hidden forever; it is only our grandiosity and self-deceiving sinful nature that would have us believe so. And the consequences only multiply when we wait. As Thomas Hobbes said, "Hell is truth seen too late." The most courageous step we can take is to say, "I'm hurting myself, I'm hurting my relationship with God, I'm hurting my loved ones, and this is going to stop—now."

It is a fearsome thing to meet God in his justice, when we first throw open the door to our secret compartments and invite him to come in and do housecleaning. But our God is a God of love as well as a God of justice. The prophet

Isaiah captures that wonderful balance in God's nature when he affirms that, yes, "He will faithfully bring forth justice." Sin has consequences and must be dealt with. But in the same verse Isaiah reassures all sinners everywhere, "A bruised reed He will not break, And a dimly burning wick He will not extinguish."[7]

For those whose wicks are sputtering and about to go out, who are carrying the self-inflicted bruises of destructive behavior, the Savior waits to bring healing, not further wounding. All he asks is that we end our isolation, come in from the cold, and drag our secrets into the light of his love. That's when our healing journey begins.

Personal Assessment:

Secret Life

Honestly reflect on the following questions to determine if there are unhealthy habits, behaviors, or relationships in your life. As you start, prayerfully read King David's response to God following the exposure of his sin with Bathsheba:

Behold, Thou dost desire truth in the innermost being,
And in the hidden part Thou wilt make me know wisdom.
Psalm 51:6

yes	no	
☐	☐	Is there a behavior, habit, or relationship in your life that you feel is wrong?
☐	☐	Is there a behavior in your life that you lie about or seek to hide?
☐	☐	Is this behavior negatively affecting your relationship with God, your wife, family, or other loved ones?
☐	☐	Do you keep this behavior secret because you feel no one would understand?
☐	☐	Do you try to hide the fact that you spend money on this habit or behavior?

yes *no*

☐ ☐ Are you filled with guilt and shame after practicing this behavior?

☐ ☐ Are you increasingly experiencing symptoms of irritability, outbursts of anger (at yourself or others), mood swings, depression, nervous tension, or insomnia?

☐ ☐ Do you use this habit, behavior, or relationship to soothe or medicate your emotional pain?

☐ ☐ Do you often feel misunderstood and taken advantage of?

☐ ☐ Are your thoughts obsessed with some person or with plans to act out with this behavior or substance?

☐ ☐ Is your preoccupation with this person or behavior consuming so much time and energy that it is interfering with your work or family responsibilities?

☐ ☐ If married, have you had sexual contact recently with someone other than your wife?

☐ ☐ Have you promised yourself repeatedly that you would quit, only to carry out this behavior again?

☐ ☐ Are you afraid of the consequences of your behavior being discovered?

☐ ☐ Has this behavior become a regular pattern in your life?

☐ ☐ Do you feel hopeless about ever overcoming this behavior?

What is this behavior or habit? _____

181

Part 2

Winning the
Secret Wars

Let us lay aside every encumbrance, and the sin which
so easily entangles us, and let us run with endurance the
race that is set before us.

Hebrews 12:1

Our God is a God who not merely restores, but takes up
our mistakes and follies into His plan for us and brings
good out of them. This is part of the wonder of His gracious sovereignty. 'I will restore to you the years that the
locust has eaten . . .' God makes not only the wrath of
man to turn to His praise but the misadventures of Christians, too.

J. I. Packer, *Knowing God*

The Rugged Journey Out

Leaving the Secret Life

Long before modern psychotherapy began trying to help
persons in stress, the Spirit was restoring and renewing,
guiding men and women through the white water rapids
of their lives to the quiet pools beyond.

Dean Merrill

The steps of a man are established by the LORD; and He
delights in his way. When he falls, he shall not be hurled
headlong; because the LORD is the One who holds his
hand.

Psalm 37:23–24

Mel looked up at me, his face contorted
with pain. Desperation filled his voice. "I didn't know it
would be this hard," he said. "I've been doing everything
my pastor told me to do, but my thought life is still driving
me crazy! I haven't been unfaithful again, but I don't know
how much longer I can hold on!"

Mel came to me at a break in one of our marriage seminars and haltingly shared his story. A long-haul truck
driver, Mel had a one-night stand with a woman about six
months earlier. He immediately went to his wife and confessed that incident as well as a lifelong addiction to pornography. Together they went to their pastor.

The pastor led Mel through a prayer of confession and repentance and gave him a list of Scripture passages to memorize. The passages dealt mainly with lust, sexual purity, and spiritual commitment. Mel had worked diligently on the passages ever since. He had three-by-five cards with Bible verses on them taped all over the inside of his cab, but his mind was still plagued with sexual fantasizing. He also confided that a couple of months ago he had begun drinking heavily because he "couldn't stand himself."

In recovery jargon, Mel was *white-knuckling* or *acting in*. White-knuckling is an attempt to curb a behavior by imposing rigid self-control without dealing with any of the underlying causes. For some situations, it may be better than doing nothing at all. Overall, though, it works about as well as the average American's diet plan. In Mel's case it merely resulted in a "migrating addiction." He stopped his involvement with pornography but began to drink to numb the pain.

I remember waking up one morning some time after my life blew apart following the discovery of my secret life. I had acknowledged my sin and was sincere in my repentance. But I felt deeply disappointed that "things weren't all better" overnight. I had naively assumed that repentance by itself would turn everything around; that my own sense of shame would be magically lifted; that those whom I'd hurt would want to become my friends again; and that God would provide some wonderful new ministry or vocational situation. But none of that happened. Indeed the next couple of years were a real wilderness period full of pain and loss.

Digging through the Layers

Looking back, I know now that my life then was like the first day on an archeological dig. I'd dug down through the first layer, but there still remained many layers of denial to work through before I even came close to the core issues that needed to be dealt with in my life. And I'm still working with my spade on that dig today.

But it's true that taking the first step of repentance begins the process of burrowing into the layers. In that sense, our initial acknowledgement of sin is the most important step we take in winning the secret wars. Motivational business speakers talk about identifying the "critical event" in the business process. For a salesman, for instance, the critical event is "the close." Everything rests on his ability to close the sale. In leaving a secret life, the critical event is repentance. Without acknowledging our sin and turning around to face the Father, we're doomed to endlessly repeat our destructive cycle.

The good news is, that first step of repentance releases all of God's power to assist us in the journey out of our secret life. The bad news is that there are still many steps ahead in the road less traveled, and more than a few potholes.

Counterfeit recovery is one-dimensional. In Mel's case, it treats the person as if he is only a spiritual being, as if he does not also possess a mind, body, and emotions. Because it doesn't deal with the whole person, one-dimensional recovery only drives the pain underground where it will later break out in some other form, as it did with Mel's drinking. Many secular psychologists have their own version of one-dimensional recovery, because they leave God entirely out of the healing equation.

During my own postcrisis healing period I moved to the beautiful Monterey Peninsula in northern California. I wanted to surround myself with the tangible evidences of God's goodness that make up that awesome combination of forests and cliffs and sea.

The first summer I lived in Monterey, a series of destructive fires broke out south of the Peninsula in the thickly forested region of Big Sur. The fires soon raged out of control. Crews flew in from around the country to assist in the fight. A call went out to the community for people to assist the teams behind the lines, and I volunteered. It was pretty dramatic stuff, with long lines of yellow-jacketed firefighters snaking up into the hills and the roar of prop jets swooping down to dump loads of red foam over the blaze.

By Monday of the second week, all the fires were out, and all the planes and some of the crews returned home. But a large portion of the firefighters stayed. I was puzzled, so when the crews came back into camp at the end of that day, I asked one grizzled old crew leader why they were staying if the fires were out.

"Son," he said, flashing a grimy grin, "don't think those fires are out just because they're covered with pink goo. Now's when the *real* work begins. We've got to go back up there with shovels and chain saws and find the hot spots under the goo. If we don't, they'll just smoulder along real quiet until the first wind comes up. And then—poof! We'll have another firestorm on our hands."

What a classic picture of leaving a secret life! A fire has ravaged our personal lives. With the help of friends, we've finally been able to put out the blaze. But now the real work begins—the grimy work of digging down under the surface day after day, looking for the hot spots that still smoulder, rooting them out one by one. Tough work. But absolutely critical. For if we assume the job is done when the obvious fires are out, it's just a matter of time before another inferno erupts.

The rooting and digging necessary for our healing following a crisis must move forward on at least four levels simultaneously: spiritual, psychological, relational, and practical. There is important work to be done in each of these areas. In my own recovery I needed to deal with issues of spiritual pride and idolatry, as well as family-of-origin issues and unhealthy relationship patterns—not to mention such practical matters as maintaining appropriate boundaries with women. All four areas have given me valuable insights into the direction my individual healing journey must take. Let's look at what's involved in leaving a secret life in each of these key dimensions.

1. The Spiritual Dimension: Reconnecting with God

Second Samuel 12 crackles with human drama. The prophet Nathan has just told King David a heartrending tale of a rich man who steals a poor man's ewe lamb. David immediately thunders, "Surely, the man who has done this deserves to die!"

Nathan whirls and points his long, bony finger straight at the king. "You are the man!"

David's secret life of murder and adultery unravels before his eyes. To David's credit, his immediate response is one of unvarnished contrition and repentance. No minimizing, no justifying. Just "I have sinned against the Lord."

From this confrontation, David goes on to pen Psalm 51, one of the most powerful descriptions of a soul in agony to be found anywhere in world literature. In it he sketches a model of spiritual restoration for everyone recovering from brokenness. He asks God to lead him through six steps toward wholeness.

Step 1: A New Depth of Honesty

Be gracious to me, O God, according to Thy lovingkindness;
According to the greatness of Thy compassion blot out my
    transgressions.
Wash me thoroughly from my iniquity,
And cleanse me from my sin.
For I know my transgressions,
And my sin is ever before me.
Against Thee, Thee only, I have sinned,
And done what is evil in Thy sight,
So that Thou art justified when Thou dost speak,

And blameless when Thou dost judge.
Behold, I was brought forth in iniquity,
And in sin my mother conceived me.
Behold, Thou dost desire truth in the innermost being,
And in the hidden part Thou wilt make me know wisdom.

Psalm 51:1–6

David acknowledges his sin and asks forgiveness. But more than that, he asks for help in being truthful on a deeper level: "in the innermost being" and "in the hidden part" of his life. Because of the self-deceptive nature of sin, it takes time to develop this kind of deep honesty. But as we remain open before the Lord, one layer of denial after another will be stripped away so we can see ourselves more clearly.

At a recent Manhood seminar, one of the elders from the host church asked if we could have lunch together. After chatting for a few minutes over lunch, the man looked at me nervously and said, "I've never shared this with anyone else, but after hearing you today, I need to be honest with someone about an area I struggle with." He paused and took a deep breath. "I've never been unfaithful to my wife, and I haven't touched a *Playboy* magazine since I was in college, but I have a problem with looking at women. You know, kind of mentally undressing them? I've been able to pretend I don't have a problem at all. But starting today I want to be honest on a deeper level. I want to take a first step by telling you about it and asking you to pray for me."

When we finally come before the Lord with the "broken and contrite heart" that David describes later in Psalm 51, we find the courage to be honest in a deeper way than ever before. Though it's scary, it's also exhilarating, for this kind of honesty before the Lord and before our brothers helps break the power of unhealthy habits.

Step 2: A New Heart and New Motives

"Create in me a clean heart, O God" (Ps. 51:10).

Once we have clearly seen our "innermost being"—our private thoughts and motives—we ask God to cleanse and purify those hidden areas. This heart cleansing, also described in 1 John 1:9 and elsewhere in the Bible, is a supernatural work of God's Spirit. We can't cleanse ourselves. It's our job to let him in to those inner rooms. It's his job to clean them up.

Step 3: A Renewed Faithfulness

"And renew a steadfast spirit within me" (Ps. 51:10).

A secret life, and the deceit that piggybacks on it like a tick bird on a rhino, steadily erodes our character in the area of steadfastness, or faithfulness. David prays here for renewal of this vital character quality, to prevent him from falling away from a close relationship with the Lord once again.

Step 4: A Restored Relationship

"Do not cast me away from Thy presence, and do not take Thy Holy Spirit from me. Restore to me the joy of Thy salvation" (Ps. 51:11–12).

One of the most chilling losses for a Christian involved in a secret life is the gradual loss of intimate contact with God. It happened for me when I continued to push into forbidden territory and violated my own conscience. There eventually came a time when the glow of God's presence that had nourished and warmed me since I was eight years old darkened and grew cold. I had always delighted in preparing and leading Bible studies for my staff team. But now even my favorite passages failed to touch me, and my prayers stuck in my throat. I was alone in a deeper sense than I'd ever experienced before.

David must have felt that same icy emptiness, for here he pleads with God to restore his experience of God's presence and of the joy of his salvation.

Step 5: A New Staying Power

"And sustain me with a willing spirit" (Ps. 51:12).

The long, dark trek into a secret life may take years; the rugged journey out involves tears, sweat, and deep resolve. When we start, we're at the bottom of a deep canyon looking up. There will be mornings when we awaken with absolutely no desire to keep walking out. It's hard work, the sun's hot, and "One day at a time" looks more like a bumper sticker than a practical philosophy. At those times we must ask the Lord to sustain us, to give us endurance.

Step 6: Ministering out of Brokenness

"Then I will teach transgressors Thy ways, and sinners will be converted to Thee" (Ps. 51:13).

After we work through the first few layers of our own healing and restoration, we find a greatly increased ability to minister to others who are in pain or bondage. This is the same principle that Paul repeats in 2 Corinthians 1:3–4: "The God of all comfort . . . comforts us in all our troubles, so that we can [in turn] comfort [others] in any trouble" (NIV).

It's unfortunate some churches relegate to second-class citizenship those wounded Christians in their midst who have failed publicly. In those congregations, contrary to David's perspective in Psalm 51 and Paul's in 2 Corinthians, failure is deemed a disqualifier for ministry, rather than a potential qualifier if responded to appropriately.

The world hungers for authentic ministry from men today—not the kind of ministry learned from a book, but ministry from those who may still have the singed smell of trial by fire about them, men who can extend a hand to the broken and say, "Here, take hold. I've been through what you've been through, and I know it's rough. But there's hope on the other side. And I'll walk through it with you." *That's* the kind of church that the gates of hell will not prevail against.

2. The Psychological Dimension: Searching the Heart and Mind

Overall, we Christians have done a fair job in applying God's truth to our external behavior; "Don't steal," "Don't lie," "Don't commit adultery" are not uncommon themes in the church today. But we have done a much poorer job in applying the truth to the vast interior areas of our hearts and minds: our thought life and self-talk, our motivations, our damaged emotions.

To use a medical metaphor, we must choose between two very different treatments: layering and lancing. We often slather layers of church attendance, Bible study, and Scripture memorization onto the surface of our lives like a topical ointment, hoping the truth will seep in and heal whatever problems lie underneath. That's fine if all I have is a rash. But if I have a cyst or a pocket of poison buried beneath the surface, I need something more. I'll probably need an X ray to determine the exact location of the cyst. And then I'll need a surgeon to lance it and drain out the poison.

Over and over, the Bible pushes us to take this deeper look beneath our surface behavior. The writer of Proverbs exhorts us to "Watch over your heart with all diligence, for from it flow the springs of life."[1] Quite clearly, the writer is saying our behavior flows out of our heart, or mind. Changing your behavior begins with taking a deep look at your heart.

But Scripture also makes it clear there are formidable obstacles blocking our ability to see ourselves accurately. It says our faults are hidden, our minds are hardened, and our

193

hearts are deceitful and hard to understand.[2] In other words, our lives are riddled with blind spots and hamstrung by entrenched denial.

King David acknowledges the difficulty of this deeper look into our interior when he prays in Psalm 139:

> Search me, O God, and know my heart;
> Try me and know my anxious thoughts;
> And see if there be any hurtful way in me [lit. "any way of pain"],
> And lead me in the everlasting way.[3]

It's not enough to deal solely with surface behavior. We need to ask God to help us identify our fears ("anxious thoughts") and our patterns of pain. As I've groped blindly in the caverns of my soul, God has used the headlamps of many Christian therapists and authors to help me see the patterns of pain that marble my inner walls.

For most of us that deeper look should include an honest examination of the patterns of pain in our family of origin. As we saw in chapter 2, we look at these early childhood influences not to blame someone else for our actions, but to better understand and thus grow out of our own unhealthy habits and flawed beliefs. A few weeks after my midnight confrontation in Europe, when I was desperately trying to understand what had happened, someone loaned me a copy of Claudia Black's book *It Will Never Happen to Me*. At that point I had never even heard the term *adult child of an alcoholic* (ACA). So I was amazed as I read the ACA profile and recognized many of the unhealthy patterns I had acted out in my life: the overachiever or Hero role, the "Don't talk" and "Don't feel" rules, the relational dependencies, and the problem with trusting others enough to be deeply honest. These insights have shown me where I most need to apply God's truth to my broken behavior—where God's lance needs to thrust to find a hidden abscess.

I have known the Bible relatively well in my adult life; I haven't known myself as well, my vulnerabilities, my Achilles heels. And in the battles that threaten our private lives as men, we need all the help we can get.

3. The Relational Dimension: Recovering in Community

The relational dimension of our journey out has two aspects: our need to rebond with those we love whom we may have hurt, and our need to surround ourselves with a healthy support structure.

Often, our secret life behaviors severely damage our relationships with our loved ones. If rebonding is to take place, trust must be restored. Our actions in life, even when we repent, still have consequences. As Stephen Covey says in *The Seven Habits of Highly Effective People*, you can't *talk* your way out of something you *acted* your way into. Especially when deceit is involved, a new track record of humility, openness, and honesty must be established. And that will take time. But for the difficult task of rebonding following a crisis, most men and their loved ones will benefit from the help of a trained counselor to chart a path through the shoals.

Ultimately, restoration after secret life behaviors is not a solo activity. Over the long haul it is essential to wage this war with the support and the objective perspective of a friend or, better yet, a support group of other men. With them you will experience the deep, nurturing fellowship that comes only from "walking in the light" with other believers.[4]

As you choose a support group to assist you in recovery, avoid two extremes that can be found in the Christian community: the moral monitors and the chronic caretakers.

The Moral Monitors

Early in my journey out, I was assigned to an accountability group to monitor my recovery. These five men took

195

on the role of my moral monitors. Every week they asked me questions about my actions, my Bible reading, and my thought life over the past seven days. In general, they took notes on my responses and dispensed advice. None of the others shared honestly about his own struggles; it was a one-sided reporting. I know the intentions of these men were good. They sincerely wanted to help me turn my life around. In fact, I'm sure I couldn't have done better if the roles had been reversed. But unfortunately, I found the method and the atmosphere shaming rather than encouraging, and I gained little from it. About a year later a friend referred me to a true recovery group. The difference was astonishing. In this group I found the companionship and encouragement of fellow pilgrims on the journey toward wholeness. There, because everyone worked equally on his own issues, I found the courage to be deeply honest.

Now, from my work with many men over the last several years, I have reservations about the effectiveness of men's groups organized around a narrow accountability function. The intentions are laudable, but I now know that many men will find that approach to be intimidating and intrusive. It reminds me of Aesop's fable and the wager between the Wind and the Sun. The Wind and the Sun saw a traveler trudging along the road below them. The Wind challenged the Sun to a contest.

"I bet I can separate that man from his coat more quickly than you can," the Wind blustered.

"You're on," replied the Sun.

So the Wind gathered all his strength and blew a mighty gale at the man. He blew and blew and blew. But with every gust, the man only pulled his coat more tightly about him. Finally, spent and humiliated, the Wind gave up.

At that point, with a mischievous look in his eye, the Sun beamed his brightest face toward the traveler. And as the warm rays cascaded down all around him, the man slipped out of his jacket, loosened his collar, and trudged on down the trail. The Sun knew the secret that the Wind did not. Men close up in response to force, but open in response to warmth.

Men's groups can indeed provide the critical element of accountability. I feel a true accountability to the men in my men's group. I've shared all my deepest secrets with them, and they with me. But we won each other's trust over a period of time—years in some cases. I now trust them to keep confidences. I trust them to accept the totality of who I am, dark side and all, and not to judge. I trust them to care about me and to actively encourage and support me in the growth steps I feel led to take. And I know that we're all equals, each there because we know we're broken and we know we're needy. Accountability is the natural by-product of a group like that.

At best, a group filled with moral monitors only intimidates us into looking good temporarily; at worst, it drives our secret behaviors further underground. True change comes from the inside out, not the reverse.

The Chronic Caretakers

While it's unsafe to be honest in a group of moral monitors, there's a sense in which it's *too safe* to be honest around those we might call chronic caretakers. Caretakers hate to see others express pain and immediately attempt to comfort anyone who expresses pain in their presence. But this often short-circuits the healing process, which requires us to *move through* pain to healing, not to skip over it. Paul, in Philippians 3, says that our loftiest goal is to "know [Christ] . . . and the fellowship of his sufferings."[5] And again in 2 Corinthians 12 he says he is "content" to go through distresses and persecutions and difficulties, "for when I am weak, then I am strong."[6] As Keith Miller says, "It is the pain of living that creates a hunger for healing that

197

only God can satisfy." Pain is actually an essential part of the Christian life.

Caretakers may also try to talk you out of your insights into your own dysfunctions. "Oh, don't be so hard on yourself," they'll say. "You're not that bad!" A few months ago my wife and I conducted a workshop in a nearby city on biblical healing and growth for Christians. During one of our discussion periods, small groups scattered all over the room to talk about "socially acceptable" addictions. They discussed the ways we use things like work, food, and control to keep us from feeling pain. They had all just taken a self-test similar to the one in chapter 5 of this book to help them think objectively about the existence of unhealthy patterns in their lives. One man, overwhelmed to see that he had marked yes to every single question in the addiction to work category, shared his feelings about this to those in his group. One of the other men, seeing his pain, tried to make him feel better by telling him that he "wasn't so bad" and that he "didn't really have a problem."

In actuality we *are* that bad. It's only when we own the extent of our brokenness that we find healing. There's a place for affirmation, but there's also a place for standing with each other while we do the tough, painful work of personal growth. So the group we choose must be safe but also committed to a new level of honesty with each other.

This new hunger for honesty and depth in relationships may result in some sifting of your current friendships. Your previous friends may not feel the same desire for deep levels of transparency and heart-to-heart sharing that you now do. If this is the case, you could certainly give yourself permission—without any shame—to find new friends who share your new values. It is absolutely essential to your journey out that you surround yourself with supportive friends who, like you, are committed to the long, hard trek toward wholeness.

4. The Practical Dimension: Know Your Triggers

Part of coming to know yourself and your potential weaknesses is to become street savvy about your triggers—those situations that tend to provoke unhealthy reactions in you.

Fault lines crisscross the emotional landscape inside each of us. A certain situation will unexpectedly trigger a reaction, and a quake rumbles through us. The reaction may be anger, fear, shame, panic, depression, or other painful emotions. These emotional reactions are unpleasant enough by themselves, but the greater danger lies in the temptation to reach for something to numb the bad feelings. That can easily lead to a relapse.

Stephen Smith is the pastor who shared the story of his recovery from sex and love addiction in chapter 6. The HALT principle helps Stephen deal with his triggers.

"HALT stands for hungry, angry, lonely, and tired," Stephen explains. "I've learned that I'm more vulnerable to temptation when I'm experiencing any of those feelings.

"So when I'm hungry, angry, lonely, or tired, I halt and try to take care of myself in a healthy way. When I'm feeling sad, for instance, I pick up the phone and call one of my friends in my support group. We'll get together and talk about what I'm feeling. It's been a lifesaver for me."

Making the rugged journey out and rebuilding our lives is not an easy task. We musn't try to do it alone, for we experience explosive growth in community, but wither alone. And above all we must carry into the journey what King David brought to his restoration experience. In Psalm 51:17 David says, "The sacrifices of God are a broken spirit. A broken and a contrite heart, O God, Thou wilt not despise."

Old Whines,
New Wineskins

Life beyond the Quick Fix

No one puts new wine into old wineskins; otherwise the new wine will burst the skins, and it will be spilled out, and the skins will be ruined. But new wine must be put into fresh wineskins.

Luke 5:37–38

How poor are they that have not patience! What wound did ever heal but by degrees?

William Shakespeare, *Othello*

I couldn't remember when I'd last heard from my arms or legs. Or my face for that matter. It felt strange not to feel my face. I could definitely feel my head, though. Some midget with a hammer was inside my skull, keeping perfect time with my footfalls up the trail. I rounded a massive boulder and willed my leaden legs to shuffle faster as I leaned into the driving snow.

America's Ultimate Challenge was what the marathon sponsors called this exercise in masochism. That slogan alone, of course, was all it took to get me to sign up. At that time, ten years ago, I still thought hero stunts were healthy. Or at least cool.

200

This was the Pikes Peak Marathon, the granddaddy of the twenty-six-milers. Every August the Peak attracted some two thousand hard-bodies (and a few guys like me) to Colorado from all over the country. The race started at an elevation of 6,000 feet at the base of the mountain and rose 7,000 vertical feet over thirteen miles of switchbacks, topping off at over 13,000 feet. During their struggle up the mountain, the runners pass through four different climatic zones. When we'd left the staging area early that morning, it was sunny and seventy degrees. But now as I slogged through the lunar landscape above tree line, it was thirty degrees and snowing.

The thin air was the worst. The blood becomes oxygen starved, sending a migraine message to the head. The muscles are swamped with lactic acid, and the legs turn into wooden stumps. To top it all off, when you finally reach the summit, you're only half done; you then turn right around and run the thirteen miles back down the trail you just came up.

Long before I had reached the crest and turned around, I knew I'd made a big mistake. My training in the last few months had been spotty; I wasn't in shape, and I was simply unprepared for a challenge of this size. I finally staggered across the finish line more than seven hours after I'd started (and behind almost everyone else, including grandmas, grandpas, and children). I had received a valuable but humbling lesson on perseverance. You don't train for a short race and expect to do well in a long race.

But then, we Americans are not known for our endurance. One of every two new marriages now ends in divorce.[1] Five of every ten new businesses run into problems and fail within two years.[2] And the relapse rate in some fields of addiction recovery tops 85 percent. Europeans look at the signs outside our businesses that boast "Continuously in business since 1962!" and just smile. In Europe, if you've only been around for three hundred years, you're still the new kid on the block.

It's not that we're afraid of problems; Americans are envied around the world for their "can do" attitude. It's just that we're an impatient people, and we expect our problems to go away quickly. When they don't, we often quit.

The result, of course, is a culture deeply wed to the concept of the quick fix. And so the bulimic woman asks her doctor for a prescription to take care of her problem and bristles when he suggests working with a therapist. And the engaged couple shops around for a minister who doesn't require weeks of premarital counseling to marry them.

Of course, if you can't find a quick fix that does the job, you can reach for its second cousin, the geographical fix. With the geographical fix, you solve your problems by moving away from them. One out of every five Americans changes residence every year.[3] And the average American worker changes jobs every 4.2 years.[4] But then, many of those new locations and jobs turn out to be worse than the ones we left. Or as Erma Bombeck said, the grass is always greener over the septic tank. But if worse comes to worst, we can simply wait another 4.2 years and change jobs again.

The problem here is, as they say, everywhere I go, there I am. I'm the heart of my problem. If I want to change in the areas of my deepest woundedness—my masculine self-image, the way I use things and people to numb my pain, my issues concerning women and sexuality—then at some point I have to plant myself like Jacob did by the river Jabbok and not move on until I've wrestled my issues through with God to the point of brokenness. Those kinds of deeper character issues are never touched by the quick fix. They require time and usually involve pain, which calls for perseverance.

Perhaps that's why the Bible emphasizes perseverance and endurance as strongly as it does. Fifteen times in the

New Testament, God prompts the writers to sound the endurance theme. Jesus said, "He that endureth to the end shall be saved."[5] The writer of Hebrews uses the metaphor of the distance race when he exhorts us to "lay aside every encumbrance, and the sin which so easily entangles us, and let us run with endurance the race that is set before us."[6] To win the secret wars over the long haul, we need to be prepared for reality. This is not a sprint; it's a marathon.

The healing of our deepest wounds demands, in Eugene Peterson's vivid words, a long obedience in the same direction.

Jesus and the New Paradigm

But deep-down change requires more than perseverance. After being down in the trenches with hundreds of men these last few years, working on the toughest issues we face, I'm now convinced that in addition to perseverance we need a new paradigm, or model, for personal change. Or, to be more accurate, we need to fully embrace the new paradigm taught by Jesus during his earthly ministry.

Jesus butted heads with the Pharisees time and again during the three short years of his ministry. And every time, Jesus used those encounters to contrast his new paradigm for personal transformation with their old one.

Luke records one such encounter in the fifth chapter of his Gospel. Jesus is still in his home district of Galilee and has not yet begun his slow journey south to Jerusalem and his appointment at Golgotha. Word of his healings has spread like a firestorm through prairie grass, and he is thronged daily by the Galilean underclass with sightless eyes and leprous hands beseeching him.

On this particular day, Jesus has called a tax-gatherer named Levi to be his follower. Out of gratitude Levi throws a party with Jesus as guest of honor. Levi invites all his friends—fellow tax gatherers (all of whom have tainted reputations), prostitutes, and others cast off by proper Jewish society.

The Pharisees observe the noisy scene in Levi's home through slitted eyes, their mouths drawn down in scorn and disapproval. This is too much for the Pharisees, whose very name means separatist.

"Why do you eat and drink with the tax gatherers and sinners?" the Pharisees sneer.

Jesus' eyes blaze as he turns to face his detractors. As he speaks, a hush undoubtedly falls over the crowd.

> "It is not those who are well who need a physician, but those who are sick. I have not come to call the righteous men but sinners to repentance."
>
> And they said to Him, "The disciples of John often fast and offer prayers; the disciples of the Pharisees also do the same; but Yours eat and drink."
>
> And Jesus said to them, "You cannot make the attendants of the bridegroom fast while the bridegroom is with them, can you?"[7]

Then Jesus makes it clear to the crowd listening to this high-voltage exchange that this is not a trivial matter, a minor difference of opinion. Rather they are witnessing a head-on collision between two competing paradigms for personal transformation. And as usual, Jesus chooses a parable to explain.

> No one tears a piece from a new garment and puts it on an old garment; otherwise he will both tear the new, and the piece from the new will not match the old. And no one puts new wine into old wineskins; otherwise the new wine will burst the skins, and it will be spilled out, and the skins will be ruined. But new wine must be put into fresh wineskins. And no one, after drinking old wine wishes for new; for he says, "The old is good enough."[8]

You can't mix the old with the new, Jesus is saying, nor the forms of the one with the spirit of the other. If you try to sew a new, unshrunken patch on an old garment, it will shrink the first time you wash it and tear the garment. If you put new wine in old rigid wineskins, when the wine expands it will burst the old skins. You have to start fresh. This is not just an improvement on the old religious system; it is a completely different system. The two are incompatible.

The parable is rich with imagery. The old paradigm championed by the Pharisees was characterized by sadness and bondage. Fasting was an appropriate symbol of that old paradigm. The new paradigm revealed in Jesus is characterized by freedom and joy. The tender relationship between a bride and a bridegroom is the symbol he chooses to capture that spirit. The old wine emphasizes ascetic ritualism and discipline as the path to righteousness and personal transformation. The new wine offers a living relationship with a loving Bridegroom as the way to change.

The two systems, in fact, are so fundamentally different that Jesus does not expect his new wine to be popular. Those who have become accustomed to the old wine of the Pharisees will simply say, "The old is good enough." Indeed we still have both paradigms present with us today. Some still feel the old wine is good enough.

At the heart of Jesus' paradigm for change is a call to a new kind of honesty and authenticity.

In a classic example of Madison Avenue doublespeak, the most popular brand of men's pants and slacks in America recently ran a national ad campaign based around the concept of authenticity. Ads in major magazines showed young men wearing the appropriate casual slacks being ogled by young women. Splashed across the two-page spread in thirty-point type was the word *AUTHENTIC.* I had to wonder when I saw it if the copywriters caught the irony of their message. Were they really trying to convince us that

205

we can achieve authenticity by wearing certain clothes? Evidently, in image-conscious America authenticity is no longer an inner issue having to do with motives and character; it's now an outer issue, a matter of how we look, how we come across.

In the religious world of Jesus' day, spiritual authenticity had become almost exclusively an outer issue. The Pharisees had a scrupulous concern with the external minutia of their legalism: the wearing of conspicuous phylacteries and tassels, observance of ritual purity, frequent fastings, and the tithing of herbs.

Jesus didn't mince words when he confronted the Pharisees' emphasis on externals.

> Woe to you, scribes and Pharisees, hypocrites! For you clean the outside of the cup and of the dish, but inside they are full of robbery and self-indulgence. You blind Pharisees, first clean the inside of the cup and of the dish, so that the outside of it may become clean also. Woe to you, scribes and Pharisees, hypocrites! For you are like whitewashed tombs which on the outside appear beautiful, but inside they are full of dead men's bones and all uncleanness. Even so you too outwardly appear righteous to men, but inwardly you are full of hypocrisy and lawlessness.[9]

In fact, the Pharisees judged the whole world on the basis of externals, dividing everyone into just two categories: us and them. That was why they were offended by Jesus in Luke 5 when he dined with Levi and the other tax gatherers and sinners. Externals were so important, they believed, that you were soiled by merely associating with the wrong people. And, of course, there was the whole question of appearances.

Jesus confronted the keepers of the old paradigm on the issue of authenticity, and he left no doubt about his view. The Pharisees were completely inauthentic and impossibly obsessed with external issues. True spirituality, Jesus made clear, is determined by internal issues.

New Paradigm Principles

1. Admit Sickness and Sinfulness

Jesus moves on to make an even more dramatic point about honesty and authenticity. When the Pharisees criticized him for befriending sinners, Jesus turned to them and said, "It is not those who are well who need a physician, but those who are sick. I have not come to call righteous men but sinners to repentance."[10] I believe Jesus used a masterful touch of sanctified sarcasm here. In essence he said, "Oh, I'm sorry I offended you, gentlemen. I didn't come for upstanding, clean-living, righteous folks like you. I only came for the sick and the sinners." I'm sure the Pharisees didn't know how to respond to that. Had Jesus just complimented them, or burned them?

In fact, Jesus had just fired off the most dramatic blast of his new paradigm: He only came for those who are willing to identify themselves as sick and as sinners!

The Pharisees were caught. They certainly didn't want to put themselves in the same category as the sinful rabble in Levi's house that night. But then again, the masses adored Jesus as the greatest prophet of all time. So the Pharisees didn't want to be viewed as being against him either.

Quite simply, Jesus was using the Pharisees' sneer about dining with sinners as an opportunity to make clear a startling new truth. His gospel is only for those who are willing to acknowledge their *fundamental brokenness;* it's not for those who feel they're generally good, upstanding people, who just want to round out their moral education a bit.

Perhaps most radically of all, Jesus here swept away the old two-category way of classifying the world: insiders and outsiders, the good people and the bad people, the saints

207

and the sinners. There is just one category: desperately needy sinners, sick people with terminal illnesses in need of the Physician.

In Luke 4 when Jesus performed the first act of his public ministry, he stood in the synagogue in his hometown of Nazareth and read from the scroll of the prophet Isaiah. As he quoted Isaiah, he announced exactly what his ministry was to be and who was to be the focus of that ministry. He had come, he said, to preach the gospel to the *poor*, to proclaim release to the *captives*, recovery of sight to the *blind*, and to set free those who are *downtrodden*. This is an amplification of what he would say later to the Pharisees. Jesus didn't come for the people with no problems. He came for those who saw themselves as poor, blind, captive, and downtrodden.

My wife and I had a revealing exchange with a pastor some time ago. We had called on him to share about an upcoming marriage workshop we were sponsoring for couples in our area. We mentioned that it would be an honest and practical workshop in which we talk about the real problems faced by real couples, ourselves included, as well as the ways to deal with those challenges.

The pastor reflected on that for a moment and then said, "I'm sorry, but if the participants have to admit to having problems, I'm quite sure none of my people will come."

Dick Bergstrom is a personal friend and president of ChurchHealth, a church consulting ministry. We meet for lunch on occasion, and at one such meeting last year Dick said, "Before we eat lunch, let me show you something. We can take my car."

Curious, I asked him what we were going to see.

"It's a giant object lesson," he said, smiling. Now I was *really* curious.

Soon we pulled up in front of a large retirement complex.

"My parents worked here one summer a few years ago," Dick said. "So I got an insider's view of this facility and how it works. Let me show you inside."

Dick led me into a lavishly appointed reception area. Pile carpeting, fine furniture, and exquisite interior decorating gave me more the feel of a Hilton hotel than a retirement home.

"Boy," I said, "retirement homes have sure changed since I last saw one."

"*This*, my friend, is not just an ordinary retirement facility. This is one of the Cadillacs of the retirement world. But," he said, holding one finger in the air, "there is just *one* requirement for entry to this facility. Well, one, in addition to money," he said, laughing.

"What's that?" I asked.

"You can't have anything seriously wrong with you," he said, a Cheshire cat grin spreading across his face. He looked at me expectantly.

"Doesn't that *remind* you of anything, Pat?"

I still didn't get it. I watched as a well-dressed couple in their seventies exited the elevator on the other side of the lobby and walked evenly down the hall toward the dining room.

"Let me give you a more complete picture," Dick said. "This is one of the finest facilities of its kind. All the apartments are top of the line. The food is excellent. It's most retired folks' dream to move into a place like this. But it's only for people with no obvious physical problems. As soon as you develop a problem—say, you have trouble walking—the rules of the facility require you to move out. They have no nursing care here. If you need that kind of help, you have to move down the street to a much less desirable facility. *Now* does it remind you of anything?" he asked.

I nodded, finally getting the analogy. "Yeah," I said, "some churches are like that."

"But I haven't told you the best part yet," Dick said. "My parents told me that when residents first begin to develop a physical problem, many deliberately try to cover it up for fear that they'll be kicked out. A lot of these folks we see strolling around here looking fine go back to their rooms and collapse, glad that they've made it through another day without anyone finding out their secret!"

Now I saw the whole picture. It's the Pharisees' paradigm, a paradigm still perpetuated by some churches. In that paradigm the church isn't a hospital for the sick; it's a club for the healthy. The only problem is, if the sin disease we all carry breaks out in some obvious way in your life, you have a choice to make. You can cover up the symptoms and continue to act healthy, or you can leave.

I could understand why people would play elaborate cover-up games to stay in the center Dick showed me. The Hilton is certainly nicer than a nursing home. It felt very pleasant to be surrounded by all that interior decorating and those attractive people. All it would cost me to stay is my authenticity.

2. Let God Heal the Wounds beneath the Sinful Behavior

This was at the heart of Jesus' challenge to the Pharisees. They were content to focus on the surface of their lives, while Jesus said the real issue is how healthy your life is inside, in the areas that are out of sight.

In an article in *Faith and Renewal* Christian counselors Rick Koepcke and E. James Wilder evaluated various aspects of the Christian men's movement today. One of their greatest concerns had to do with the danger of underestimating the wounds within men.

> The assumption that men can change simply by "trying harder" is rather demeaning to the many men who feel they *have* been "trying harder" without success. More important, it ignores

the issue of the wound within the man that may be rendering him incapable of making the desired changes in his life. Men struggling with sexual addictions or unwanted homosexual tendencies, for instance, have a wound underneath needing to be healed, of which the troubling behavior is a symptom. When the wound is uncovered, allowing the real need to surface and be tended to, the behavior can be dealt with.

If the leaders of the fledgling Christian movement attempt to avoid the wounds that men suffer and move straight to exhortation and admonition, the church may find itself with fewer men, and with those that are left being even more damaged and more incapable of succeeding as men than before.[11]

In twenty years of ministry prior to my own broken-world experience, I received significant amounts of training, Bible teaching, and practical ministry experience. But I only applied that training to certain superficial levels of my life. I ignored the wounded areas beneath my outward behavior. I was, in essence, ignorant of my own neediness.

Like many Christians, I placed too much emphasis on my salvation experience, on having been a Christian since I was a child, and on having been raised in a good church environment. In Pharisee terminology, I was an *insider*, and insiders, by definition, don't have problems. But of course, we do. Having eternal life is indeed an indescribable gift. But our salvation experiences are no substitute for "cleaning the inside of the cup and the dish," as Jesus told the Pharisees.

In my own inner work I've identified at least four levels of woundedness that we must address if we are to stay healthy.

- The false self we present to others
- The socially acceptable dependencies we use to treat our emotional pain

211

- Our secret life behaviors
- The core pain and core issues we carry into adulthood from childhood

The diagram below captures those four levels of brokenness.

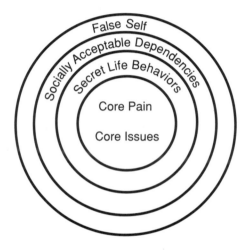

Most of us will need to work on these layers sequentially—from the outside in. The first step requires giving up the false self and the Hero role, and admitting our neediness. And because we use our socially acceptable dependencies (on food, work, spending, etc.) as well as our secret life behaviors to medicate our emotional pain, it is generally necessary to deal with our unhealthy habits next, for one simple reason: We will not be in touch with our core pain as long as we numb that pain with addictive behavior.

Ultimately, we must deal with our core issues. These issues are generally rooted in our childhood experiences and include things like toxic shame (who I am is never good enough), mother wounds and father wounds, and lifescript issues that have imprinted us with unhealthy rules, roles, and recordings.

Until we deal with these core issues, our attempts at change will probably result in little more than addiction swapping; we manage to give up, say, alcoholism, but because we didn't treat the underlying pain, we simply replace alcohol with another pain deadener such as workaholism.

In chapter 8 we heard the story of Gary, who voluntarily ended his secret struggle with alcoholism. That one step started a positive ripple effect in his life. It took away the narcotic he was using to numb his pain. It stripped away a major part of his false self as he leveled with his wife and with his friend at work about his drinking problem. And it ended his secret life behaviors involving alcohol. That didn't mean Gary's problems were all gone, however. In fact, those steps helped Gary to see other problems that had been there all along but were masked by alcohol.

"After I took the Pleaser Profile test I saw why I was having so many problems at home and at work," Gary said. "I realized I had made my boss my father, and my wife my mother—and the results were just as disastrous as when I was a kid! I felt the same anger and frustration I did back then. When I was growing up, my parents were always on my case, always critical. So I had a flinch reaction as an adult when my wife or my boss even implied a criticism.

"Now that I see the source of the problem—my own lack of self-worth—I've stopped blaming my boss and my wife, and both of those relationships are much less conflicted. And those Scriptures about God's unconditional love have been incredibly healing for me. I have a couple of them taped to my dashboard, and I let them roll around in my heart to and from work."

Gary could never have taken the steps required to deal with his core issues if he was still numbing them with alcohol.

In one seminar my wife and I gave in a local church last year, we talked about socially acceptable dependencies like workaholism and their negative effect on our lives. I noticed a lady near the front who became more and more agitated as the session went on. As soon as the session ended, the lady charged the podium, radiating anger.

"How dare you suggest I cut back the hours I work?" she said, close to tears. "My marriage is a living hell, the church has told me I can't get a divorce, and I would go absolutely insane if I couldn't escape into my work every day." And with that she burst into tears.

We didn't have any easy answers for that woman. The primary reason any of us develop unhealthy behaviors or addictions is that we can't stand the inner pain we're carrying, and we're desperate for a pain killer. It's also true that as we give up the habits we've developed to defend against our core pain, we may be flooded with overwhelming levels of distress.

If the thought of facing that raw pain without the narcotic of your unhealthy habits daunts you (and it does me), you can draw a kind of back-door courage from this fact: If you leave your toxic habits in place, they will ultimately cause you even greater pain. They could cost you—as they have me—many of the relationships that mean the most in life.

The woman who confronted us in the church seminar was terrified by the prospect of stripping away one problem, only to be confronted by an even scarier one, a highly conflicted marriage, underneath. But that is how Christians grow. God has promised to flood us with his grace if we ask him and to give us the courage to do what looks impossible. As we yield one area after another to God's gracious Spirit, we experience the real payoff: Peace and serenity gradually replace the chaos and fear that have terrorized our interior landscapes for so long.

3. Embrace Pain

Over and over, Scripture reminds us that without pain, there's no gain. The psalmist tells us, "Those who sow in tears shall reap with joyful shouting. He who goes to and fro weeping, carrying his bag of seed, shall indeed come again with a shout of joy, bringing his sheaves with him."[12]

Of course, when we're in the middle of pain, we want to run from it. Everyone loves Easter more than Good Friday. But confronting our areas of fundamental weakness will not be accomplished easily or painlessly.

I was sharing my feelings about all that recently with my friend Jon. Jon mulled it over for a moment and then said, "The process of change is scary. We're talking about God changing the core of who we are. There are bound to be many painful feelings during that process. That's why it's absolutely crucial not to try to work through the process of change alone. We'll never make it without a strong support structure. The pain is just too great." That support structure, of course, includes God himself, who has promised never to leave us or forsake us. Ideally it should also include a support group of other men dedicated to change, and possibly the help of a Christian therapist.

4. Be Honest in Communication

John Bradshaw captures the way our society has developed phoniness into an art form.

We are taught to be nice and polite. We are taught that these behaviors (most often lies) are better than telling the truth. [Our society] is rampant with teaching dishonesty (saying things we don't mean and pretending to feel ways we don't feel). We smile when we feel sad; laugh nervously when dealing with grief; laugh at jokes we don't think are funny; tell people things to be polite that we surely don't mean.[13]

215

Breaking these patterns means going against a lifetime of training. It involves the kind of honesty that doesn't say "I'm fine" when I'm really full of pain. It's the kind of honesty embraced by the early church, where the emphasis was on "speaking the truth in love,"[14] where believers were exhorted to lay aside falsehood and speak truth to their neighbors,[15] where lying to each other was seen as a serious offense, as it was with Ananias and Sapphira in Acts 5.

Dishonesty only cuts us off from the help of those who could support us in our journey toward wholeness.

As you make a commitment to increase the level of honesty and authenticity in your life, you may find challenges even from those who are closest to you. Early in my own restoration journey, I was in a support group with several other men. All of us had been in some form of full-time ministry, and all of us had gone through some kind of broken-world experience.

One of the other men in the group had struggled with a lifelong addiction to pornography. He had also been involved with prostitutes, all without the knowledge of his wife. His wife was a well-known Christian author and hostess of her own syndicated radio show. Greg told the group he felt God prompting him to tell his wife about his struggle. He knew his keeping secrets had damaged their intimacy, and he wanted her encouragement in his ongoing fight to stay clean. We all affirmed him and prayed for him that week.

The next week we all asked Greg how it had gone.

"Well," he said, "as soon as I said, 'Honey, there's something I want to tell you about me,' my wife cut in and said, 'If this has something to do with that men's group you go to, I don't want to know anything about it. I'd rather not know at all.' And that was it. She didn't want me to share anything."

Greg looked discouraged and disappointed. Evidently his wife didn't want anything—including the truth—to mar her image of her husband or her image of her marriage. But intimacy in marriage can only be achieved if both individuals are working to build greater honesty into their relationship. I felt sad for Greg and his wife.

The Process of Transformation

So far we've seen that the process of change requires perseverance, a willingness to let God heal the wounds beneath the unhealthy behavior, as well as a new kind of honesty and authenticity. But there are two other crucial truths to understand about the process of personal transformation. Without understanding these two truths, you will almost certainly grow discouraged and drop out.

Change Is a Process with Phases

In his excellent book *Transitions: Making Sense of Life's Changes,* William Bridges says that whenever we attempt to make a life-change (as opposed to a quick fix) we can expect to go through at least three phases. First there's an ending, followed by a transitional period of confusion and lostness, and then a new beginning.

The ending phase is what Jesus refers to in Matthew 16:25, "Whoever wishes to save his life shall lose it."

What was new for me was Bridges' main point, that the *transitional* phase—despite its chaos and distress—is essential for change to take place.

As I reflected on that, some lights came on for me about my own restoration experience. When I first bounced out of my crisis nine years ago, I expected my ending (the sin and the secret life) to be immediately followed by a new beginning, complete with a new set of behaviors and attitudes. What I didn't expect and wasn't prepared for was that messy, middle, muddle-through phase called transition.

I've never liked transitions. I've never even liked waiting at traffic lights. I prefer it if things move from black to white, preferably overnight while I sleep. When I have to go through a messy transitional period, progress seems so slow and I wonder if I'll ever really get there. It's at those times that I'm most vulnerable to sniper attacks from the platoon of doubting Thomases in my head.

"Recovery and restoration are scams!" one such voice used to mock regularly. "You're supposed to feel better now. But you feel worse than you did before!"

But that's where the insights from William Bridges are helpful. "Distress is not a sign that something has gone wrong," Bridges says, "but that something is *changing*." Change includes sifting out old behaviors and attitudes and embracing the new. All of that involves hard work and pain.

Since then, as I've studied the Scriptures I've seen more clearly that God often takes his children through long, messy transitions on the way to a new life. It took the children of Israel a full generation to conquer all their enemies *after* they'd moved into the Promised Land. God was at work in the process.

Moses spent forty years learning lessons in the wilderness after killing the Egyptian before God called him at the burning bush. And the apostle Paul had to cool his heels for fourteen years on the backside of the desert after his conversion. All of that was essential preparation for his ministry. God definitely values process and struggle in the business of changing lives from the inside out.

Change Is Not Linear

I grew up during the Sputnik era in America. The U.S. was racing the Russians to get a man into space. Every week, it seemed in those early days of NASA, there was another report of a rocket exploding on the pad at Cape Canaveral, or lifting off for a few seconds only to do a one-eighty into the ocean. And every time a rocket exploded, NASA would issue a press release saying that the launch had been a "partial success." As an all-wise teenager at the time, I can remember thinking how humorous it was to call a multi-million-dollar fireball a partial success.

But I see it differently now. Sure, those early setbacks were discouraging to the scientists. But they learned from each one of them. And the net result *was* progress. NASA *did* go on to put a man in space and a man on the moon.

It's the same in our personal growth. It's simply not realistic to expect that our progress will be linear, as in the graph below. Because we're human, we'll have setbacks and failures and occasionally revert to our old behavior. As Chuck Swindoll says, our growth is usually "three steps forward, and two steps back." (Or sometimes *two* forward and *three* back!)

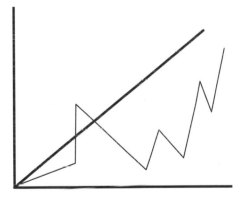

When we expect unbroken linear growth, our first setback can fill us with shame and intense self-criticism. It's one thing to repent of your mistakes and move on, feeling loved and worthwhile. It's quite another to punish yourself for being a "failure," to decide that you'll never see growth in this area, and to give up. Jesus' exhortation to Peter in Matthew 18:22 to forgive his brother "up to seventy times seven" captures God's gracious attitude toward us. He *knows* our progress heavenward will involve zigzags. Lots of them. Maybe seventy times seven. He has pledged to be there every time we stumble to help us get back on our feet and to get on with the journey.

The spirit of our forward-and-back journey toward healthiness is captured whimsically in a recovery classic by Portia Nelson:

Autobiography in Five Short Chapters

1. I walk down the street.
   There is a deep hole in the sidewalk.
   I fall in.
   I am lost . . . I am hopeless.
   It isn't my fault.
   It takes forever to find a way out.
2. I walk down the same street.
   There is a deep hole in the sidewalk.
   I pretend I don't see it.
   I fall in again.
   I can't believe I am in the same place.
   But . . . it isn't my fault.
3. I walk down the same street.
   There is a deep hole in the sidewalk.
   I see it is there.
   I still fall in . . . it's a habit.
   My eyes are open.
   I know where I am.
   It is *my* fault.
   I get out immediately.
4. I walk down the same street.
   There is a deep hole in the sidewalk.
   I walk around it.
5. I walk down another street.[16]

For all of us, the walk down that street begins with a decision. That's where it began for one of the characters in C. S. Lewis's novel *The Great Divorce*. In this whimsical account of a fictional bus ride from hell to heaven, the passengers are allowed to walk freely around the outskirts of heaven for a day and decide whether they'd like to stay on permanently.

One of the passengers is an oily looking man who has decided to leave and is headed back to the bus. Sitting on his shoulder is a little red lizard, twitching its tail like a whip and whispering things in his ear. The man turns his head to the reptile and snarls, "Shut up, I tell you!"

Just then one of heaven's radiant angels sees the man. "Off so soon?" he calls.

"Well, yes," says the man. "I'd stay, you know, if it weren't for *him,*" indicating the lizard. "I told him he'd have to be quiet if he came. His kind of stuff won't do here. But he won't stop. So I'll just have to go home."

"Would you like me to make him quiet?" asks the angel.

"Of course I would," says the man.

"Then I will kill him," says the angel, stepping forward.

The man panics at the thought of permanently losing the lizard and the sweet fantasies the creature whispers in his ear. But he *is* tired of carrying him around. He dithers back and forth between the two choices. Solemnly, the angel reminds him he cannot kill the lizard without his consent. And yes, it will be painful for the man; the angel refuses to soften the truth. Finally, in anguish, the man gives his consent, then screams in agony as the angel's burning hands close around the lizard and crush it.

"Ow! That's done for me," gasps the man, reeling back.

But then, gradually but unmistakably, the man begins to be transformed. Bright and strong he grows, into the shape of an immense man, not much smaller than the angel. And even more surprisingly, something is happening to the lizard, too. He grows, rippling with swells of flesh and

muscle, until standing beside the man is a great white stallion with mane and tail of gold.

The new man turns from the horse, flings himself at the
feet of the Burning One, and embraces them. When he
rises, his face shines with tears. Then in joyous haste the
young man leaps upon the horse's back. Turning in his seat
he waves a farewell. And then they are off across the green
plain, and soon among the foothills of the mountains. Like
a star, they wind up, scaling what seem to be impossible
steeps, till near the dim brow of the landscape, they van-
ish, bright themselves, into the rose brightness of that ever-
lasting morning.[17]

That remarkable journey stretches out to the horizon in
front of each of us as well, beckoning us to an experience
of personal transformation. The journey starts as we let God
have the issue we are struggling with. Pain will be involved
in that exchange; he never said otherwise. But there also
will be the ascent toward something magnificent—the discovery of our redeemed manhood as we allow our Creator
to take the broken pieces of our lives and fashion them into
something that reflects his own glory.

"But we all, with unveiled face beholding as in a mirror
the glory of the Lord, are being transformed into the same
image from glory to glory."[18]

-11-

Stumbling Heavenward

Shame and Grace

Hoping together, forgiven and loved,
As we're stumbling heavenward.
Ray Salmond, Mike Mulder
"Growing Richer"

Justice: We get what we deserve.
Mercy: We do not get what we deserve.
Grace: We get what we do not deserve.
Sam Wilson

The sixteen-year-old girl stood awkwardly in the front of the church, twisting a handkerchief in tight little coils in her hands. Tears ran down her cheeks and dripped unnoticed onto her prim white blouse. A teenage boy stood to her left, shifting his weight from foot to foot, his face drained of all color. The pastor stood grim-faced to their right behind the pulpit.

The girl glanced back at him, and he nodded. She turned back to face the congregation and locked her eyes on a patch of carpet in front of her. A sob rose in her throat and she stifled it.

"I've committed a moral sin . . ." Another struggle. "And I'm here tonight to confess that sin to you, and to ask for your forgiveness. We're really sorry . . ." Great racking sobs choked off her words completely now. She covered her face with her hands as a deaconness rose to lead her off the platform.

Jenny's eyes were moist as she described this scene to me from twenty years ago. Her husband, Jim, squeezed her hand and studied her closely. Jim and I had worked in a mentoring relationship together the last several months.

"She had nightmares about that scene for a couple of years afterwards," Jim said. "The thing was, the pastor told us we had to stand up in front of the church that way, or we wouldn't be allowed to come to the church anymore. We knew we'd sinned, and we just did what they told us to do. But I know now if any of our kids ever made a mistake like that, I'd never, ever let them go through something like we did."

"We were already wounded," Jenny said, shaking her head. "It was like adding scars to the wounds."

Shame is making a comeback today. Long popular in certain parts of the religious community as a method of controlling behavior, public shaming is now being adopted by various governmental agencies to help carry out policy. Law enforcement agencies in several cities across the country are buying space in local newspapers to run the names, ages, and photos of men arrested for soliciting prostitutes. Some sociologists are recommending that misbehaving school children be forced to wear dunce caps in front of their classmates in hopes of motivating them to shape up. Others are looking for ways to publicly shame pregnant teens as a way of curbing unwed motherhood.[1]

Not everyone, however, agrees that shaming is a good idea. Former Wisconsin commissioner of corrections Walter Dickey says that public humiliation "tends to harden people." And Reverend Timothy MacDonald of the First Iconia Baptist Church in Atlanta says of shaming techniques, "It only produces a negative stigma that cannot have any redemptive quality at all."[2]

We cannot talk intelligently about our ongoing journey toward spiritual healthiness without addressing the issues of shame and grace. Is shame an appropriate tool for us to use in our warfare with sin? Is grace just a silk-and-lace disguise for coddling our weaknesses?

Shame

There is a substantive difference between shame and guilt. Guilt has to do with our behavior, what we do; shame has to do with our identity, who we are. When we do something wrong, our God-given conscience rings an alarm. That pang we feel is guilt. Guilt is not destructive to our person because we can do something about it. We can acknowledge our wrongdoing, change our behavior, experience forgiveness, and we no longer have to feel guilty. (The fact that some of us do feel guilty even after taking those steps is not the fault of guilt; it is the result of our inability to forgive ourselves in the same way God has forgiven us.)

Shame, on the other hand, goes beyond the sense that "I did bad things" to the sense that "I am bad, through and through." John Bradshaw says, "Toxic shame . . . is experienced as the all-pervasive sense that I am flawed and defective as a human being. Toxic shame is no longer an emotion that signals our limits, it is a state of being, a core identity. Toxic shame gives you a sense of worthlessness."[3]

Of course, as Christians we believe we *are* flawed in one sense—we are each afflicted with a sinful nature. We are fallible. But that is not the same as saying we are worthless.

We are flawed, we are fallible, but we are of great worth, and we bear the image—marred but clearly recognizable—of the Master Designer of the universe.

But shame is the very atmosphere of our fallen world. It pools and swirls outside the fringes of our lives like a poisonous nerve gas, waiting for us to open the door a crack and let it seep in to paralyze and destroy. Shame, in this sense, is a demotivator for ongoing growth. It usually results in self-condemnation, discouragement, and the urge to give up. ("I'm bad. I blew it. There's no hope for me ever getting better.")[4]

Let's look more closely at what Scripture says about shame and grace.

Satan, Condemnation, and Shame

In Revelation 12:10 Satan is described as "the accuser of [the] brethren . . . who accuses them before our God day and night."

You might say Satan has the "ministry of condemnation" as he ceaselessly accuses us. It is this ministry of condemnation that Jesus came to dismantle. The eighth chapter of Romans bursts with life as Paul describes how Jesus triumphed over the forces that would condemn us. Paul opens with a flourish of trumpets as he proclaims, "There is therefore now *no condemnation* for those who are in Christ Jesus."[5] And he ends the chapter in the same spirit of triumph: "If God is for us, who is against us? . . . Who will bring a charge against God's elect? God is the one who justifies; who is the one who condemns?"[6]

God has not taken away Satan's weapons of shame and condemnation. But God has given us our own armaments so that we can protect ourselves. Every fiery dart of shame and accusation that the enemy hurls at us can be deflected by that amazing promise from Romans 8: "There is therefore now *no condemnation. . . .*"

The key to long-term staying power, the key to not losing heart, is to surround ourselves with God's mercy and grace, and to fend off Satan's messages of shame and condemnation.

This becomes especially important for us following our failures, when the line between healthy guilt and toxic shame becomes the most blurred. To clarify this critical area, we need to understand God's view of us when we fail. We need to understand grace.

Grace

The God of the Second Chance

Scripture is rife with the images of a God who is full of compassion for those who have struggled and fallen on the field of battle. David, who committed murder and adultery, was still entrusted with the kingship of the nation and was still called a man after God's own heart.[7] Rahab, the prostitute, is praised for her faith and her good deeds and is included in the royal lineage of Jesus himself.[8] Moses murdered a man and ran away but was later given responsibility for all the children of Israel.[9] Peter denied Jesus and fled like a coward, but he was still appointed leader of the early church.[10] Jesus, in fact, knew beforehand that Peter would fail, but still entrusted him with the leadership role. Our failures do not surprise God. John the Baptist, despite knowing Jesus personally, expressed doubt at the end of his life about Jesus being the Messiah. Jesus still praised him, saying, "Among those born of women there has not arisen anyone greater than John the Baptist."[11]

The testimony of Scripture is clear from Genesis to Revelation: God has compassion, he knows we're made of dust; he forgives our sin and remembers it no more; he causes *all things,* even our failures, to work together for good.[12] He knows our failures beforehand and still trusts us with important responsibilities. He is, in short, the God of the second chance.

Haddon Robinson tells the memorable story of Roy Riegels to illustrate God's attitude toward those of us who make big mistakes.

On New Year's Day, 1919, Georgia Tech played University of California in the Rose Bowl. Shortly before halftime, a man named Roy Riegels recovered a fumble for California. Somehow he became confused and started running—sixty-five yards in the wrong direction. One of his teammates, Benny Lom, outdistanced him and downed him just before he would have scored for the opposing team. When California attempted to punt, Tech blocked the kick and scored a safety.

The men filed off the field and went into the dressing room. They sat down on the benches and on the floor, all but Riegels. He put his blanket around his shoulders, sat down in a corner, put his face in his hands, and cried like a baby.

If you have played football, you know that a coach usually has a great deal to say to his team during halftime. That day Coach Nibbs Price was quiet. No doubt he was trying to decide what to do with Riegels.

The timekeeper came in and announced that there were three minutes before playing time. Coach Price looked at the team and said simply, "Men, the same team that played the first half will start the second."

The players got up and started out, all but Riegels. He did not budge. The coach looked back and called to him again; still he didn't move.

Coach Price went over to where Riegels sat and said, "Roy, didn't you hear me? The same team that played the first half will start the second."

Roy Riegels looked up, and his cheeks were wet with a strong man's tears. "Coach," he said, "I can't do it. I've ruined you; I've ruined the University of California; I've ruined myself. I couldn't face that crowd in the stadium to save my life."

Coach Price reached out and put his hand on Riegels' shoulder and said to him, "Roy, get up and go on back; the game is only half over."

Roy Riegels went back, and those Tech men will tell you that they have never seen a man play football as Roy Riegels played that second half. . . .

We take the ball and run in the wrong direction; we stumble and fall and are so ashamed of ourselves that we never want to try again, and He comes to us and bends over us in the person of His Son and says, "Get up and go on back; the game is only half over."[13]

The Scandal of Grace

But the picture becomes even clearer in the New Testament. The Gospels in particular are a veritable photo album full of snapshots that capture the response of Jesus Christ to sin and sinners from all walks of life. Jesus was referred to as the friend of sinners.[14] When he met the Samaritan woman at the well, he said he knew about her serial marriage syndrome, but never used the information to shame her.[15]

Similarly with the woman caught in the act of adultery, he faced off with the Pharisees by telling them that the one who was without sin could cast the first stone. The obvious message: The knowledge of our own fallibility should temper our rush to judgment. The scene closed with that remarkable exchange between Jesus and the woman, who was undoubtedly sprawled before him in the street, her clothes and hair disheveled, tears streaking little rivulets of mud down her dusty cheeks.

Straightening up, Jesus says, "Woman, where are they? Did no one condemn you?"

Eyes downcast, afraid to meet his gaze, the woman says, "No one, Lord."

Jesus, speaking gently, says, "Neither do I condemn you; go your way; from now on sin no more."[16]

"Neither do I condemn you"—a scandalous response from God's holy Son. How could he not condemn her? She had just been caught in an ugly act of sin. Could the Son of God himself be soft on sin? But his response is consistent with all we've seen about Jesus' mission. Satan uses shame and condemnation as weapons to enslave men and women. Jesus came to free us from shame and condemnation, and he refuses to use those methods even when sin

229

has clearly been committed. It is scandalous. But grace has always been scandalous.

Nowhere is the scandal of grace—and the heart of the Father toward those who have failed—painted more poignantly than in Jesus' parables of the laborers in the vineyard and the prodigal son.

THE GENEROUS LANDOWNER

In the parable of the laborers, from Matthew 20, a landowner goes out early in the morning to hire laborers for his vineyard. He hires a group of workers for a denarius for the day's work and sends them off. Three hours later he hires a second group of laborers and sends them off. He does the same at the sixth and the ninth hours. Then very late in the day, at the eleventh hour, he notices another group of men lounging around in the marketplace. He hires them as well and sends them off to work.

One hour later the end of the workday comes, and the workers trudge back in to be paid. The owner has the groups line up in order, beginning with the last ones hired. To those whom he hired in the eleventh hour, he gives a denarius each.

That's okay with everyone until those who were hired first get paid. To these, who've put in a long day indeed, he also gives just a denarius. These early workers become angry. When they saw what the late workers were paid, they thought they would receive more.

"These last men have worked only one hour, and you have made them equal to us who have borne the burden and the scorching heat of the day," the men grumble.

But the landowner answers one of them, "Friend, I am doing you no wrong; did you not agree with me for a denarius? Take what is yours and go your way, but I wish to give to this last man the same as to you. Is it not lawful for me to do what I wish with what is my own? Or is your eye envious because I am generous?"

Then Jesus ends the parable by saying, "Thus the last shall be first, and the first last."[17]

This parable shows better than any other that the rules and the values of the kingdom of God are completely different from those here on earth. The laborers' grumbling reflects the value system of the world. The value system of the world says you are paid what you deserve to be paid based on the amount of work you've done. If somebody else is paid more for the same work, then the principle of fairness says you should be paid more too.

But the kingdom of God doesn't fit in any of our earthbound categories. It's not a democracy. It's evidently not even a union shop, from the sound of this parable. God hasn't set his kingdom up according to our values of fairness and equality. We don't get what we deserve in God's kingdom. If we did, we'd all get hell. We get precisely the opposite of what is considered fair on earth—we get what we don't deserve. That's grace.

Jesus operated with kingdom values when he interacted with men and women here on earth. With the adulterous woman, the Pharisees operated with the world's normal values. This woman sinned; let's give her what she deserves. Jesus responded out of a different set of values: Yes, this woman sinned. I know what she deserves. But I'm giving her what she doesn't deserve; I'm giving her grace.

THE PERFECT FATHER

In the story of the prodigal son, Jesus dresses the same truth in a different set of clothes. With one significant addition. In Luke 15 we are also given a glimpse into the heart of a perfect father, a father who loves and yearns for the restoration of the relationship with his younger son.

231

We see God's attitude toward prodigals everywhere in the father's eager searching of the horizon for the return of his son, in his quickness to shower gifts and honor on his son, cutting short the son's well-rehearsed confession. The father could have told his servants to keep the boy in the stockyards away from the house for a few days to make sure his repentance was genuine. But no, the joy is too great to be bottled up and parceled out in cautious dribs and drabs. The father's joy is lavish, his showering of gifts and blessings once again scandalous.

And like one of Pavlov's dogs, right on cue the elder brother storms in full of sound and fury about the unfairness of it all. Like the laborers in the vineyard we saw earlier, he is offended by his father's gesture of extravagant grace toward his younger brother. The elder brother is, of course, reacting out of the world's value system: Everyone should be dealt with according to what he deserves, according to what he has earned.

But the father's heart beats to a different celestial rhythm. And God, speaking through him, says once again, I know what you deserve, but I have come to give you what you don't deserve. I've come to give you grace and to smash Satan's weapons of shame and condemnation.

We have all been prodigals in one way or another and can feel the almost too-good-to-be-true sense of hope blooming inside us as we let the truth of this story wash over us. But we all have been elder brothers too, focused on "what's right" and judgmental of others—usually of those whose area of weakness is one that has never been a problem for us. It's a sad truth about our fickle human nature that we are so changeable. We quickly swing from a call for justice to a call for grace, depending on whether we happen to be the one who has failed at that particular moment.

Grace can give us forgiveness. Grace can give us blessings we don't deserve. But there are some things grace cannot do for us. Grace cannot relieve us of our responsibility for our sin, nor excuse it. We are still responsible and must own that, no matter how painful it is.

And grace may not deliver us from the consequences of our sin. David experienced God's forgiveness and grace but still lost his son by Bathsheba. Moses was honored as one of God's great heroes, but he was still not allowed to enter the Promised Land because he had struck the rock in anger, against God's command. Grace is God's greatest gift, but there are some things grace cannot do.

In any case, God's stance toward us today does not waver. It's rooted solidly in kingdom values, values that say, No matter what the offense, I know what you deserve, but I'm here to give you what you don't deserve and to smash Satan's weapons of shame and condemnation.

There is only one exception to be found to this compassionate stance during Jesus' earthly ministry. When Jesus debated with the scribes and Pharisees, the religious leaders of his day, his tone was decidedly ungracious. Jesus called them vipers, blind, hypocrites, serpents, white-washed tombs with the stench of dead men's bones and, last but not least, children of the devil. This last term of derision, from John 8:44, may hold the key to Jesus' starkly different manner with the religious leaders. Jesus had one enemy he came to confront and to war against during his earthly ministry. That enemy was the devil. In John 8 Jesus identifies the religious leaders as having sided with Satan and accuses them of taking part in the same evil acts as their father. They were, in essence, actively fighting against the establishment of a new kingdom of God based on the principle of grace. As such, the Pharisees were also the enemy.

God's attitude today toward us as sinners is the same gracious attitude Jesus took with all the broken people he befriended during his years on earth. We have nothing to fear—unless, of course, like the Pharisees, the vineyard workers, and the elder brother, we're offended by the concept of grace.

Growing in Grace

In 2 Corinthians 4:1 Paul writes, "Therefore since we have this ministry, as we received mercy, we do not lose heart, but we have renounced the things hidden because of shame." The results of steeping in God's mercy and grace are that we will not lose heart in our battle to keep growing, and we will keep on giving up our secrets, renouncing "the things hidden because of shame." But how do we "detox" our minds from the shame that binds us? How do we continue to grow in grace? There are several key steps.

1. Deepen Your Commitment to Both Grace and Truth

The apostle John describes Jesus as full of glory, "glory as of the only begotten from the Father, full of grace and truth."[18] Jesus embodied the perfect balance between a commitment to all that *truth* connotes—holiness, righteousness, discipline, dying to self—as well as a commitment to all that *grace* implies: love, a forgiving spirit, believing in someone, kindness, mercy, patience. To continue growing as men we must also deepen our commitment to both grace and truth.

Grace provides the motivation, the spirit, the atmosphere of encouragement. Truth provides the direction, the north star for our journey toward wholeness and holiness.

Jesus modeled this balance between grace and truth over and over. With the adulterous woman, he gave grace when he said, "Neither do I condemn you." And he emphasized truth when he said, "Go and sin no more." Grace does not relieve us of our responsibility to be obedient, to pursue holiness. But without grace we do not have the long-term motivation to keep on yielding and submitting and relinquishing.

So did the Pharisees have at least half of the truth? Did they do a good job with the righteousness side of the gospel and just neglect the grace side? No, not at all. Grace and truth cannot be isolated and separated from each other, or they become counterfeit. God's grace has been flavored with his truth. The only genuine grace is his truth-loving, righteousness-seeking grace.

The same goes for truth. God's truth has been flavored with his grace. The only kind of truth that is genuinely God's truth is grace-full truth, righteousness that is pursued with the spirit of grace. The Pharisees had false truth and false righteousness, just as some Christians do today. Their righteousness had none of the flavor of grace permeating it, and was therefore bogus.

The scene with the adulterous woman is a classic example of how the two different philosophies work in real life. The Pharisees practiced graceless righteousness: The woman had sinned, she deserved to be stoned. Justice demanded it. Jesus' righteousness was impregnated with grace: Yes, she'd sinned; no, he didn't condemn her; yes, he exhorted her not to sin again.

This is the same spirit we find in Galatians 6:1. "Brethren, even if a man is caught in any trespass, you who are spiritual, restore such a one in a spirit of gentleness; looking to yourselves, lest you too be tempted."

In the scene with the woman caught in adultery, the Pharisees delivered justice on the point of a spear. There was no gentleness, and certainly no humble reflection on their own vulnerability.

God calls us to the kind of balance in the Christian life in which grace and truth are simmering together in the same delicious stew, the flavors of each so commingled that we cannot tell the difference.

2. Make Space for Grace

Grace happens when we finally reach brokenness, when we hit bottom, whatever that might be for us. Brokenness simply means coming to the end of whatever it is we're relying on to make it through life successfully. That might be money, reputation, physical strength, control. For the apostle Paul it meant losing his prestige as a Pharisee of the Pharisees. When we find ourselves without the commodity or quality we have always prized the most, our first reaction is panic.

My prized commodity was reputation. My lifelong efforts to play the Hero role had resulted in an obsessive concern with image and reputation. Then my bad behavior blew apart my carefully crafted reputation. Post-pedestal, divorced, and out of a job, I found myself stripped of all the props that had helped me deal with life. I sent out scores of resumes and pounded the pavement in search of a job. Most of the applications to Christian organizations were returned with a form letter saying, "I'm sorry. Our policy prohibits hiring divorced people."

Finally in despair, I sank to my knees in my apartment and told God I'd be willing to do anything he wanted; I'd come to the end of my own resources. That was a turning point with me. None of my circumstances changed immediately on the outside, but I had reached a new level of submissiveness to God's will on the inside.

I had always planned carefully as a way of controlling my life; now I began to learn how to live just one day at a time. And like the children of Israel depending on God for their daily manna, I began to learn the link between grace and dependency. I'd been so full of my self, my strengths, and my dreams for all those years, I didn't have room for grace. I see now that if we want a deeper experience of God's grace, something always has to go to make room. The process is humbling, but humility is the price of admission. "God is opposed to the proud," James tells us, "but gives grace to the humble."[19]

3. De-shame Your Inner Dialogues

In *The Road Less Traveled* Scott Peck says that when people find themselves in conflict with the world, two extreme reactions are possible. The neurotic person automatically assumes he is at fault. The person with what Peck calls a character disorder automatically assumes the world is at fault. The neurotic assumes too much responsibility, too much blame, for what goes on around him; the person with the character disorder, not enough.[20]

Those of us with a neurotic streak will tend to be more vulnerable to feelings of toxic shame. We actually have an adversarial relationship with ourselves, that is, we don't like ourselves and are quick to judge ourselves. This kind of constant, critical inner dialogue leads to discouragement and undercuts our motivation to keep working on our issues. If this is true for you, a big first step would be to not automatically assume you're to blame the next time something goes wrong around you.

4. Forgive Yourself

What do you do with your old memories of past failure? What if you feel what David expressed in Psalm 51:3— "My sin is ever before me"? How do you get over feeling guilty?

I went to a therapist to help me with guilty feelings similar to David's some two years after my crisis. I explained that I'd gone over and over the old events, trying to sift meaning from the patterns and to learn from the mistakes. I also told him I was struggling with depression and guilt.

I genuinely liked and admired my therapist. Dr. C. was a Christian man in his seventies who still rode his motorcycle to the office every day and went dancing with his wife every Friday evening. He leaned back in his chair, looked at the ceiling, and mussed his white hair while he thought. Finally he spoke.

"I want to paint an image for you. I see you upstairs in a dusty old attic. You're kneeling in front of an old, antique trunk. The lid's open on the trunk, and it's stuffed full of old, dirty rags. You're taking each of these rags out and fingering them, inspecting them closely. You've been through all the rags several times, but you're still sorting through them, over and over.

"I think you need to close the lid of the trunk, walk out of the attic, close the door, and come downstairs and outside into the sunshine. You need to forgive yourself and move on with your life."

I told him I'd tried, but I didn't feel any different.

"So," he said with a twinkle in his eye, "let me get this straight. God himself, who is perfectly holy, has forgiven you, but you aren't able to forgive yourself. Do I have this right?"

I smiled slightly and nodded.

"You know what Jeremiah 31 says, right? That God forgives our iniquity and will remember our sin no more? Well, if *God* has forgotten your sin, and *he* wants you to move on with your life, why can't you give the same gift to yourself?"

In the years since, I've thought often about what Dr. C. said that day. Some days I'm able to experience it; other days I'm not. The part that helps me the most is to know that when I'm able to forgive myself, I'm aligning myself with God.

The apostle Paul exhorts us in Ephesians 4:32 to "be kind to one another, tender-hearted, forgiving each other, just as God in Christ also has forgiven you." In the previous verse, Paul encourages us to put away a pungent package of attitudes that poison our relationships. Among them are bitterness, slander, and malice.

It struck me recently that we could profit from applying these verses not only to our relationships with others but to ourselves as well. For most of us who have been through failure, we are our own worst critics. Our minds are often filled with bitterness and slander toward ourselves. That saps our energy and our hope. And we need all the hope we can get for the journey ahead.

Jesus' message to each of us is: "Don't side with Satan in his ministry of accusation. Forgive yourself for the ways you've failed, just as God in Christ also has forgiven you."

Keith Miller tells the story of a nun who was reported to have visions in which Jesus Christ personally appeared to her and talked with her. Her bishop heard these stories and determined to find out for himself if the stories were true. So one day when the bishop visited the convent where the nun lived he asked if he could meet with her.

"Is it true, sister, that Jesus appears to you personally?" he asked.

"Yes it is, father."

"And he talks to you?"

"Yes."

"In that case I have a question I'd like you to ask him for me. The next time Jesus visits you . . ." The bishop paused nervously. "The next time, I want you to ask him what was the worst sin your bishop committed before he became bishop."

The nun agreed, and a few weeks later the bishop returned and summoned her once again to a meeting.

"Well, has Jesus appeared to you again, sister?" he asked.

"Yes he has, father."

"And did you ask him the question I mentioned last time?" the bishop asked.

239

"Yes I did, father."

"So," the bishop said, leaning forward intently, "What was the worst sin committed by your bishop? What did Jesus say?"

The nun met his gaze and answered quietly, "He said, 'I don't remember.'"

I've always been deeply warmed by the account in Genesis 28 of Jacob's flight from the murderous rage of his brother Esau, whom he had cheated. There on the journey to Haran, God appeared to him in a dream (the famous "Jacob's ladder" dream) and promised to bless him mightily wherever he went the rest of his life. And God gave Jacob that incredible blessing while he was fleeing from the consequences of his sin, with no outward indication of his repentance!

In many ways, I've seen God do the same for me. I was still reeling from the consequences of my sin when he began blessing me—with new friends, then with a wonderful wife and partner on life's journey, and a chance once again to reach out and extend grace in his name to others. I was still raw, headstrong, and unbroken when he began doing that. Like Jacob, I didn't deserve any of it. But I'm just beginning to understand that "deserving" doesn't have anything to do with our Father's grace.

Restoration
The sheep goes now
Toward the distant slope
Where taller, tastier grass awaits.
Let the ninety and nine stay bleating and bumping one
    another—
The horizon calls.

He's one of your flock, Good Shepherd,
And he's heading for the ravine.
He doesn't understand drop-offs

And wolves
And how soon darkness will fall upon the land.
Call him back! Stop him!

The meadow shrinks in the gathering dusk
And the Shepherd's ram,
Full but unsatisfied,
Edges toward the rim
Until in a clatter of gravel and dust
He plummets into the gorge
Brambles clawing at his wool—
He lies stunned upon his back.

He cannot rise; he cannot reverse
The steps that brought him to this dreadful place;
He can, in fact, do nothing at all.
A cold moon stares down at him
While sounds of night intensify;
He is trapped—but more
He is alone.

A flickering lamp, footsteps in the underbrush,
The chill and darkness are foiled this time
As muscled arms encircle the fallen one
And hoist him from the stones and mud
To ride upon tall shoulders
Back to the village fold.

Had you nothing else to do this night, Good Shepherd?
Should not this rebel sheep of yours be ousted
From care and food and drink for this?
He chose his independent path—
Will he yet be welcome in your flock?

He answers not; he is too busy
Calling friends and neighbors,
The young and old about the town,
And even angels hear his shout:

"Rejoice with me! I have found
My sheep which was lost!
He was mine before; he is mine tonight;
He shall be mine forever!
Rejoice, rejoice."

The villagers cheer,
And light years distant,
The cherubim slap each other
On the back—
Both earth and heaven are awake tonight
For the jubilee that crowns
The restoration of a single sheep.

Dean Merrill[21]

Appendix

Mentor Leadership Training
Personal Growth Plan for Men ©

For it is God who is at work in you, both to will and to
work for His good pleasure.

Philippians 2:13

┌ ▬ ▬ ▬ ▬ ▬ **Welcome to the adventure of personal**
transformation! It is possible to see true change around our
tough issues and unhealthy behaviors. I've seen it in my own
life and in the lives of many other men. The Mentor Leadership Training Personal Growth Plan for Men is a practical tool for applying the biblical principles contained in
this book to the areas you most want God to change in you.
May God's Spirit give you strength and encouragement as
you step out on the journey toward spiritual wholeness.
Know that many other men walk with you on that journey.

Note: You'll find it helpful to make an enlarged copy of
the two-page Personal Growth Plan diagram following
page 250. Enlarge it to the size you need to comfortably
record your answers in each box.

Step 1

The following is a list of issues we have considered. Reflect
on them, referring to the relevant exercises or sections in the
book. Then circle a number from 1 to 10 to indicate how
negatively you feel this issue is affecting your life. (1 = minimal disruption. 10 = serious disruption of my life or relationships; needs urgent attention.) If there are issues you are
concerned about other than those listed below, list them at
the bottom of the column and rate them on the same scale.

243

Appendix

1 2 3 4 5 6 7 8 9 10   Shame profile/shame core (p. 27)

1 2 3 4 5 6 7 8 9 10   Fatigue and burnout (p. 31)

1 2 3 4 5 6 7 8 9 10   People pleasing and approval (p. 30)

1 2 3 4 5 6 7 8 9 10   Lifescript: rules (p. 39)

1 2 3 4 5 6 7 8 9 10   Lifescript: roles (p. 39)

1 2 3 4 5 6 7 8 9 10   Lifescript: recordings (p. 41)

1 2 3 4 5 6 7 8 9 10   Father wound (describe) (pp. 66–67)

_____

1 2 3 4 5 6 7 8 9 10   Mother wound (describe) (pp. 126–28)

_____

1 2 3 4 5 6 7 8 9 10   Adrenaline addiction/stress (pp. 122–24)

1 2 3 4 5 6 7 8 9 10   Workaholism (p. 122)

1 2 3 4 5 6 7 8 9 10   Spending/finances (p. 123)

1 2 3 4 5 6 7 8 9 10   Dependency on women's approval (p. 144)

1 2 3 4 5 6 7 8 9 10   Sexual addiction (p. 132)

1 2 3 4 5 6 7 8 9 10   Relationship styles: Controller (pp. 149, 162)

1 2 3 4 5 6 7 8 9 10   Relationship styles: Caretaker (pp.150, 163)

1 2 3 4 5 6 7 8 9 10   Relationship styles: Isolator (pp. 152, 165)

1 2 3 4 5 6 7 8 9 10   Unfinished grieving/unresolved loss (p. 100)

1 2 3 4 5 6 7 8 9 10   Secret life behaviors (p. 180)

1 2 3 4 5 6 7 8 9 10   Alcohol or drug abuse (pp.108, 159–60, 171–72)

1 2 3 4 5 6 7 8 9 10   False self (posturing, lack of openness and vulnerability) (pp. 72–73, 169)

1 2 3 4 5 6 7 8 9 10   Nonintimate marriage (pp. 146–49, 172)

1 2 3 4 5 6 7 8 9 10   Healthy versus unhealthy core (p. 116)

1 2 3 4 5 6 7 8 9 10   Other

_____

Step 2

Pick two issues or behaviors you most want to see God change in you. In the Personal Growth Plan at the end of this appendix, you will have an opportunity to answer questions in eight categories for each issue you have selected. Your answers to those questions will become your personal growth plan for that specific issue. The following is a detailed explanation of the eight components in the plan along with examples of how one man in our mentoring program (Bob) answered the questions as he worked through his own secret life behavior involving alcohol abuse (shared with his permission).

1. Behavior/Issue

List one of the areas of your life in which you feel the greatest need to change. This could be an unhealthy behavior, such as workaholism, or a core issue, such as toxic shame or unresolved grief or loss. If you are still using certain behaviors to significantly medicate your emotional pain, it's generally best to work on eliminating those first.

Bob's example: Alcohol abuse

2. Symptoms/Patterns

There are three important questions in this area. (1) What triggers this behavior? (2) What does the behavior look like? What pattern does your behavior take? How does it manifest itself? (3) What negative consequences does the behavior produce?

Bob's example:

Triggers? *For me the trigger is usually fear, stress, or anger. The most common situations that trigger feelings of fear or stress are marital strife, perceived criticism from my wife, or experiences I interpret as failure, which trigger shame attacks. Other triggers include financial pressure and job stress.*

245

What does it look like? *Typically I stuff my negative feelings inside after one of these triggers, say, an argument with my wife. I let the feelings build to the breaking point and then secretly purchase and consume the alcohol to numb the feelings. The whole cycle might take two or three hours from the trigger to the drinking.*

Negative consequences? *The primary negative impact is on my relationships. I usually become quiet and withdrawn after drinking—emotionally unavailable. Occasionally I become angry and emotionally abusive.*

3. Need/Core Issue

What need are you trying to meet through this behavior, or what is the core issue underneath the behavior?

Bob: The surface need for me is relief from my painful feelings of fear and failure. I am also afraid of my feelings of anger and numb them to neutralize them. The core issue is my shame core. The overwhelming feelings come from never feeling good enough, never able to do enough to earn acceptance and approval from others (or from myself).

4. Changes/Action Steps

What steps of growth have you already taken in this area? List these first. Then list what additional changes or action steps you plan to take in the coming weeks and months to break your unhealthy pattern. Use the Serenity Prayer as a model as you think this through: "God, grant me the serenity to accept the things I cannot change, the courage to change the things I can, and the wisdom to know the difference."

Bob: Steps of growth already taken are:
1. *Owning my problem with alcohol abuse*
2. *Making myself accountable to my support person and to my support group*

3. *Improving communication in my marriage, resulting in less conflict and less temptation to numb feelings*
Continued action steps are:
1. *Continue to reduce stress.*
2. *Continue to talk openly about my feelings of fear and failure and shame when they occur, rather than holding them in and being tempted to numb them with alcohol; specifically, to talk openly and without shame about my problem with alcohol to my wife, to my support person, and to my men's group.*
3. *Take time for something I really enjoy once or twice a week.*
4. *Work on my core issue of shame and "lack of acceptability" by replacing all my old critical self-talk with God's view of me.*
5. *Stay away from critical or destructive relationships and work on building a network of encouraging, affirming friends.* (Note: List names of men you'd like to deepen friendship with.)

5. Roadblocks

Identify the main obstacles or temptations that might hinder your growth in this area. What things in the past have sabotaged your steps toward new behavior? After each roadblock, describe what you can do to overcome it. Use the back of the worksheet if necessary.
Bob: My roadblocks are.
1. *"Give-up-itis," feelings of hopelessness, that the pain will always be more than I can handle, that I may as well give in to it. (To overcome this: call a friend, ask for help.)*
2. *Out-of-control lifestyle. When I jam too much into my schedule, my serenity and my personal growth program are usually the first casualties. (To overcome: Say no more often. Turn down new opportunities when my plate is already full. Give up trying to please everyone when to do so means violating my own limitations. Do the best*

247

job I can of balancing the demands of work with my personal needs and marriage and family needs.)

3. Self-pity, which leads to self-indulgence, thinking, "I
deserve to have a drink because of how bad things are."
(To overcome: Take responsibility for meeting my real
needs in legitimate ways. Put together the kind of life and
weekly schedule that is as nurturing as possible. For the
hard parts of my life that I cannot change, I will seek to
let go of my anger and frustration over those and ask God
for grace to accept them.)

4. The strength of my core pain and core issues, overwhelming my ability to handle it. (To overcome: Do some tough
inner work with the help of a therapist.)

5. Lack of availability of support people at times. (To overcome: Arrange to meet more regularly with my support
person, not wait to see if he's available on the spur of the
moment.)

6. Accountability

To whom will you be accountable as you work on changing these behaviors? Who can function as your confidant,
support person, or sponsor in this personal growth process?
Whom do you trust enough to share your struggles with,
knowing you won't be judged and that he will keep confidential all that you share? Write the name of that man or
group of men and when you will meet. (If you have no one
who ideally fits this profile, list the names of men who have
that potential. Plan to develop closer relationships with
these men in the weeks ahead.)

Bob: Support person: Bill. Men's group: Ken, Frank, Caesar.

7. Resources

What outside resources would help you as you work your
Personal Growth Plan? A Christian therapist? (Who? Or

if you don't know a therapist, who will you ask for a referral?) Who can you enlist for prayer support? (Remember to pick only those who can keep a confidence.) What books on this issue or related issues do you want to read? What Scriptures would you like to study or meditate on? Are there conferences you can attend or magazines you could subscribe to that would help you in the healing journey?

(One excellent resource is STEPS magazine, the quarterly publication of the National Association for Christian Recovery. The NACR also sponsors high quality conferences on personal growth issues. Write to, STEPS/NACR, P.O. Box 11095, Whittier, CA 90603.)

Bob: For prayer support: my men's group. Books: Margin. Meditate: Psalm 103, Jeremiah 29:11–14.

8. Vision

Picture yourself five years from now after having worked diligently on this particular behavior or issue. In what ways will you be stronger? Are there ways your life in general will be healthier? What kind of person would you like to be in five years? Describe yourself inside and out.

Bob: I hope I'll be carrying much less pain inside and will feel less need to medicate. I'll have worked on some of my tougher issues (including my marriage) with a therapist and made progress on my critical self-talk and my shame reactions. I want to experience fewer things as "failures," and more things as lessons to be learned. I will be more accepting of myself as fallible, and not perfect. I'm really going to try to cut back on how busy I am—I know I'm a workaholic—and work on reducing my stress. In the area of alcohol abuse, I will continue to stay on guard, meeting regularly with my support person and my men's group. I hope to be closer to God and to my wife, and to be handling life better.

Step 3

Fill in the MLT Personal Growth Plan on the next two pages. If necessary, use extra paper or a journal to record your longer answers; summarize them on the MLT plan diagram. As you work, claim this promise: "For I am confident of this very thing, that He who began a good work in you will perfect it until the day of Christ Jesus" (Phil. 1:6).

The Mentor Leadership Training Personal Growth Plan ©

Behavior/Issue	Symptoms/Patterns	Need/Core Issue	Changes/Action Steps
	Triggers? What does the behavior look like? Negative consequences?	What need are you trying to meet? Core issue underneath?	What steps of growth have you already taken? What additional changes or action steps do you plan to take?
1.			
2.			

Wholeness

Roadblocks	Accountability	Resources	Vision
Main obstacles, temptations? What can you do?	Confidant/support person—who? Men's group? When?	Therapist? Who? Prayer support? Books, Scriptures, conferences, magazines?	Who do you want to be in five years? Describe yourself inside and out.

© 1996 by Mentor Leadership Training

Notes

Chapter 1: White Knights, Black Hats

1. *Newsweek*, June 3, 1991, 56.
2. *Parade Magazine*, April 14, 1991, 4.
3. Verses 15–16, emphasis added.
4. Rev. 3:17.
5. 2 Cor. 12:9.
6. 2 Cor. 12:9–10.
7. Eph. 4:22.
8. 1 John 1:8.
9. Rom. 7:19, emphasis added.
10. John Fischer, *Dark Horse: The Story of a Winner* (Portland: Multnomah, 1983), 13–19. Adapted with permission.
11. Jeffrey Van Vonderen, *Tired of Trying to Measure Up* (Minneapolis: Bethany, 1989).
12. Matt. 5:48.
13. Charles Perry Jr., *Why Christians Burn Out* (Nashville: Thomas Nelson, 1982), 41–42.

Chapter 2: If the Genes Fit

1. Alvin Toffler, *Future Shock* (New York: Random House, 1980), 167–68.
2. John Bradshaw, *Healing the Shame That Binds You* (Deerfield Beach, Fla.: Health Communications, 1988), 184.
3. Neh. 9:2.
4. Isa. 6:5.
5. James 1:23–24.
6. For further insight on how to develop the discipline of journaling, you might want to read one of the following books on the subject: Ron Klug, *How to Keep a Spiritual Journal* (Minneapolis: Augsburg, 1993); Leanne Payne, *Listening Prayer* (Grand Rapids: Baker, 1994); Richard Peace, *Spiritual Journaling* (Colorado Springs: NavPress, 1996).
7. Rom. 12:2.
8. Phil. 3:5; Rom. 1:1.
9. Acts 14:11–12.
10. Acts 14:15.
11. The voices we must quiet in our minds are the toxic messages, amplified by the "accuser of the brethren," that tell us we are unloveable and defective as persons. These are not the voices of our Spirit-led conscience, which convicts us of our sinful behavior. We can confess our sinful behavior (1 John 1:9) and experience forgiveness and cleansing. Any accusatory voices that remain *after* confessing our sin are those old toxic tapes that must be rebuked and replaced by God's affirming messages.
12. Matt. 22:39.

Chapter 3: The Elusive Father Blessing

1. David Blankenhorn, *Fatherless America* (New York: Basic Books, 1995), 1. Used by permission of HarperCollins Publishers.
2. Matt. 3:17; I am indebted to Pastor Van Savell for these insights into Matthew 3.
3. Eph. 6:4.
4. Cited in "Healing Your Father Wounds" by Gordon Dalbey, *Today's Better Life*, fall 1992, 48.

Notes

5. Mal. 4:5–6.
6. 1 Peter 3:8–9.
7. Ken Druck and James C. Simmons, *The Secrets Men Keep* (Garden City, N.Y.: Doubleday, 1985), 73–74.
8. Interview with Daryl E. Quick, Ph.D., *STEPS* magazine, spring 1992, 9.
9. Rick Koepcke and E. James Wilder, "The Men's Movement," *Faith and Renewal,* May/June 1994, 8.
10. Ps. 68:5.
11. Gen. 25:27–28.
12. Gen. 32:27–28.

Chapter 4: You Can't Heal What You Don't Feel

1. Jack McGinnis, "The Gift of Grieving," *STEPS* magazine, spring 1992, 12–15.
2. Matt. 26:39.
3. Jer. 6:13–14.
4. Matt. 5:4.
5. Ps. 147:3.
6. Joe Dominguez and Vicki Robin, *Your Money or Your Life* (New York: Viking Penguin, 1992).
7. Reprinted from Karen Dockrey, *When a Hug Won't Fix the Hurt* (Wheaton: Victor Books, 1993 SP Publications, Inc.), 89–90. Used by permission.
8. McGinnis, "The Gift of Grieving."
9. Ibid.

Chapter 5: When the Hits Don't Keep On Coming

1. Keith Miller, *A Hunger for Healing* (San Francisco: Harper San Francisco, 1991), 22. Used by permission of HarperCollins Publishers.
2. LynNell Hancock, "Breaking Point," *Newsweek,* March 6, 1995, 58.
3. Ibid., 59–60.
4. Archibald D. Hart, *Adrenalin and Stress* (Dallas: Word, 1986), 86–92.
5. Ps. 103:13–14.
6. Hart, *Adrenalin and Stress,* 89, 92.
7. Ibid., 154.
8. James Dobson, *Dr. Dobson Answers Your Questions* (Wheaton: Tyndale House, 1982), 27.
9. Swenson, *Margin,* 155.
10. Ibid., 150.
11. Ibid., 165.
12. Ibid., 168.
13. 1 Tim. 6:6–11.
14. Rom. 13:8 NIV.
15. Rosalind Forbes, *Corporate Stress and Life Stress* (Garden City, N.Y.: Doubleday, 1979), 136–38.

Chapter 6: The Search for the Magic Wand

1. 1 Kings 11:4.
2. *Leadership* magazine's 1992 national survey of pastors showed that 20 percent of the 356 responding pastors acknowledge having had intercourse or inappropriate sexual contact outside of marriage. (Source: "Leadership Family and Ministry Survey Summary"; Christianity Today, Inc., Research Dept.,

July 1992). In a 1992 survey of *Christianity Today* readers (one-third pastors, two-thirds laymen; 80 percent active in church leadership), of the 810 respondents to the questions on marital infidelity, 15 percent of the men and 11 percent of the women admit to having been unfaithful to their spouses; just less than half (49 percent) have viewed pornography in the past year. (Source: "Christianity Today Marriage and Divorce Survey Report"; Christianity Today, Inc., Research Dept., July 1992). In addition, the 1991 survey sponsored by the Fuller Institute of Church Growth revealed that 37 percent of pastors surveyed confessed to having been involved in "inappropriate sexual behavior with someone in the church." (Source: H.B. London, Jr. and Neil B. Wiseman, *Pastors At Risk* [Wheaton: Victor, 1993], 22.)

 3. Cited in Anonymous, "The War Within," *Leadership*, fall 1982, 31.
 4. Prov. 6:27–29.
 5. Stephen M. Smith, "'Love' in the Shadows: Sexual Addiction in the Church," *STEPS* magazine, winter 1991, 8ff.
 6. James 5:16.
 7. Job 31:1 NIV.
 8. Patrick J. Carnes, *Out of the Shadows* (Tucson: CompCare, 1983), 146–49.
 9. Ibid., 13.
 10. Ps. 51:16–17 NIV.

Chapter 7: When Your Happily Ever After Isn't

 1. Robert A. Johnson, *HE: Understanding Masculine Psychology* (King of Prussia, Pa.: Religious Publishing Co., 1974; Harper Perennial Library Edition, 1977), 28–29.
 2. Matt. 7:1–5.
 3. 1 Cor. 13:12 KJV.
 4. Gal. 6:4–5.

Chapter 8: The Long, Dark Trek into a Secret Life

 1. Heb. 3:13.
 2. Charles Colson, "The Pedestal Complex," *Christianity Today*, February 5, 1990, 96.
 3. Druck and Simmons, *Secrets Men Keep*, 19–20.
 4. Jer. 17:9.
 5. Eph. 4:2.
 6. Prov. 20:17 KJV.
 7. Isa. 42:3.

Chapter 9: The Rugged Journey Out

 1. Prov. 4:23.
 2. Ps. 19:12; 2 Cor. 3:14; Jer. 17:9.
 3. Ps. 139:23–24.
 4. 1 John 1:7.
 5. Phil. 3:10.
 6. 2 Cor. 12:10.

Chapter 10: Old Whines, New Wineskins

 1. Judith S. Wallerstein and Sandra Blakeslee, *Second Chances: Men, Women, and Children a Decade After Divorce* (New York: Ticknor & Fields, 1989), 303.
 2. Louis E. Boone and David L. Kurtz, *Contemporary Business* (Fort Worth: Dryden Press, 1985), 78.

Notes

3. Toffler, *Future Shock*, 78.
4. Ibid., 109.
5. Matt. 10:22.
6. Heb. 12:1.
7. Luke 5:27–34.
8. Luke 5:36–39.
9. Matt. 23:25–28.
10. Luke 5:31–32.
11. Rick Koepcke and E. James Wilder, "The Men's Movement," *Faith and Renewal*, May/June 1994, 10.
12. Ps. 126:5–6.
13. Bradshaw, *Healing the Shame*, 70.
14. Eph. 4:15.
15. Eph. 4:25.
16. Portia Nelson, "Autobiography in Five Short Chapters," from *There's a Hole in My Sidewalk* (Hillsboro, Oreg.: Beyond Words Publishing, 1993), 2–3. Copyright © 1993 by Beyond Words Publishing. Used by permission.
17. C. S. Lewis, *The Great Divorce* (New York: Macmillan, 1946), 98–103.
18. 2 Cor. 3:18.

Chapter 11: Stumbling Heavenward

1. Jonathan Alter and Pat Wingert, *Newsweek*, "The Return of Shame," February 6, 1995, 24–25.
2. Ibid., 23–24.
3. Bradshaw, *Healing the Shame*, 10.
4. Some authors make a distinction between healthy shame and unhealthy shame. Those authors generally use those terms the way I use *guilt* and *shame*. But because so many Christians have been wounded by shaming techniques, I believe it would be a barrier to communication to attempt to link the concepts of health and shame. For that reason I will use *shame* with exclusively negative connotations.
5. Rom. 8:1, emphasis added.
6. Rom. 8:31, 33–34.
7. Acts 13:22.
8. Heb. 11:31; James 2:25; Matt. 1:5.
9. Exod. 2ff.
10. Luke 22:31–34, 54–62.
11. Matt. 11:1–6, 11.
12. Ps. 103:13–14; Jer. 31:34; Rom. 8:28.
13. Quoted in Dean Merrill, *Another Chance: How God Overrides Our Big Mistakes* (Grand Rapids: Zondervan, 1981), 123–24.
14. Matt. 11:19.
15. John 4:7–42.
16. See John 8:1–11.
17. Matt. 20:1–16.
18. John 1:14.
19. James 4:6.
20. Cited in Bradshaw, *Healing the Shame*, 9.
21. Taken from *Another Chance*, by Dean Merrill, 11–12. Copyright © 1981 by The Zondervan Corporation. Used by permission of Zondervan Publishing House.

Leader's Guide

> Wise people learn not to dread but actually to welcome
> problems. Most of us are not so wise. Fearing the pain
> involved, almost all of us, to a greater or lesser degree,
> attempt to avoid problems. We procrastinate, hoping that
> they will go away. . . . Problems do not go away. They must
> be worked through or else they remain, forever a barrier to
> the growth and development of the spirit.
>
> M. Scott Peck,
The Road Less Traveled

The Mentoring Process

— — — — Welcome to the twelve-week Men's Small
Group series based on *Men's Secret Wars*. Peck is right, of course.
Problems don't just go away; they require work. As you work
through the material in *Men's Secret Wars* over the next several
weeks, you and the men you meet with in a mentoring relationship will have the opportunity to address the problems all of you
would most like to see changed in *your* lives.

In one of the first acts of Jesus' public ministry, he attended
synagogue in his hometown of Nazareth. He was handed the
scroll of the Book of Isaiah to read. He stood, and in a moment
of pure drama, read, "The Spirit of the Lord is upon me,
because He anointed me to preach the gospel to the poor. He
has sent me to proclaim release to the captives, and recovery of

sight to the blind, to set free those who are downtrodden . . ." (Luke 4:18).

But it is becoming apparent today that many of us Christian men are *not* experiencing the release and the freedom that Jesus came to bring. The Men's Confidential Survey I took with several hundred Christian men nationwide—primarily men in leadership positions in the church—revealed that a fifth of the men have gone through serious burnout, 64 percent struggle with some form of sexual addiction or pornography, 20 percent have a problem with substance abuse, and 25 percent of the married men admit to having had an extramarital affair since becoming a Christian. (For more information on the Men's Confidential Survey, see pp. 132–33, and 254–55 in *Men's Secret Wars.*)

We need help to avoid these crises, the kind of help Proverbs 27:17 talks about: "As iron sharpens iron, so one man sharpens another" (NIV). In working with hundreds of Christian men in the last few years, I have concluded that true change in our lives cannot be accomplished without the help of some kind of Christ-centered support structure like mentoring. It's too difficult to accomplish alone. That's why James exhorts us to "Confess your sins to one another, and pray for one another, so that you may be healed" (5:16). And John, in his first letter, describes true fellowship as "walking in the light" with one another. Over and over, we are urged in the New Testament to "encourage one another" and to "bear one another's burdens."

The good news is, you *can* see real change in your life in the weeks ahead—new freedom from many of the fears and temptations that have plagued you for years and a new and deeper relationship with God. Of course, everything worthwhile in life has a price, and this is no exception. The price in the mentoring process is a commitment to work hard and to be honest. That's the ticket that gets us in the front gate. In addition, here are four group guidelines essential for a successful small group experience.

Group Guidelines

1. Safety and confidentiality. In the Old Testament, God allowed for "Cities of Refuge" in the nation of Israel. These cities were places of sanctuary for individuals pursued by vengeful relatives in blood feuds. The guilty individuals were safe as long as they stayed in the City of Refuge; no one was allowed to harm them.

We men also need a "City of Refuge," a safe place to be honest about our struggles and failures without fear of being judged or attacked. No criticism of one another is acceptable in our groups. (If a particular area of your life needs to be discussed in more depth, it should be done apart from the group meeting—just you and your mentor—and done in a sensitive manner, in the spirit of Galatians 6:1.) This creates an atmosphere in which you and the other men will feel free—often for the first time in your lives—to be deeply honest.

You and the group must also strictly adhere to a policy of confidentiality. What is heard in that room must remain in that room. No one else, not even your spouse, should be told what men share in the group.

2. Respect and being considerate. The group needs to listen respectfully to whomever is speaking and refrain from interrupting. And each man, when he shares, should show consideration for the group by sharing briefly and staying on the topic. You're all there to grow and to encourage the others in their growth.

3. Commitment. When you commit to the mentoring process you are taking on a serious commitment. Genuine, Spirit-led change takes work. You must be conscientious in attendance and do the assignments that are given between meetings.

4. Daily communication with another man. Spiritual growth will be accelerated and old harmful habits best broken when we develop a close accountability relationship with another man. One of the most important goals for you during the twelve weeks of the mentoring series will be to find another man to be a Growth Partner, preferably from within the mentoring group. Growth Partners are peers who are committed to encouraging one another to persevere and overcome the daily challenges and temptations of life. Ideally, Growth Partners will call each other daily. Until each of you develops his own Growth Partner, you may need to call your group mentor daily, to begin building the habit of staying in touch each day with another Christian brother.

Above all, know that God *does* want you to experience a new freedom and joy in your daily walk with him in the weeks ahead. Welcome to the adventure!

The Mentor Role

The Christian men's movement has exploded today in an unprecedented way. And yet, despite the numbers of men involved, there is a desperate need for mentors—men committed to Christ, who are walking solidly toward spiritual maturity and who are willing to serve as models and encouragers to other men. It is my hope that *you* will be one of God's mentors to stand in the gap in our generation. The material in *Men's Secret Wars* will lay an important foundation within you for that ministry as you deal honestly with the critical issues we will cover in the weeks ahead.

There is no doubt that many Christian men are being impacted by stress and temptations in a variety of forms. What can we do? We can climb down into the trenches beside these men where the warfare is being waged, where, every day, men are being wounded and their families devastated. We can work with them and walk with them on a journey of healing and growth. That's what the ministry of mentoring is all about—coming alongside another man and helping him grow. But not every man is ready to be a mentor.

What are the qualities of an effective mentor? Among others, there are four especially important ones.

1. Authentic. The mentor needs to have done the work he is asking his men to do. And each of us who serves as a mentor also needs a mentor of our own. As the Men's Confidential Survey makes clear, none of us is above needing the guidance and encouragement of another and the accountability that comes from being honest and open with a brother on a regular basis. Our walk must match our talk.

2. Honest. The impact of these next twelve weeks will be determined largely by the level of honesty that is developed among the men in your group. And that group honesty, in turn, is largely a function of how honest *you* are able to be as a mentor. As the old saying goes, if you want others to bleed, you have to hemorrhage. Being an example of honesty and vulnerability may be your most important leadership contribution.

3. Humble. There is no place for pedestals in the mentoring ministry. We are not better or worthier or less human than the men we are called to serve. In Galatians 6:1 Paul says it well: "Brethren, even if a man is caught in any trespass, you who are spiritual, restore such a one in a spirit of gentleness; each one looking to yourselves, lest you too be tempted." The adage that "The ground is level at the foot of the cross" must be lived out in a mentoring ministry.

4. Servant leader. Mentoring is most effective when we adopt a servant leadership style. This is the kind of non-authoritarian leadership style Jesus taught his disciples. On the road to Jericho, the disciples got in a squabble about privilege and position in the kingdom of God. Jesus overheard the ruckus and called them together. This is what he said: "You know that those who are recognized as rulers of the Gentiles lord it over them; and their great men exercise authority over them. But it is not so among you, but whoever wishes to become great among you shall be your servant; and whoever wishes to be first among you shall be slave of all. For even the Son of Man did not come to be served, but to serve, and to give His life a ransom for many" (Mark 10:42–45).

There is potential for great good in the mentor relationship, but there is also potential for abuse. If you have a need to control the people around you, if you see yourself as almost always right and others wrong, you're not ready yet to mentor someone. (To assess this area in your own life, complete the exercises in *Men's Secret Wars*—the Stress Test on pp. 123–24 and the Controller Test on pp. 162–63.) Men grow best in an atmosphere that is non-judgmental and non-coercive. You are simply a brother in Christ who is able to offer your own experience, strength, and hope to another brother. God then brings the increase. We are peers with those we mentor, and the relationship of accountability we establish is a two-way relationship.

There are, of course, many other elements to be considered in facilitating an effective small group for men. We can't go into all of those elements here. But there are in print a number of resources for small groups. I'd recommend you visit a bookstore and peruse some of these as part of your preparation.

Inside the Group Session

Following is the suggested content for each of the twelve group sessions.

- Opening prayer
- Introduction: a brief overview of the topic for that session
- Wealth from the Word: discussion of one or two Scripture passages pertinent to that week's topic
- Written exercise: a personal assessment exercise from *Men's Secret Wars* (to be completed by the men prior to the session)
- Discussion of the written exercise
- Assignment for the coming week
- Closing prayer

The sessions are geared to take about an hour and a half and to cover one chapter per week from *Men's Secret Wars*. Feel free to take more than one week on a particular subject, however, if the group seems to need it.

━━ ━━ ━━ ━━ ━━ ━━ ━━ ━━ ━━ ━━ ━━ ━━ ━━

Session 1: Men and the Hero Subculture

Prior to session 1, each of the men should have purchased a copy of *Men's Secret Wars* and read the introduction and chapter 1.

Opening Prayer

Introduction to the Series

(After a welcome and group introductions, share your own hopes and expectations for this time together, that God would use it to speak deeply to you about areas in your own life, and to each of the men as well. Then you may want to say something like this:

"To get the most out of the next twelve weeks, each of us needs to ask God for openness and teachability. It would be easy to let these mentoring meetings turn into debate sessions, where we toss around ideas and opinions and never let God speak to our hearts. Our lives will not change for the better in that atmosphere. Let's all commit to approach these twelve weeks prayerfully, asking God to do whatever it takes to break through our defenses and make significant changes in our lives."

Go over the Group Guidelines from the material above. Discuss them as necessary, and when it's appropriate, ask the group for a specific response indicating their acceptance of the guidelines. The "Safety/Confidentiality" guideline is absolutely crucial. The group cannot continue effectively without it.)

Introduction to Session 1

This first session is on "Men and the Hero Subculture." According to the book, what is the basis upon which men are judged in our society? *(Success, as measured by money, power, or prestige)* And how are women judged? *(Beauty)* We're going to look at a couple of passages from the Bible to get God's perspective on success versus failure, and strength versus weakness.

Wealth from the Word

(Read 2 Chronicles 26:15. Summarize 26:1–14, especially emphasizing how talented and successful Uzziah was.

Ask someone to read from the last sentence of 26:15 through verse 16.)
What happened to King Uzziah when he became successful ('strong')?

Group Discussion

Read 2 Corinthians 12:7–10.

What does Paul mean when he says, "When I am weak, then I am strong"? Why is being strong dangerous? How are our personal lives impacted by our society's emphasis on success and strength for men?

Written Exercise

One of the dangers of trying to be successful in the world's eyes is that we become People Pleasers. Let's take a look at the results of the exercise in the book on People Pleasing and Approval (pp. 30–31).

(If someone has not yet completed the written exercise, take time for it now. Ask them in the future to complete the exercises for that chapter before *coming to the group.*

Then ask each one to share what insights about himself he got as a result of the "People Pleasing" exercise. Stress that there aren't any right or wrong answers and that we shouldn't compare ourselves with anyone else. Remind the men again not to interrupt each other, to listen respectfully to each person, and to not criticize or give feedback. An atmosphere must be created where each man's insights are respected and each man takes responsibility before the Lord for his own journey toward spiritual maturity. We're there to encourage and to work on our own growth, not *someone else's.*

Complete and discuss the results of the "Signs of Burnout" exercise in the same way.)

Assignment

1. Meditate this week on Psalm 139, found on pages 32–33. *(Suggest that the men write the passage out on an index card and meditate on it during their quiet times, while driving to work, or on breaks at work. The goal should be to begin to see ourselves the way God sees us—as precious, lovable, and valuable—not needing any man's approval to help us feel like a worthwhile human being.)*

2. Read chapter 2 on "Rewriting Your Lifescript."

3. Page 39 in the book contains a section on the unwritten family rules you may have grown up with. Try to identify some of your family's unhealthy rules. Write down two or three. Remember, this is not about blaming our parents. We're actually trying to see our own weaknesses more clearly by understanding the influences on us in our childhood. Once we see ourselves more clearly, we can take responsibility before God for our weaknesses and set about changing them with God's help.

How do you think those rules have impacted your life as an adult?

4. From the information given on pages 39 and 40, try to identify which role or roles you may have been assigned to play in your childhood family.

Closing Prayer

━ ━ ━ ━ ━ ━ ━ ━ ━ ━ ━ ━ ━

Session 2: Rewriting Your Lifescript

Opening Prayer

Introduction

Our session today is on rewriting our lifescripts. We'll look at some of the excess baggage we've brought with us into our adult lives—baggage like bad habits or character defects. We picked up some of these character defects in our original family through certain unhealthy rules and roles we learned there. These rules and roles make up our lifescript. Our lifescript affects the way we approach marriage, parenting, work—almost everything we do.

Once again, our purpose is not to blame but to better understand why we have some of the bad habits and mental attitudes that we do as adults, so that we can change and be more conformed to the image of Christ.

Wealth from the Word

Read Exodus 20:5. In the book, several biblical examples were given in which the character defects of one generation affect the next. What were some of those? (See pp. 36–37.)

Read Romans 12:1–3. Blindly following the unhealthy aspects of the lifescript we grew up with is the same as "being conformed to the world." How do we "renew our minds" in order to rewrite our lifescripts?

What does it mean in verse 3 to "not . . . think more highly of [yourself]" than you ought but rather to think about yourself with "sound judgment"? *(Not to be puffed up about who you are, because all we are is a gift from God, but neither to think of ourselves as worthless, because "God has allotted to each a measure of faith.")* That's our goal in rewriting our lifescript—to see ourselves as God sees us, not as our parents saw us or as the world sees us.

Sharing from Written Exercises

What are some of the unhealthy family rules you identified in our exercises this past week? *(Let each man share who wants to. Remind the men about no interrupting, no advice-giving, and no criticism. What we each need is respectful, supportive listening.)*

What role or roles were you assigned to play in your family? You may want to refer to page 40 in the book. When you're ready, separate into groups of two and share with one another any insights you got into yourself, and the way you see yourself today as an adult.

Group Discussion

As you think about the unhealthy rules, roles, and recordings you grew up with, which of these affects your adult life and relationships the most right now?

Quiet Time/Application

Take a couple of minutes to reflect on what God might be saying to us here. Pick an area you've identified in this session that you'd most like to see changed.

Write down one negative behavior pattern you've identified. Then write down one action step you can take this week to replace the unhealthy behavior with healthy behavior. *(Take a couple moments of quiet time.)*

Share that action step with your Growth Partner so you're accountable to someone else and so you will have his prayers behind you. *(Offer to play that role for those who have not yet chosen a Growth Partner.)*

In conclusion, let's each read one of the passages of Scripture listed on pages 50 and 51. These reflect the truth about us—God's view as opposed to the shame messages we may be carrying inside. *(Read through the passages. Encourage the men to copy these verses down and carry them around this week to meditate on.)*

Assignment

1. Read chapter 3 on "Manhood without Models."
2. Do exercises 1 and 2 on pages 66–67.

Closing Prayer

▬ ▬ ▬ ▬ ▬ ▬ ▬ ▬ ▬ ▬ ▬ ▬ ▬

Session 3: Manhood without Models

Opening Prayer

Introduction

Our session this week deals with the biblical concept of the Father Blessing. We'll be examining our relationship with our earthly fathers and how that affects our own sense of manhood. *(At this point read the quote from David Blankenhorn on the top of page 53.)*

More than anything else, God created boys to need the approval or blessing of their fathers as part of their healthy transition to manhood.

Wealth from the Word

Let's look at the model of the Father Blessing given by God the Father to Jesus at his baptism.

Read Matthew 3:17. What are the elements in the Father Blessing? *(1. The son is "much loved." 2. The Father is "well pleased" with him—accepts him. 3. That love and acceptance is unconditional, not based on what the son has done or accomplished [Jesus had not yet begun his ministry].)*

What are the three kinds of harmful fathering styles described in the book? *(1. Abusive father. 2. Absent father. 3. Controlling father.)* Have the men define or describe the three styles.

Sharing from Written Exercises

Pair up and share your answers to exercises 1 and 2 on pages 66–67. Share any insights about yourself you may have gotten.

Group Discussion (whole group)

Wealth from the Word

Read Malachi 4:5–6 and 1 Peter 3:8–9.

What do these passages tell us? *(We need to attempt to reconcile our relationship with our fathers. We are not responsible for making the reconciliation happen, for we cannot control our father's response. But we are exhorted to deal with our own negative attitudes and try to bridge the gap.)*

Have any of you had the experience of attempting a reconciliation with your father that you'd like to share with us? *(Discuss.)*

At the very least, we can begin praying about reconciliation. And for those who have already lost their fathers or who have attempted to reconcile and failed, we can ask God himself to give us the Father Blessing we never received from our earthly fathers. *(See pp. 75–79.)*

Another major way to strengthen our authentic manhood as Christian men is to deepen our relationship with other men. What are some reasons we tend to avoid deep relationships with other men in our society? *(See p. 69.)*

Let's look at a couple of reasons the Bible gives for developing close friendships with other Christian men.

Read Proverbs 27:17. *(Discuss.)*

Read Ecclesiastes 3:9–12. *(Discuss.)*

Personal Assessment Exercise

Who can explain the diagram on page 72? *(Discuss.)* Let's take some time right now in the group to do exercise 3. *(Take quiet time.)*

Group Discussion

This is probably the most important step we can take during this entire mentoring series. Each of us needs to develop a close relationship with at least one other man—someone we can be honest with and pray with regularly. *(Read James 5:16.)* Without a close brother to confide in, we won't experience the healing James talks about. If you don't yet have a Growth Partner, pray for God to direct you. Take action on it this week, if possible.

Assignment

1. Read chapter 4 on "Pain, Grief, and Anger."
2. Complete the grieving exercise on page 100. If you have questions about the exercise, call me this week. You'll need to set aside a couple of quiet hours to complete it, so plan ahead, and be prepared for a blessing.

Closing prayer

━━ ━━ ━━ ━━ ━━ ━━ ━━ ━━ ━━ ━━ ━━ ━━

Session 4: Pain, Grief, and Anger

Introduction

This session has to do with experiencing pain, grief, and anger and has a lot of potential for healing. Let's ask God to make this a sacred time.

Opening prayer

Wealth from the Word

In Matthew 14:12–13, Jesus grieved the death of John the Baptist. He modeled for us the healthy response to significant loss in our lives—to grieve the loss, to work through the sadness to a place of comfort and healing on the other side.

Read Matthew 5:4. What does God promise to those who grieve their losses?

Group Discussion of Written Exercise

We are to bear one another's burdens, to support each other in the difficult issues of life. We have an opportunity here to support one another as we do the tough work of talking about a loss from childhood or from some other time in life. Let's share the answers we wrote out in response to the grieving exercise on page 100.

(This is generally one of the deepest and most powerful experiences during the mentoring process. Allow as much time as is necessary for each man to relate his painful experience and to share his answers to the questions from page 100. Encourage an atmosphere of compassionate supportiveness, but remind the men that there is to be no cross talk—no advice giving or sermonizing—even if the intent is to encourage. You are all there to listen respectfully and compassionately and thus silently, and through your non-verbal expressions of love, to let him know you care.

If there is not enough time for all the men to share before your session time is up, this may be one of those instances where it would be wise to carry over the topic to the next week. Use your own judgment.)

In closing, read the last two paragraphs on page 102.

Assignment

1. Read chapter 5 on "Adrenaline Addiction."
2. Complete all the exercises on pages 122–24.

Closing prayer

━━ ━━ ━━ ━━ ━━ ━━ ━━ ━━ ━━ ━━ ━━ ━━ ━━ ━━

Session 5: Adrenaline Addiction

Introduction

In this session we will be addressing adrenaline addiction and our overly busy lives. Men are especially impacted negatively by this. The rate of stress-related disease, such as heart disease and stroke, is much higher for men than for women. We're going to be taking a hard, honest look at our own work habits in this session. We must not create a critical or shaming atmosphere around this issue, because there aren't any easy answers. And what represents a balanced life for one man might not for another. We're not here to compare ourselves with each other; we're here to ask God to shine his light into the habits and motivations of our lives and speak to us individually about these issues. Let's ask God for honesty and openness.

Opening Prayer

Wealth from the Word

Read Matthew 11:28–30. What are the two qualities that Jesus says characterize his heart? *(Gentleness and humility)*

He said we can find rest by learning from him and his gentleness and humility. Is it possible to be driven and competitive and simultaneously be gentle and humble? *(Allow a full discussion on this.)*

Read Hebrews 4:15–16. Is Jesus sympathetic of our weaknesses? Do you suppose that includes our physical and mental and emotional weaknesses?

Read Psalm 103:13–14. What does it mean that God "knows our frame" NASB) and that he is "mindful that we are but dust"? *(The key conclusion for the group to reach is that God knows we are not unlimited in strength, that we have limitations—he created us with limitations! And, as a general rule, he expects us to respect those limitations. He may, of course, ask us and empower us at some time to step outside those limitations. But that is to be the exception, not the rule.)*

Discussion of Personal Assessment Exercises, pages 122–25

Ask the men to break up into groups of two to share their results from both of the exercises. After this discussion, call the group back together for a general discussion.

What insights did any of you get from the exercises? *(Some men get defensive about their high scores. They compare themselves with*

271

someone with a relatively low score and feel they need to defend their lifestyle. Assure the men that this is a matter between them and God, that no one can tell someone else what is "balance" for him; it's an individual matter. These are merely tools to help him reflect on his own life. There is no one "perfect" score.)

Remind the men again during this discussion that there is to be no advice-giving. We are here to focus on our own life, not someone else's. Men clam up when they feel they're being preached to or talked down to. Respectful listening is the rule.

Discussion on Solutions

Can someone explain the concept of "The Box" found on page 113?

What are ways you have found effective to stay inside your time limitations—to find the time for personal quiet time for yourself, or for family time? *(Again remind the men that they share their experiences with reference to themselves alone, not as a way of giving indirect advice to anyone else.)*

If there is time (and there may very well not be), ask the men the same question about finances—what ways they have found effective to stay inside their financial limitations.

Assignment

1. Read chapter 6 on "Women and Sex."
2. Complete the exercise on "Dependency on Women's Approval" on page 144.

Closing Prayer

▬ ▬ ▬ ▬ ▬ ▬ ▬ ▬ ▬ ▬ ▬ ▬ ▬ ▬

Session 6: Women and Sex

Introduction

This chapter in *Men's Secret Wars* begins with the following quote from Frank Pittman in "The Masculine Mystique": "At the heart of the problem of [men with wounded masculinity] is our society's bizarre attempt to raise sons without fathers. . . . So our boy marches forth to find a female whose magic wand will turn him into a man. The quest is fraught with doubts and dangers."

We're focusing on women and sex in this session, and it's one of the most important topics we can tackle as men. As we've learned before, 64 percent of Christian men admit struggling with pornography or some form of sexual addiction; 25 percent of married men have had an extramarital affair since becoming Christians. When you add in the men who have had "emotional affairs" and those who have had "inappropriate sexual contact with women short of intercourse," more than half of Christian men have had some type of affair outside marriage.

In general, we men need help when it comes to dealing in a healthy way with women and sex. Let's ask God to give us honesty and insight.

Opening Prayer

Personal Assessment: Dependency on Women's Approval

Let's begin this session by discussing the written exercise in the book on "Dependency on Women's Approval" on page 144.

Small Group Discussion

Break up into groups of three and each of us in turn will share the insights we got on our own behavior from completing the exercise. Remember not to cross talk or give advice, but be a respectful listener as each one of us shares.

Group Discussion

Let's get back together as an entire group. Would any of you care to share any insights about yourself you received? And remember, everything you hear in this room is to be kept in confidence. *(Our goal should be to foster the kind of honest atmosphere in which men can own the various ways they try to gain women's approval, from dressing a certain way, to talking to women in ways that are intended to charm, to flirting, etc. The whole issue of overreacting to women's criticism is worth exploring also. The first step toward spiritual health in this area is to break our denial and own our unhealthy behavior and motivations. Set the pace by acknowledging whatever part of this unhealthy pattern you can see in yourself.)*

Wealth from the Word

Let's see what God's Word has to say to us. First, a warning. Read Proverbs 6:27–29. What are some ways we men can have our "clothes . . . burned" and our "feet . . . scorched"?

Now let's read a passage that's full of practical instruction—Proverbs 4:23–27.

Heart. There are parts of the body Solomon uses to give us guidance. First is the heart (which to the Hebrews means roughly the same as "mind.") What have you found to be either helpful or discouraging in your battle with lust and the mind?

Mouth. Solomon encourages us to put away "a deceitful mouth" and "devious lips." What has been your experience with being honest about sexual matters? Has honesty helped lessen the power of lust for you?

Eyes. The author talks about his built-in "antenna" toward women—how he would immediately notice when a woman entered a room or would quickly find the most attractive women in a room he would walk into. What has been your experience with your own antenna toward women?

Feet. What are the places that you've found to be out of bounds for you? Do you have a plan for avoiding these? Have you made yourself accountable to someone about avoiding these places?

Conclusion

Ultimately, we need to acknowledge that no plan, no matter how elaborate, will save us from falling to sexual temptation. That's something only God's grace can do, as we daily acknowledge our powerlessness and ask God humbly to give us the strength one day at a time to say no to temptation. We need to come to a place of total brokenness on this issue before we will begin to see growth.

Let's acknowledge that brokenness now in prayer together.

Closing Prayer

Assignment

1. Read chapter 7 on "Relationship Styles."
2. Complete the exercises on relationship styles on pages 162–65.

■ ■ ■ ■ ■ ■ ■ ■ ■ ■ ■ ■

Session 7: Relationship Styles

Introduction

It's tough to be objective about our relationship with the special woman in our life—our wife or girlfriend. It's the relationship that we're closest to, the one that affects us most deeply, the one that's most apt to expose our character flaws. As we move through our material in this session, we once again need to ask God for openness, teachability, and freedom from defensiveness.

Opening Prayer

Wealth from the Word

As we read in chapter 7, God's intention for our marriages and committed relationships is deep intimacy—a relationship in which you feel loved and accepted unconditionally. That kind of intimacy grows in certain kinds of environments. Let's look at a couple of those.

Read Matthew 7:1–5. How does this passage apply to our relationship with our wives? What are examples of how you've applied this principle in your marriage? What are examples of when it is tough for you to apply this principle? Let's try to refrain from making this a "gripe session" about our mates but to keep the focus on the work we ourselves need to do. *(Discuss.)*

Read Ephesians 5:21. What does it mean to be "subject" or submissive to one another in the marriage relationship? When there is no mutual submission in a relationship, how is intimacy eroded? Can you give an example from your own relationship? *(Discuss.)*

Personal Assessment Exercises

Let's break up into groups of three to discuss our exercises from pages 162–65. Each man should share what the exercises revealed to him about his own relationship style. This is an especially important time for each of us to be supportive of one another and to be good listeners. We should not be critical, nor should we attempt to talk a brother out of the insights he has gained about areas of his character he needs to grow in.

Group Discussion

Let's gather back together. Do any of you have insights or comments you'd like to share with the rest of us?

Conclusion

New habits generally develop slowly. They need a lot of encouragement. If God has spoken to you about areas in your own relationship behavior that you would like to see changed, share these with your Growth Partner. Then, as you're challenged in these areas, or as you see victories, you will have someone to talk to about them.

Assignment

1. Read chapter 8 on "The Secret Life Syndrome."
2. Complete the Personal Assessment Exercise on pages 180–81.
3. If you have not yet picked a Growth Partner from within this group, it's important that you do so before next session.

Closing Prayer

▬ ▬ ▬ ▬ ▬ ▬ ▬ ▬ ▬ ▬ ▬ ▬ ▬

Session 8: The Secret Life Syndrome

Opening Prayer

Introduction

According to recent surveys, the majority of Christian men—including men in leadership positions in the church—have a secret life of some sort. As we saw earlier, for almost two-thirds of the men that secret life involves pornography or some other sexual behavior or habit. For about 20 percent, the secret life involves a struggle with alcohol or drugs. For other men the problem is gambling, or overspending, or illegal activities in business.

Your secret life could be something that is hidden within your mind, a thought life not visible to anyone else. A secret life can involve almost anything—anything that an individual is embarrassed by or wants to keep hidden for any number of reasons.

Let's review the diagram on page 72 to define a secret life another way. *(Read the last paragraph, bottom of p. 72, through the first paragraph, top of p. 73.)*

If there is no one in our lives right now who knows everything that we're struggling with—even if our area of struggle would be considered minor by most people—then, by definition, we have a secret life. Or more accurately, we are a secret. We are not allowing ourselves to be fully known by anyone.

Group Discussion

Why are we afraid to let another person really know us?

Read the six benefits of acknowledging our secrets from the top of page 171. Which of these appeals to you the most?

Wealth from the Word

Read Psalm 51:6.

What does this verse have to say about the way out of a secret life? What does David mean when he says to God, "[You] desire truth in the innermost being"?

Who needs to know the truth about us—God? *(No; obviously God already knows the truth about us. We need to know the truth about ourselves—not just know it intellectually, but know it and apply it.)*

The verse says, "In the hidden part Thou wilt make me know wisdom." Wisdom is truth *applied* to life. So it all starts with our acknowledging the truth about our secrets.

Read James 5:16. How do we gain healing? Is it enough just to confess our sins to God? *(The verse is not advocating some sort of regular or formal confessional practice, as is done in certain churches. Rather, it is simply saying some sins are so toxic, so harmful to our lives and the lives of those around us, that we need the healing that comes from confessing those sins to another human being, in addition to God.)*

Personal Assessment Exercise

Let's break up into groups of two with our Growth Partners. Share with each other, to the extent you feel comfortable, the results of your assessment exercise on the "Secret Life."

I would encourage each of you to be completely honest. But I also don't want anyone to feel pressured to talk about something he's not ready to disclose yet. It's okay, if you're not ready to be completely honest, to choose a level of disclosure that is comfortable for you.

Two guidelines:

1. Each group of two go someplace where no one will overhear you.
2. Everything you hear today is to be kept in strictest confidence and not shared with anyone else without the individual's permission.

We'll gather back here in one hour.

Conclusion

Was your time helpful? *(Allow the men to share any feelings they have to help them bring closure to the experience. To help ward against shame attacks from the "Accuser of the brethren," you might ask various men to read the affirming Scriptures at the end of chapters 1 and 2.)*

Assignment

1. Meditate this week on those Scriptures at the end of chapters 1 and 2, or similar passages that remind us of God's love.

2. Arrange to meet again with your Growth Partner early in the week to encourage each other and to pray together about the areas you discussed tonight. This will help prepare you to overcome any shame attacks that sometimes are a natural result of

sharing the totality of ourselves with another person. *(Remind them of the promise of James 5:16 and encourage them to claim that healing.)*

3. Read chapter 9 on "Leaving the Secret Life."

Closing Prayer

▬ ▬ ▬ ▬ ▬ ▬ ▬ ▬ ▬ ▬ ▬ ▬

Session 9: Leaving the Secret Life

Opening Prayer

Sharing

Who would like to share how the past week has gone, especially in light of last week's topic? Have you felt any new freedom? Have you experienced counterattacks from the Accuser of the brethren?

(It's important to allow as much time as is necessary for the men to process their "post-disclosure" feelings. Encourage them from your own experience, if you can. Share how difficult it was for you to be that honest, but also share the positive results you've experienced. Remind them that Jesus never said it would be easy to be his disciples, but that the freedom and inner joy that results cannot be experienced any other way. And remind them that one day, after they have walked through this process themselves, they will be able to reach out and help other men who are still enslaved to their secrets.)

Introduction

Can someone tell in his own words the story in this chapter about the forest fire? How is it an analogy of the secret life? *(Key idea: we must look for the hidden "hot spots" or weaknesses to guard against the behavior breaking out again. The battle isn't over just because this first, very important step has been taken.)*

It was an act of courage to honestly share with another man last week about our areas of struggle. This week we'll focus on how to begin to bring God's healing to all four dimensions of our wounded

places inside. What are those four dimensions? *(Spiritual, psychological, relational, practical.)*
Let's look at each of these four areas.

Wealth from the Word

1. THE SPIRITUAL DIMENSION

Read Psalm 51:17. What does it mean to have a "broken and contrite heart"? Why is this absolutely essential to true change in our behavior?

(Key thought: "contrite" means "truly and deeply sorry"; a "broken spirit" means we have completely given up—we're out of options to fix ourselves, we've accepted the hopelessness of our condition aside from God's grace. We must come to the end of ourselves and surrender to God in a new and deeper way before his healing can sweep in. Encourage anyone who wishes to share an example of "coming to the end" in some area of his life. Be prepared to share one of your own.)

2. THE PSYCHOLOGICAL DIMENSION

Read Proverbs 4:23. We looked at this verse earlier in the series. What does "heart" mean to the Hebrews? What does it mean that "the springs of life" flow from it? *(Wrong behavior begins with wrong thinking, with looking at life in a distorted way, a way other than the way God looks at it.)*

Can someone explain the medical metaphor used in the chapter about the difference between "layering" and "lancing"? Give an example of "lancing" some actual problem area of your own—i.e., identifying and acknowledging it as a problem, coming to a place of brokenness about it, and offering that area up to God, asking him to change it.

(Many of the issues we looked at earlier in this mentoring series—playing a hero role, listening to the critical inner voices playing inside our heads when we make a mistake, our people-pleasing motivation—are potential breeding grounds for secret life activity to break out again. These are the kinds of areas we need to be aware of and be offering up to God for his healing.)

Read Proverbs 23:7, the first part of the verse. What does this verse mean?

3. THE RELATIONAL DIMENSION

Some wise person said, "Relationships are the stage on which our recovery is played out." When we begin to surrender some behavior or habit that's had a hold on us for years, we can expect resistance. Usually, this behavior has negatively affected those closest to us. Certain patterns of relating to one another in less-than-healthy ways have probably been established in most of our primary relationships.

In short, our newfound commitment to change will probably be tested most severely in our marriage or other committed relationship.

Do any of you have examples of this you'd like to share? *(Be prepared to share one from your own life or marriage. Do a brief summary of the main points from chapter 7 on "Relationship Styles." These are the areas we all need to work on us men.)*

4. THE PRACTICAL DIMENSION

Can someone explain the "HALT Principle?" *(See p. 199.)* What are other triggers? Take a few minutes to jot down the things that can trigger you. If you have trouble thinking of some, reflect on the times you've been angry, irritated, or discouraged in the past week. *(After five minutes, call time.)*

Group Discussion

What are some of the triggers you came up with? *(Write them on the board as they offer them.)*

What are ways you've discovered to blunt the effect of these triggers, so that you don't react in an unhealthy way that may be a setback for your new growth?

(Make the point that calling their Growth Partner, or if he is unavailable, any of the other men in the group, and simply talking about the incident is one of the most important steps they can take. Encourage them to get over the macho attitude that it is unmanly to reach out for help. That's what the body of believers is for. Encourage

the men to exchange phone numbers for this purpose, if they have not already done so.)

Assignment

1. Read chapter 10 on "Life beyond the Quick Fix"
2. Read pages 243 through the first paragraph on the top of page 245. Pick five issues or behaviors you would most like to see changed from the list on page 244. You will later narrow this list down to two, but pick five for now.

Closing Prayer

━━━━━━━━━━━━━━

Session 10: Life beyond the Quick Fix

Opening Prayer

Questions/Answers

Does anyone have any questions about last week's assignment to begin working on the Personal Growth Plan in the appendix?

Introduction

We Americans love the quick fix—from our fast food to our sixty-minute photo development. We want our needs met *now* and our problems solved now. But the kinds of behaviors and habits we've been addressing in this mentoring series didn't develop overnight, and they won't go away overnight. We need to develop perseverance, and set our minds for a long-distance race.

Wealth from the Word

Read Hebrews 12:1–3, plus verses 11–13. Let's list all the ways these passages exhort us to develop perseverance. *(List them on the board.)*

What are the main obstacles we face in running this race with endurance, with perseverance?

(Look for both general obstacles—like "our sin nature" or "laziness"—as well as specific obstacles like "changing my work schedule

to allow for thirty minutes of quiet time and meditation in the morning.")

But deep-down change requires more than perseverance. It requires a new paradigm, or model, for personal change. Can someone explain what a paradigm is, or give an example?

Read Luke 5:33–39. What is Jesus talking about here? What are the "old wine" and the "new wine," the "old wineskins" and the "new wineskins"? *(The Pharisees represented the old paradigm, characterized by legalistic adherence to external rules. Jesus' new paradigm is characterized by grace, and by a supernatural change from the inside out, not the outside in.)*

How does this emphasis on what's inside versus what's outside apply to the areas we want to see changed in our lives?

Read Luke 5:30–32. Do you see yourself as one of the righteous or one of the sinners? If the latter, how do you feel about putting yourself firmly in the "sinner" category? *(Note: When we think we've become so good that we've "graduated" from the sinner category, that's when we're most in danger of falling back into a secret life.)*

Group Discussion

Who can tell the story about the retirement home in his own words?

In your opinion, are there ways the church today fits that retirement home analogy? How specifically? Do you feel free to let the other Christians in your church, including those in authority, know that you still struggle with issues, that you have character weaknesses and bad habits? Why or why not?

What can we do to promote Jesus' new paradigm among the Christians we know and fellowship with?

Conclusion

Someone read the C. S. Lewis story, beginning the top of page 221, through the end of the chapter.

That's what lies ahead for us, as we ask God for perseverance and trust him to turn our weaknesses and failure into something to glorify himself.

Assignment

1. Read chapter 11 on "Shame and Grace."

2. Narrow your list of five needy areas to the two you most want to see changed.

3. On a copier, enlarge the diagrams on pages 251–52. Make them big enough that you can fit all your writing inside the squares.

4. Read pages 245–49. For your first issue or habit, answer all eight of the questions under step 2. Copy your answers in pencil onto your enlarged Growth Plan. The examples from "Bob" should help clarify what is expected. *(Have them call you if they have questions. It's strongly recommended that you have already completed the Growth Plan yourself before leading them through it.)*

Closing Prayer

━━━━━━━━━━━━━━

Session 11: Shame and Grace

Introduction

It's easy to begin living the Christian life by grace and then to slip back into a modern-day Phariseeism. Someone has called that "Avis" Christianity—"We try harder." We can't change ourselves in the areas of the secret wars by trying harder. If we could have, we all would have changed by now, after innumerable sermons, retreats, altar calls, and Christian books.

True change requires that we work hard and persevere, but it all must be done in the spirit and power of God's grace or it will come to nothing.

So that's the issue for this session—do we grow more by a process of shaming or by a process of grace? This requires real wisdom. Let's ask God for it.

Opening Prayer

Wealth from the Word

How do you define *grace?*

Who can summarize the parable of the generous landowner from Matthew 20?

Can you identify with the attitudes of the grumbling workers? Is there a fairness issue at work here? How do the grumbling workers' attitudes reflect the value system of the world we live in every day? *(See p. 231.)* Is there part of you that resists, perhaps even is offended by, the uneven treatment by the landowner?

Now could someone tell the story of the prodigal son from Luke 15, please?

How is the response of the elder son like that of the grumbling workers in Matthew 20? How does the elder son's response again represent the value system of the world?

What does the father's response reveal about God's attitude toward us and our failures and weaknesses?

Group Discussion

If God truly has an attitude of grace toward us such as Jesus described in these two parables, how does that make you feel as you contemplate tackling the secret wars in your life? Reflect on his attitudes for a moment, put yourself in those parables, think about your weaknesses and the things you struggle with—how do you feel?

Split off in your Growth Partner teams and pray for each other, seeing each other through God's eyes of grace.

Assignment

1. Complete step 2 in the Growth Plan for your second issue or behavior—i.e., answer in writing all eight questions in step 2.

2. Transfer those answers in pencil onto your enlarged Growth Plan worksheet. Come prepared next week to share your Growth Plan with the group.

Closing Prayer

Session 12: Going On Growing

Introduction

This is the final week in our mentoring series. We've covered a lot of ground, done a lot of soul-searching and honest sharing of our lives with one another. In the process, we've discovered much about ourselves and about God and his grace; we have also deepened our relationships with other men. In this final session, we'll share with each other the plans we've put together for our ongoing growth in at least two areas. Let's ask God to speak to us tonight.

Opening Prayer

Wealth from the Word

Let's begin by looking briefly at two passages on spiritual growth—first, a passage that reminds us that we never arrive, Philippians 3:12–14. Comments?

Now let's look at Philippians 2:13. What part does God play in our growth, according to this verse?

Sharing

Let's each share about one of the issues or behaviors we picked for God to work on. I'll begin by sharing what I wrote in the eight boxes on my worksheet for my first issue.

(Ask each of the men to share in turn about one of his two issues. Reassure them that they don't have to share everything on their worksheet if they're uncomfortable doing so. This is primarily an exercise between each man and God. The rest of us are just witnesses.

It's fine for the men to change some of their answers because they get new ideas from the other men; that's why we encouraged them to write in pencil. Again, the atmosphere should be affirming, with respectful listening the norm, rather than cross talk or advice-giving.

If you have time to do a second round with the men in which they share about their second issue, we'd encourage that.

You have several options for the future to discuss with the men:

1. If you wish, you can extend the group for a few more weeks. This would allow for working on their plans and coming together weekly to share about their progress and challenges. Or you can end the series now.

2. Many groups have found it fruitful to run a second mentoring series soon after the first. The "graduates" of the first series return, paired with new men as their Growth Partners. The graduates thus have the chance to work through the material a second time and have the stretching experience of working with a new man as well.

3. In either case, we'd strongly recommend that the Growth Partners continue to meet and encourage each other on a weekly basis. We all need this kind of encouragement and accountability!)

Closing Prayer

Pat Means is the president of Prodigals International, cofounder of the National Association for Christian Recovery, the former U.S. director of Campus Crusade for Christ, and a frequent speaker to men's groups. Pat and his wife, Marsha, live and work in Seattle, Washington. For more information on Prodigals International, visit their web site at www.iProdigals.com.

Also Available from Revell

Living with Your Husband's Secret Wars

Marsha Means

When a woman discovers her husband is involved in sexual sin—whether it's the sin of lust, pornography, infidelity, or some other behavior—pain whips through her like a tornado. Yet in the midst of incredible hurt, she can find God's healing with help from *Living with Your Husband's Secret Wars*.

Written by Marsha Means, who along with her husband works with couples coping with sexual sin, this book offers specific, proactive steps readers can take in their journey toward wholeness. They'll learn how to find the support they need, grieve the losses of sexual betrayal, focus on their own spiritual growth, and move toward forgiveness and moving on—whatever the outcome of their marriage.

Marsha Means, M.A., is a marriage and family therapist and a frequent speaker to women's groups. Marsha is cofounder, with her husband, Pat, of Prodigals International, a Seattle-based ministry to individuals and couples impacted by sexual addiction. For more information on Prodigals International visit their web site at www.iProdigals.com.

0-8007-5710-6   224 pages $12.99p